Forensic Psychologists

Forensic Psychologists: Prisons, Power, and Vulnerability

BY

JASON WARR

De Montfort University, UK

emerald
PUBLISHING

United Kingdom – North America – Japan – India – Malaysia – China

Emerald Publishing Limited
Emerald Publishing, Floor 5, Northspring, 21-23 Wellington Street, Leeds LS1 4DL.

First edition 2021

Reprints and permissions service
Contact: www.copyright.com

British Library Cataloguing in Publication Data
A catalogue record for this book is available from the British Library

ISBN: 978-1-83909-961-8 (Print)
ISBN: 978-1-83909-960-1 (Online)
ISBN: 978-1-83909-962-5 (Epub)
ISBN: 978-1-83909-963-2 (Paperback)

INVESTOR IN PEOPLE

This book is dedicated to … all those who were kind enough to take part in the study.

To Dr Ruth Mann, the first of the nine, who died on 25/04/2020. In her absence Forensic Psychology is diminished.

To those dynamic educators who got me started on this path – Yvonne Hurlow, Bill Macdonald, Alan Smith. If not for you this road would not have been walked.

To those Criminologists that I met at the Cropwood Conference on the Effects of Imprisonment in 2004 who encouraged me to this career, and those who have supported me ever since. Special mentions to Shadd Maruna, Jo Phoenix, Barbara Owen, Fergus McNeil, Bethany Schmidt, Borah Kant, and Alice Ievins.

To my Doctoral supervisors, Adrian Grounds and Ben Crewe. Your patience, kindness, support, advice, friendship, and patience(!) saw me through. Thank you.

To my Doctoral examiners Alison Liebling and Odd Lindberg your advice and guidance made this a much better book than it would otherwise have been.

Most importantly, and as ever, to Dr Kate Herrity (the Sound Lady Under the Stairs) – for everything.

Table of Contents

List of Figures

Glossary

AI	Appreciative Inquiry
AII	Appreciative Informed Inquiry
BPS	British Psychological Society
GOAD	Good Order and Discipline
HMIP	Her Majesty's Inspector of Prisons
HMPPS	Her Majesty's Prison and Probation Service
HMPS	Her Majesty's Prison Service
IEP	Incentives and Earned Privileges
IPP	Imprisonment for Public Protection
IRAS	Integrated Research Application System
ISPP	Indeterminate Sentence for Public Protection
KPTs	Key Performance Targets
MoJ	Ministry of Justice
NOMS	National Offender Management Service
NPM	New Public Management
NRC	National Research Committee
OASys	Offender Assessment System
OBPs	Offending Behaviour Programmes
OM	Offender Manager
OMU	Offender Management Unit
OPDP	Offender Personality Disorder Pathway
PCL-R	Psychopathy Check List (Revised)
PIPEs	Psychologically Informed Planned Environments
PSI/O	Prison Service Instructions/Orders
SMT	Senior Management Team
SOTP	Sex Offender Treatment Programme
VP	Vulnerable Prisoner
YOI	Young Offender Institute

About the Author

Dr Jason Warr is a Senior Lecturer in Criminology and Criminal Justice at De Montfort University, UK. He has a wide range of research interests which include penology, sociology of power, sensory criminology, and the philosophy of science. He has conducted research in a number of criminal justice settings and has written on the emotional geographies of prison, the pains of imprisonment, prison staff, and narrative criminology.

Preface

Its funny, someone like you, interviewing someone in my position.
                                        –Psychologist during this study

Prisons often act as impenetrable fortresses. Behind their stony edifices lie hidden worlds of social life, organisational practice, and working realities. To this day, after hundreds of years of thought and word, after examination and description, the lived and occupational realities that occur within these Leviathans is still marred with an agnotologic air. They remain mysterious and, to some extent, barely known. We, the outsiders, remain largely ignorant of what these places of punishment, these places of control, do, how they are constructed, what makes them tick. We only occasionally become aware of the horrors and deprivations, the pain and suffering, the trauma that exists within. We know even less of the joys, triumphs, victories, humour, and camaraderie that also defines these hidden worlds. This shrouded reality makes them essential sites of research, of inspection. Yet herein lies a fundamental problem. Prisons have traditionally been, and remain, bloody difficult places to access. As Alisa Stevens (2019) notes, for researchers, gaining access to prisons has never been an easy enterprise but has become, sometimes, a Sisyphean task.

A number of factors have conspired to move this abstract impenetrability into a palisaded reality. There exists in this epoch of penal risk and image control both a politicised penal and carceral fetish as well as a desire to hide the reality of the institutions in which that fetish is embodied. This overt political charge has created a situation in the last two decades whereby gaining access to the Prison Service in England and Wales to conduct any sort of research is fraught, and can sometimes elicit Ministerial wrath. It also, now much more so than ever, involves a careful negotiation of a bureaucratic labyrinth, at the heart of which lies the much feared (and oft maligned) National Research Committee. The research project upon which this book is based suffered, as many others have suffered, the same trials that is now common to the prison research milieu. However, there were two compounding variables that rendered this research somewhat more difficult. Firstly, the fieldwork for this project began during a period when psychological services within Her Majesty's Prison Service (HMPS) were under a further burden of heavy criticism from prisoners, prison reform campaigners, and legal advocates. This combination of institutional pressure and professional critique resulted in a population and a service that were embattled and defensive. This compounded the problems of gaining access, securing trust, and recruiting an adequate sample. Secondly, there was the small problem of my background as a former Life/HMP sentenced prisoner who had been subject to the power, assessment, and reportage of forensic psychologists working within the prison service.

Plan A was to conduct a systematic and empirical account of the role of the forensic psychologists within the modern prison, the effect of the risk assessment process on both prisoners and psychologists, and the power differential that exists between these two parties. However, the Area Psychologist with whom I liaised prior to beginning the hazard strewn *Pathway to Access* informed me that given my history as an HMP sentenced prisoner such a research project, given that it would require access to formal sensitive data, was unlikely to gain ethical approval. This necessitated the reformation of, and a change in outlook to, the study. Plan B. The decision was made to focus not so much on the risk assessment process and the power of psychological expertise in the modern prison but instead on the forensic practitioners themselves. The reason for this decision was twofold: firstly, it avoided the ethical problems relating to case data and physical access to prison sites making the research more likely to be approved centrally. The second reason was that at inception, and subsequently (see Brown et al., 2015; Crewe, 2009; Shingler et al., 2017), there existed a small body of literature, and numerous articles and letters in the prison newspaper 'Inside Time', which covered prisoners' experiences of the risk assessment process and of specialist services such as probation and psychology. However, little beyond the brief attention given by Brown et al. (2015) and Crighton and Towl (2008, 2015) focused explicitly on either the experiences of those specialist practitioners themselves nor on the personal/subjective specificities of conducting psychological work in the prison. What was missing was an exploration of what impact such work may have on the practitioners themselves.

However, the point made by the Area Psychologist regarding my history, and thus positionality, is worthy of further consideration. As previously stated, I had been an HMP sentenced prisoner who was incarcerated for 12 years in 14 different establishments. During that period of time, I had numerous interactions, both formal and informal, with forensic psychologists employed within Her Majesty's Prison Service (see Warr, 2008). I had been both witness and subject to their power. For much of my incarceration, the interactions and experiences I had with forensic psychologists were both negative and profound. Despite a degree of separation between these interactions and my beginning this project, I held some enmity towards forensic psychologists. To some degree I still do. Therefore, not only had these experiences shaped my initial interest in conducting this research but my consequential positionality had imbued my approach, unwittingly, with a particular bias. This was echoed when the research design was reviewed by two independent Professors who pointed out to me that the actual design of the study, specifically the structure of the provisional interview schedule, was not concomitant with the stated aims of the research.

Kochan (2013) argues that emotion in and of itself is a necessary aspect to the development and process of science but nevertheless must be guarded against – especially if the shaping emotion is one that is negative. One of the fundamental duties of the qualitative researcher is to ensure that their personal interest, or 'positionality', does not negatively bias their research (Marshall & Rossman, 2006). The main danger of positionality is when it is carried through, from informing the initial interest in a subject to the point where it becomes operationalised in the structure of the study, and infects the analysis and communication of findings. When discussing the philosophical problem of the Rosenthal Effect in social science, whereby the assumption and value laden nature of research and theory construction can shape the very results that are discoverable, Martin (1994) argues that mitigating strategies are necessary in order to prevent these forms of overt bias. In order to mitigate one's positionality, the social scientist must engage in multiple processes of reflexivity and methodological introspection and peer review – processes which force the researcher to inspect their approach, theory, method, analysis, explanation, and communication (Hopkins, 2007). Immersion within this bias-focussed process, coupled with honest and critical peer input, will (hopefully) enable the researcher to discover their own assumptions and 'subjectivities' thus taking account of them when constructing/ analysing/communicating their study (Mason, 2002).

I had been aware that my positionality may have flavoured my approach to the research subject and as such had attempted to construct the study in such a way as to minimise whatever negative bias may yet have lingered. Unfortunately, though I had managed to achieve this in the scope and focus of the project, the timbre of the interview schedule was tainted by the negativity towards the prison environment, and more explicitly, the power of forensic psychologists, that my experiences had left me with. This had resulted in a somewhat hostile interview schedule that, instead of focussing on what psychologists experienced in their occupational lives, focussed on eliciting negative responses that affirmed my bias. It seemed obvious once highlighted but up until that point I had been unaware of it. This is the curse of researcher bias, whilst you can be aware that it exists, the specifics of it always remain just slightly beyond your own sight. It teases you from the shadows of your own enquiring mind and lays in wait, ready to pounce, ready to trip you up when you are least prepared. An academic addendum to the Laws of Infernal Dynamics if you will. There are many positionalities that the wary researcher needs to consider: ethnicity, class, gender, sensory and embodied processing (Herrity et al., 2020; Pink, 2015), neurotypicality or neurodiversity, theoretical and disciplinary perspective, etc. Each and all require some examination and reflexivity. Qualitative research does not have the luxury of the simplicity of quantitative research – it often requires a more profound examination of self, process, method, methodology, analysis, and communication. However, to return to the problem as was, both Professors mentioned above noted that this sense of negativity with which my approach was imbued might be a contributing factor to the hesitancy of the prison authorities in granting me access to the requested population. They recommended that in order to further eradicate this aspect of my 'positionality', and to alleviate the fears of those prison gatekeepers (an issue I shall return to), I should restructure the research project in terms of an Appreciative Inquiry (AI) and adopt methods of Appreciative Interviewing. Whether I have been successful in achieving this will be up to the reader to decide.

There have been a number of formulations of AI as various academic disciplines and industrial discourses have adapted it for their own ends. However, as Cooperrider et al. (2007) note, the process is designed to be a force for effective organisational change. As a method of research it is based upon a number of central assumptions: firstly, that organisations are co-constructed social realities; secondly, that organisational processes are dependent upon what meaning those who are involved ascribe to their interactions, and not so significantly on the dedicated application of official techniques; and thirdly, that both effective knowledge and change is best bought about by focussing on and engendering what is positive and successful as opposed to focussing upon that which is negative. Whitney and Trosten-Bloom (2010) further note that perhaps the most powerful aspect of AI is its ability to allow researchers to know and comprehend their participants through the direct relationships, and forms of sociality that they have to their profession and peers, as opposed to solely knowing them through the organisational roles they perform. The purpose of this method is to facilitate an understanding of a 'culture, society or organisation through the eyes of its inhabitants' (p. 50) and not the superficial perspectives sometimes gained by external observers. It allows those working with an organisation to be heard in the context in which they live, work or operate. In many regards, the methodological approach of AI is similar to, and shares many facets with, both Ryle's (1968) and then subsequently Geertz's (1994) notions of 'thick description' and the best means by which a researcher can attempt to capture the experiential realities of a lived culture where in-depth ethnography is not possible.

It must be noted, however, that coming from a perspective external to the organisation and profession with which I was concerned meant that I was obviously not conducting a strict, by the books, form of AI. Rather my method was an Appreciative Informed Inquiry (AII). By adopting the methodological ethos in the development of my interviewing models (Kvale, 1996), it allowed me a way out of the bias that I found myself ensnared by. This is, really because of the third precept described above

> that both effective knowledge and change is best bought about by focusing on and engendering what is positive and successful as opposed to focusing upon that which is negative.

This also happens to be the most misunderstood element of AI. Many people take this as the view that you are trying to discover 'only' the good in an institution/organisation. A particularly troublesome practice when exploring the realities of such contentious sites as prisons. In this regard, it can be seen to be a mechanism of justification or legitimation – something that we criminologists should, given the power laden nature of those disciplinary monuments, be extremely wary of. I have seen this allegation made towards a number of prison scholars who have utilised the AI method and seen their work dismissed exactly in this manner. However, this is a misunderstanding of the process and method. The purpose of exploring the positive is that it gives you a contrast to the negative elements of organisational life, and thus a fuller picture of the social world of that organisation. In a typical interview if you ask someone 'what it is like to work here?' you will get a partial answer that resembles

> It's not bad, it's okay I suppose ... bit stressful sometimes, there's not enough of us and we're understaffed. Actually, it's gotten quite bad at the moment the workload is getting on top of us and the cracks are beginning to show. It doesn't help that our line manager is really awful and really unhelpful. Also, someone keeps on stealing the milk out of the fridge and others won't wash the cups or the microwave ... and as for Susan in accounts ...

Now, there is some good information in that made-up(ish) vignette which could tell you a lot about the organisational culture in which such an interviewee worked. However, it is partial. This is because structuring interviews in this way allows the person to focus on a closed set of elements (Crow & Semmens, 2008) which are negative or bring dissatisfaction to them. However, there is no account about what works well, what they enjoy doing, where they get their job satisfaction, what makes the environment survivable, where the humour is, who they like, etc. In order to have a fuller picture of life in that office, you would need that side of the story. Asking for the positive gives you that. People will still tell you everything that is wrong, problematic, and disturbing but before they do you will have gotten the flipside of that narrative coin. I have now conducted 100s of interviews in multiple criminal justice settings and, if you do not explicitly ask for the positive, all you end up with is the negative. All you end up with is a partial account. All you end up with is data that hamper your explanation and theorising.

After reformulating the project in terms of AII, the process of gaining access became more straightforward. However, once access was granted, I then ran into a second problem. Hardly any of the psychologists working in prisons were willing to talk to me. As expected, the response to the initial call was minimal but a small number of psychologists (four) responded. It took some negotiation with those individuals to find a suitable location in which to conduct those interviews. For some, it was decided that the best locale was Stirling House, a Prison Service training and conference centre, whilst for others there were facilities outside of, but attached to, their home prisons. Once these locations were decided upon, the interviews were arranged and conducted. Then a scandal broke. It was discovered that a serving forensic psychologist was having a sexual relationship with a prisoner. Informally, I was told that my topic and the nature of my research may cause concern for some in light of this development. Whether that was the reason I do not know but the respondent well, as it were, dried up at that point.

Plan C. As a result of these concerns, when I resent the introductory emails to the contact list to see if any more people would be interested in participating, I was at pains to explain my neutrality and point out that this was an opportunity for them to speak to those issues which concerned them. Again, a small number of people came forward and with whom negotiations began in order to arrange times, dates, and locations. However, uptake was extremely low. It was also at this time that a number of psychologists responded by saying that though they were interested in participating time constraints and work schedules prevented them from doing so. A few more were polite enough to respond and say that they were not interested in taking part. However, the majority did not respond at all. This was a pattern that became repeated (not the scandal but the not responding) throughout what became a long, torturous, bout of fieldwork.

I had been aware that, as a body, forensic psychologists were an embattled group but thought that the study would, at the very least, be an opportunity for them to put their side of the story forward. One potential issue beyond the matter of interest may have been my history. One of the early participants had been very forthright in pointing out that they had found my background as a prisoner to be a stumbling block. They explained that they had found the prospect of being interviewed by a former prisoner '*extremely uncomfortable*' and '*daunting*'. However, they also felt that as they '... *were supposed to be in the business of rehabilitation it would be hypocritical for them not to participate*' solely on those grounds. It is difficult to gauge how widespread these concerns were as few others spoke of this and, obviously, the position of those who either did not respond or declined to participate is impossible to know. A further potential issue was the fact that psychological services were undergoing a national remodelling at the time that the fieldwork was being conducted. This may also have contributed to the insecurity that some may have felt during this period and thus may have prevented some from volunteering. However, this is guesswork. Why people did not want to be involved is something that I have still not fully been able to get to the bottom of.

What is certainly true though is that there was a great deal of hesitancy from this population which was difficult to overcome during the initial fieldwork (which involved Plans D through G). Over a period of 30 months, I managed to convince only 21 individuals to sit down with me in interview. One of these formally requested that their interview be terminated and any information gleaned not be used. This was of course honoured. This meant that the effective sample consisted of 20 forensic psychologists all of whom were in the current employ of the Prison Service at the time. The shortest of these interviews was 85 minutes and the longest nearly three hours (it involved a bad bout of food poisoning and vomiting but no one needs to hear about that). Though a small sample, given the population of forensic psychologists working in HMPS (currently just over 500), they were both sufficiently culturally knowledgeable (Rubin & Rubin, 1995) and represented a purposive sample where those interviewed were able to provide sufficiently significant data (Silverman, 2010) on the occupational realities of forensic psychologists in prisons. The 20 main interviewees were drawn from various regions around the country, were employed at various grades (psychological assistants, trainees and qualified), were engaged in various forms of psychological work, and included both men and women of varying ages. It must be noted that none of those interviewed were employed within PIPE units, which is still something of a fringe practice in terms of the core psychological work undertaken by forensic psychologists. These practitioners were not deliberately excluded from the sample but none of those who wished to participate happened to work in these environments. This means that I have no substantial data on this type of working. The sample that were drawn, however, were considered to be sufficiently knowledgeable regarding the delivery of the quotidian psychological services in the Prison Service, able to offer a range of perspectives that would be representative of the wider population and were minimally sufficient in number and range of views that a larger respondent pool was not deemed necessary (Gordon, 1992).

A further nine people were interviewed in order to gain an understanding of the historical context in which the recent era of forensic psychology arose. These interviewees consisted of former high-ranking psychologists and Prison Service personnel who were involved in the recruitment, training, and delivery of psychological services over the last 25 years. Informal conversations were held with a number of Prison Service psychologists throughout the duration of the study and these played a part in shaping the interviews and analysis. Since the completion of the doctoral thesis, I have had further conversations with another 20 + forensic psychologists about my research. In many ways, these conversations have given weight to my findings and allowed me to be slightly bolder in setting out the conclusions discussed in the following chapters. However, it is important to note that the data used to inform the substantive chapters of this book are, unless otherwise noted, based solely upon the 20 original participants mentioned.

Before beginning in earnest, a further point has to be raised both about the research that underpins this book and the way that this has shaped the writing process. This point is concerned with ethics. Usually there are four core areas of ethical concern when conducting qualitative research. These tend to relate to voluntary participation, subject well-being, anonymity, and confidentiality. The first two of these issues were not concerns for this research. The forensic psychologists who were involved were adults and trained professionals who understood the parameters of the research, their role, and my responsibilities to them. However, the latter two issues were something of a problem. A problem that arose during the fieldwork and which now shapes how I write about it.

In terms of anonymity and identity disclosure, there were a number of issues that had to be addressed, some of which only arose as the study continued. Due to the nature of the research questions, there was a possibility that identifying and/or sensitive, incriminating or individually harmful, information could be supplied by the participants. Fortunately, no direct or actionable information arose during the course of the interviews that concerned illegal activity and as such no action was necessary in this regard. However, this consideration dictated that, as far as is possible, the participants would not be identified in person during the course of the research and that everything would be done to try to ensure anonymity. For this reason, it was initially intended that the participants would be assigned pseudonyms based upon obscure Star Wars characters (yes, I am a geek) and that any information that could result in the identification of the respondent would be altered or removed. However, a problem quickly arose which smacked down those carefully laid plans. At the time of the fieldwork there were, within the psychologist population of prisons in England and Wales, very few men compared to women. It was thus felt that if participants were given gendered pseudonyms it might still be possible for those men who participated in the study to be identified. Even obscure names from a galaxy far far away would not have solved this issue. Alas. Along the same lines, it was noted early on that because of the relatively small number of chartered psychologists within the Prison Service at the time of the fieldwork if a respondent was referred to as such it may, again, be possible to identify them. Therefore, it was decided that nongendered and nonrank-specific titles would be used when quoting directly, so it will be 'a' psychologist said X or Y.

One ethical issue, which had not been anticipated but which also impacts on how I write about this population, arose in part due to the bureaucratic nature of the Prison Service and the manner in which recruitment emails were cascaded down through the hierarchical management structure of the service. During the early stages of the study, it came to my attention that some of the people who were interested in participating in the study had in fact been asking their line managers for permission to participate, who then forwarded the request on to various departmental heads and Area Psychologists/Managers. This obviously compromised their anonymity, especially if they were to be the only person from a particular region who volunteered. From that point on I made sure that when first contacting individuals I emphasised the importance of their anonymity to the ethics of the research. However, at a later stage, I had a one respondent inform me that they knew I had previously interviewed two others, from different regions, whom they then went on to name. AGHHHHH. This had arisen after they had been cc'd into an email exchange between their line manager and one of the two identified psychologists where participation in the study had been discussed. At least two others 'outed' themselves by talking about their participation in the study on social networking sites. Yet another prefaced a question to me whilst I was presenting at a conference by identifying themselves to the room as someone who had participated in the study. This reinforced the decision not to provide pseudonyms of any description throughout this thesis and to avoid the gendered pronouns 'he' and 'she'. It was also decided that this method would satisfy any issues concerning confidentiality.

This gives you some understanding of the method, sample, and research that was conducted in order to provide the material discussed. More information on these issues will be littered throughout this book. However, I also hope that this preface gives you some indication to the type and nature of the discussion that will exist herein. I take my responsibilities seriously and will present, what is I hope, a robust and theoretically sophisticated discussion on the working realities of forensic psychologists in prisons. It is my aim that the discussion here will extend our understanding of the prison, the matrices of power that exist there, and how those who wield a significant amount of power within carceral settings can also be professionally vulnerable. I am, however, also hoping that this book is easy and enjoyable to read. I believe wholeheartedly that in order for this type of discussion to have resonance, we need to move somewhat beyond the cold, literary conventions of traditional academic texts. We need to attempt to bring such texts alive, to take our readers into these worlds with us.

That is my intention.

Welcome to the prison world of forensic psychologists.

J Warr (2020).

Chapter 1

Introduction: Forensic Psychology and Her Majesty's Prison Service

> The control of individuals, this sort of punitive penal control of individuals at the level of their potentialities, could not be performed by the judiciary itself; it was to be done by a series of authorities other than the judiciary ... a whole network of institutions of surveillance and correction ... the psychological, psychiatric, criminological, medical and pedagogical institutions for correction.
>
> –Foucault (1994a, p. 57)

> I think from a psychology point of view, working within a prison, you have got a range of role conflicts that you have not necessarily got in other institutions.
>
> –Participant Forensic Psychologist

Prisons stand boldly as a totem of a state's control and dominance. Whilst the blue line of the police and the green shield of the military are also emblematic of a State's coercive potential, they still do not come close to the symbolic power of the stony morality of the prison. Those high walls and barely glimpsed barred windows shout a clear and profound message to all those who witness them. Here be power. Awful power. Yet that power is not singular. Within the prison there exists a confluence, a complex matrix, of differing forms of power designed to both restrain and constrain. Those in our society deemed to have breached the tenets of our social contract are consigned to these institutions. In England and Wales, with its neo-liberal political economy, we demand that the prison not only take these individuals and keep them away from us, the public, we also demand they remake those civic ghosts into conforming and contributing citizens. Labourers. It is within the confines of these penal monoliths that we, as a society, expect, or even demand, that prisoners be both punished and remade. Forensic psychologists have in the last two decades come to inhabit a central role in these conflicting processes. They are tasked, utilising a nascent and flawed disciplinary power, with both serving the punitive and disciplinary interests of the prisons in which they serve, and bringing about the reformation of prisoners that society demands. As a

Forensic Psychologists, 1–10
Copyright © 2021 Jason Warr
Published under exclusive licence by Emerald Publishing Limited
doi:10.1108/978-1-83909-960-120200002

profession they have become both harbingers of change and adjuncts of penal power.

Examining how psychological power manifests within, and influences experience of, the carceral habitus allows us to gain a greater understanding of the prison as an entity and its role in our lives. However, forensic psychologists in prisons and their staff culture are overlooked in terms of contemporary prison sociology. Little is known about this specific subgroup of prison staff. Other staff groups such as prison officers (Crawley, 2004; Liebling, Price, & Shefer, 2011; Nylander, Lindberg, & Bruhn, 2011; Tait, 2011), prison governors/managers (Bennett, 2016; Bryons, 2008; Liebling & Crewe, 2013) and even prison health and drug workers (Kolind, Frank, Lindberg, & Tourunen, 2015; McDonald & Fallon, 2008; Walsh, 2009) have been subjected to an investigatory gaze the prison psychologist has not. There is a distinct lack of knowledge regarding their culture, how they interact with the wider institution, how they perform their multiple roles, how they experience the prison, and what role they play in prison's confluence of power. The aim of this book is to redress this particular lacuna of knowledge and to highlight how an examination of this staff population can tell us so much more about the contemporary prison.

Between 1992 and 2007, there was a significant increase in the demand for, and expansion of, psychological services within prisons in England and Wales. This established a psychological status quo within our modern prisons. As one prisoner in Crewe's (2009, p. 118) study of the prisoner social world noted '*psychologists have taken over the prison in the last ten years*'. Overwhelmingly, this psychological demand has been met by specialist forensic practitioners (Crighton & Towl, 2015; Towl, 2004). I bore witness to this expansion, and its consequence, first hand. As discussed in the Preface of this book in 1992, at the age of 17, I entered the prison system of England and Wales as an HMP sentenced prisoner.[1] At that time, especially in Young Offender Institutions, the only psychologists you encountered were those who had a counselling, or a clinical, role. They were, from a prisoner's perspective, on your side. They were there to help. The very first conversation I had with a psychologist, in the dim and distant carceral past, was related to whether I was sleeping okay and if they could be of any assistance? At that time their power was minimal and reflective of other nonuniformed and health-related staff. What power they had derived from the coercive matrices of control produced by the institution itself and conferred on all those who wield keys. It was not unusual. However, the next 12 years saw psychological services shift from a minor institutional entity concerned with helping prisoners and providing the odd pretrial report to an entrenched and powerful discipline that influenced all aspects of the carceral life world.

I witnessed first hand the growth in numbers, the expansion of role, and the embedding of this professional practice into the very fibre of the contemporary prison. By the time of my parole in 2004, they were no longer a benign entity. They had become a group of staff who wielded a great deal of unchecked power.

---

[1]Her Majesty's Pleasure. An indeterminate sentence given to juveniles.

Unchecked, because unlike with other prison staff who have formal systems of check and balance to mitigate their power, there is no recourse to the power of psychology in prisons, nor is there any avoiding it. It is pervasive. So pervasive that the very discourse of forensic psychology now infuses the very narrative habitus (Fleetwood, 2016) of prisoners and shapes all aspects of their identity performance (Warr, 2019). Psychological terms have come to infest the day-to-day language and points of reference that prisoners utilise to discuss their own carceral lives (I shall return to this point). However, their power is not only pervasive but is also profound. One example I have discussed elsewhere (see Warr, 2008) was where a forensic psychologist perceived a relationship between a personal officer and myself as unhealthy (the officer accepted that I may have been telling the truth over my continuing appeals against conviction) and thus the psychologist recommended that my personal officer be reassigned. This recommendation, this act deprived me the succour of a single person within those monstrous walls who thought I may be telling the truth. The power of that psychologist went so deep that it could affect the very relationships that I could have with other staff in the prison, and shaped my penal life for many years afterwards. Their power, in only a short number of years, had infiltrated every aspect of the prison so much so that on the say so of a forensic psychologist your relationships with other prisoners and with staff, your role and activities within the prison, and your very future could be disrupted and destroyed. Psychological pronouncements carry a great deal of symbolic weight and can have devastating and unescapable consequences for prisoners, especially indeterminately sentenced prisoners.

When it came to forensic psychologists and their power within the contemporary prison, my lived experience made me an ideal candidate to conduct the research that follows. It allowed me to identify questions that needed to be explored. However, we need to be careful when it comes to how much we privilege lived experience, or insider knowledge. Over the last decade, we have seen something of a fetishisation of lived experience. It has, in some regards, come to be elevated in such a way as that it, in and of itself, can confer expertise and authority. We see, especially within the criminal justice commentariat, a wealth of people trading upon their lived experience. Of course, lived experience can provide someone with unique insight into the criminal justice system (or whatever phenomena they happen to be discussing) but it is also a double-edged sword. As I discussed in the Preface, it can imbue someone with a profound bias that is difficult to overcome and which, if care is not taken, can cloud every judgement and pronouncement they make. Furthermore, whilst the individual with lived experience may be an expert on their own subjective experience, this does not necessarily mean that person has any great insight into the lived realities of others. This extrapolation from the subjective to the general is a particular inductive danger of the lived experience fetish. We must not make the mistake of assuming that lived experience, whilst profound and important, makes anyone an expert on the realities of others or the phenomenon that they discuss. It does not. We sometimes forget this in our rush and desperate need to hear the voices of those traditionally silenced within criminal justice discourse.

However, I soon discovered that my lived experience was not unique. In every prison in England and Wales that I visited I heard the same stories being told. So much so that it became a frequent lament, a constant of the modern prison, this tale of psychologists and their power. In some regards, the forensic psychologist has become the folk devil of the modern prison and many a wary prisoner has a cautionary tale of their encounter with these maleficent and mysterious creatures. An illustrative example of this is a young man whom I met at HMYOI Neverland.[2] He had been convicted over a gang-related homicide in South London. A forensic psychologist had noted that despite doing all recommended offending behaviour courses, his risk remained high, and thus they should not progress to a lower category prison, due to the fact that he maintained a close connection, and friendships, with a number of co-defendants in the prison.[3] This maintenance of relationships was perceived as maintaining gang ties.

Given that 3 of the 5 co-defendants in the prison (one of whom he shared a cell with) were family members, the implications of such a report were clear. Maintaining his relationship with those family members meant that his perceived 'risk' would not reduce and he would not progress through the system. Family or freedom. Those were seemingly the choices being imposed upon him. His anger at that psychologist was immediately palpable and, given that soon after showing me this report he was moved from HMYOI Neverland to a high security prison in the North of England, would be long lasting. That move, predicated on that report, will add years to that young man's time in prison. His was not a lone tale. Why would this happen? Forget for a brief moment the (at best) cultural insensitivity or (at worst) naked racism inherent to the interpretation of the life of this young man. The reason is that the proclamations of forensic psychologists can condemn these prisoners to years of extra, or even permanent, incarceration. Given that there are currently about 10,000 indeterminately sentenced prisoners in England and Wales (Ministry of Justice, 2020), forensic psychologists wield a particular, pervasive and potent power over a significant number of our prisoners.

There is a considerable need for a grounded understanding on the role and influence of forensic psychologists in prison (see Crewe, 2007; Liebling, 2004). Their power over the future lives of prisoners means that forensic psychologists have, in the eyes of many prisoners and prison staff, come to be central to an absolutist yet partial nexus of soft power (Crewe, 2007, 2009). Indeed, some forensic psychologists themselves have expressed discomfort about the changing nature of their role, the demands placed upon them, their colleagues and indeed their profession (Brown, Shell, & Cole, 2015; Crighton & Towl, 2008). Witnessing the infestation of this power into the contemporary prison, and the effects that it has on so many, left a lasting impression on me and a desire to understand both the source of their power and the influence of this professional

---

[2]Not the establishments real name but a place where I conducted field work for 30 months between 2011 and 2014 and have referred to in a number of publications.
[3]He showed me the report and I read it in full. Basic details were recorded in field notes.

group. Coupled to this motivation was a growing awareness that although we had some understanding of other prison staff, and how they experienced power and the institution, this particular staff group were absent from the wider story. This struck me as a glaring omission, and one I hope to redress here.

The expansion in numbers of forensic psychologists employed within our prisons is an outcome of several interrelated factors. Firstly, since 1993, the number of people being committed to prison has almost doubled (Ministry of Justice, 2020) and the number of people serving indeterminate sentences has also increased in the wake of the Criminal Justice Act of 2003 (Cavadino, Dignan, Mair, & Bennett, 2019). These factors have created greater case-loads, and thus more bureaucracy, for psychology departments throughout Her Majesty's Prison and Probation Service (HMPPS). A further factor has been an overt commitment to the ideals of public protection that have come in the wake of the 2003 Criminal Justice Act and the report into the case of Anthony Rice, a paroled life sentenced prisoner who went on to kill whilst under probation supervision (HMIP, 2006). This shift, and the corresponding expectations of the Ministry of Justice, the Parole Board and the Prison Service authorities, has impacted directly upon psychologists employed in our prisons. The duties and procedures of risk-monitoring, risk-assessment, and programme delivery have now overtly supplemented existing responsibilities for the majority of psychologists employed in our prisons. In 2011, the development of an Offender Personality Disorder pathway (NOMS, 2015) involving both the Ministry of Justice and the Department of Health also involved some changes to psychological practice in prisons – especially the Psychologically Informed Planned Environments. These changes in ethos and practice have affected the nature and level of work faced by psychologists in prisons and have directly resulted in a new range of occupational, institutional, and individual pressures.

Fitzgibbon (2007), as well as Towl (2004), have noted the importance of understanding both the risk-assessment process that is central to modern penal practice (Litwack & Schlesinger, 1999; O'Malley, 2005) and the impact that it has on those who are responsible for administering it. It is inevitable that an increased and altered workload, set against the backdrop of a constrained and austerity focused prison, will impact on the occupational and professional lives of those psychologists who work there. Further to these issues is the continuing 'bad press' that psychologists working within the prison system of England and Wales and their 'treatment industry' receive through the national prisoner newspapers *Inside Time* and *ConVerse*.

The almost constant negative rhetoric and vitriol contained within these pages, which often relates to the folk devil status I mentioned earlier, can be both incredibly personal and intense. Given the nature of psychological power in the prison and the numbers subject to it, this is perhaps understandable. However, at the time that this research began, many psychologists felt besieged by the negativity that was being directed towards them (Maruna, 2011; Warr, 2008). For every one of those stories reproduced in those papers, there is a personal referent – a forensic psychologist who is being excoriated. Many felt they were under personal attack. Many felt that their work was misunderstood, misrepresented, and much maligned. As one noted

> I feel like they are deliberately trying to undermine not only what we do, but the skills and expertise we have, by attacking us personally and ... that's not fair as we can't answer back.

Another noted that reading such stories in print made them feel *'vulnerable'* and *'got at'*. This is a situation that has, in some senses, only been compounded as critiques of the 'treatment industry' have become more profound and vociferous. In October 2019, a former Director General of the Prison Service, Sir Martin Narey, publicly attacked the 'treatment industry' that had overtaken British prisons.[4] This garnered a great deal of backlash by forensic psychologists and others on varying social media sites.

However, there were other factors that seemed to play a significant part in this sense of vulnerability. Right at the start of this research, at a wine soaked social function, I was introduced to a former forensic psychologist who had recently left the Prison Service. After some awkward conversation (the person who introduced us said that I was *'investigating you lot'* ... thanks!) the psychologist explained that they had left the service after being stalked by a married uniformed officer. They noted that, although this was an extreme circumstance, it was nevertheless an extension of their wider experiences of the uniformed body. Experiences that were tainted with sexism, misogyny, bullying, and harassment. At the time I thought this was an extreme example. However, soon after, another former prison employed psychologist who I met at a conference, also relayed a number of negative and related experiences with uniformed members of staff, across a number of prisons, that had resulted in them also leaving the Prison Service for private practice. These experiences, which were rapidly corroborated by those I interviewed, made me aware that work place relationships, and the dynamics which underpinned them, were indeed one of the defining factors in how individuals perceived their role and professional life. They also played a significant part in an overarching ontological vulnerability that many psychologists felt.

This factor highlights that though wielders of incredible power these psychologists also felt vulnerable within the context of the prison. They seemed to occupy mutually exclusive positions – being both central to a wide reaching, pervasive, unchecked, and inescapable penal power whilst simultaneously being vulnerable and powerless. How can such a situation be explained? This question highlights the need to understand this population, their experiences, and how they manage their carceral employment in far greater depth than has hitherto been achieved. This question forms the foundation for this book.

Despite these concerns being both evident and a source of much discussion between practitioners, much of the literature surrounding forensic psychology, which is largely practitioner-authored, misses this. This extant, and increasingly exhaustive, literature tends to fall into two broad categories. The first focuses largely on the development, mechanics, and tools of risk-assessment, programme

---

[4]See article: https://www.theguardian.com/society/2019/oct/29/prisoner-rehabilitation-does-not-work-says-former-prisons-boss.

delivery, training, and creating rehabilitative ways of working (e.g., Clarke, Simmonds, & Wydall, 2004; Friendship, Blud, Erikson, & Travers, 2002; Mann, Howard, & Tew, 2018; Mann & Riches, 1999 etc.). Even a critical text like *Bad Psychology: How Forensic Psychology Left Science Behind* (Forde, 2018), which is an excoriating exploration of forensic psychology in the United Kingdom, largely falls into this category. The second comprises evidence-based investigations into both the efficacy of varying assessments, programmes, interventions, and the best practice for their delivery (Adler & Gray, 2010; Andrews & Bonta, 2003; Clarke et al., 2004; Friendship et al., 2002). What has been lacking from this academic discourse is any in-depth, sociological, and generative studies which focus upon the practitioners themselves, their role in the contemporary prison, their motivations, their perspective on their relationships with the prisoners whom they assess, and the impact of the environment and work on their emotional selves. Brown et al. (2015) in their book *Forensic Psychology: Theory, Research, Policy and Practice* and the Ministry of Justice's (2018) promotional videos exploring the experience of forensic psychological work in prisons come closest to addressing some of these issues. However, as the Brown text is introductory many of these issues are only afforded a brief examination and the MoJ videos are promotional and thus of limited value. Therefore, it remains the case that, in both the practitioner and wider psychological and criminological literature, the experiences of the psychologists themselves have had limited attention. There is still a need to understand how forensic psychologists in the employ of the Prison Service[5]experience their professional world.

Given this need, the core aim of the research was to explore the following questions: firstly, how is psychological power formulated, what recognition is there of the power inherent to their role and profession, and how do psychologists experience the power of the institution to which they belong? Secondly, just who are the psychologists who are employed within our penal institutions and what motivates them to join this profession? Thirdly, how do these psychologists derive occupational satisfaction and what are the barriers to doing so? Fourthly, what impact does performing psychological work in the prison have on their personal and emotional lives? Lastly, how do these psychologists experience the relationships they have with those whom they work on, and alongside?

Inevitably, given the nature of these questions, there are a wide range of interrelated themes discussed in this book. However, these themes really coalesce around four sociological issues: Power, Occupational Morality, Emotion Work, and Gender Relations. Firstly, I discuss how disciplinary discourses, via symbolic interactivity, both inform and shape penal power. Also, how those who wield extensive penal power can also be extremely vulnerable to other forms of penal power within the contemporary prison. Secondly, I discuss how a typology of values and professional perspectives for this occupational group allows us to understand variance in professional practice. Thirdly, I discuss the necessary distinction between emotional and emotive labour. Here the former is defined as

---

[5]From here on in referred to as prison psychologists.

the process of working with one's own emotions; the latter is the processes of working with the emotions of others. This involves an exploration of how the occupational vicissitudes that this population face, given the variant moral positions, result in differing ways of experiencing and coping with the prison. This provides a hitherto unknown account of how these prison staff members perceive and derive job satisfaction and conversely experience stress. Fourthly, I provide an explanation of how these distinct 'types' both respond to the power of the establishments in which they work, the manner in which they wield their own professional power, and how their discipline creates and promulgates a form of symbolic capital I refer to as disciplinary capital. As psychologists sit at the intersections of varying power relations in terms of the prison and wider criminal justice system, this provides a novel understanding of modalities of power and discourse. Finally, the manner in which the gendered nature of the prison can impact on female forensic psychologists is elucidated. This adds to the wider literature on gender relations within the prison and provides a greater understanding of how many female staff can be unprotected, and indeed victimised, within the confines of penal spaces designed around, and dominated by, varying forms of masculinity.

This is the part of any academic text where the author typically sets out the structure and contents of the succeeding chapters. This always strikes as somewhat superfluous given the discussion above and as you have probably read the contents page. Nevertheless, the book is split into two broad sections which separate the explication of the history of psychological services in the prisons of England and Wales and the wider theoretical legacies that inform this discussion and then the setting out of the substantive findings. The first section (Chapters 2 and 3) establishes the theoretical framework upon which the research is built, a description of the historical events, policies and practices that have given birth to modern psychological practices within the British penal system and discusses the issues and foundations of forensic psychology as a structure of expertise. As such, Chapter 2 explores psychological expertise and the concept of disciplinary capital and its exchange within the contemporary prison. It will detail how this symbolic interaction lies at the heart of forensic psychological expertise. This chapter will also explore how this symbolic capital is central to both ideations and manifestations of varying forms of power, especially soft power, within the penal habitus. Chapter 3 is concerned with the genealogy of psychological, and then later forensic psychological, services within the Prison Service of England and Wales. This will include a broader discussion of the medicalisation of deviance within society (Conrad, 2007; Conrad & Schneider, 1992) and how these positivistic discourses have shaped the contemporary penal landscape. This chapter also explores the literature on prison staff cultures, defines Emotional Labour and the specifics of the emotional labour that psychologists engage in.

The second broad section details the substantive findings. Chapter 4 describes the varying psychologist types that can be found working within the modern prison system and establishes a central hypothesis. The moral and occupational positions of those interviewed, whilst an unintended area of exploration, became immediately evident and could be categorised in terms of four distinct 'types'.

These types, Humanists, Functionalists, Utilitarians and Retributivists, correspond to a particular moral and occupational outlook. This analysis also sets the groundwork for later discussions as each type (other than when issues of gender experience arise) responds to and perceives the prison, their profession, occupational satisfaction, and their role and power in type-specific ways.

Chapter 5, on 'Occupational Experiences', explores the emotional and emotive labour that underpins both positive and negative aspects of forensic psychological practice in prisons. Relating to each of the types described in Chapter 4, this explores how each type derives job satisfaction and what constitutes a good day or experience. This chapter will explore the day-to-day working life of psychologists and elucidate their relationship to the products of their labour, the intellectual and professional challenges they enjoy, and the forms of prosociality and support that psychologists experience. The chapter will also explain the negatives of occupational and ontological ambiguity, occupational pressures that arise from working within the Prison Service, and the hindrances to job satisfaction. This will involve some analysis on work place stress and the associated emotion work (Mann & Cowburn, 2005; Nylander et al., 2011). Lastly, the chapter will explore and analyse some of the more harmful occupational experiences reported by participants and the impact of such experiences on the emotional lives of psychologists beyond the prison.

Chapters 6 and 7 explore the core contention of the thesis and explicate how forensic psychologists are both incredibly powerful within the penal landscape yet also vulnerable adjuncts of power. Specifically, it analyses psychologists as both wielders of a particular, discursive form of penal authority and as subjects of the wider authority of the establishments in which they work. The first of these two chapters examines psychologists as wielders of power and the ways that the various types perceive and respond to this reality. It will also involve a discussion on the psychologist as an expert and net producer of disciplinary capital, the bureaucratic forms of power associated with psychology in prisons, and the coercive nature of psychology in prisons and how this can create issues of ethical and moral blindness. Chapter 7 explores how psychologists experience the power of the institution itself, the way this constrains their practice, and how this can further affect them. This involves a discussion on the issues of territoriality in relation to other expert groups within the prison. This chapter will also explore the problems, such as bullying and intimidation, which psychologists can encounter from the uniform staff. Lastly, this chapter examines how the problems of impositional and isolational uniform staff dominance affect the occupational environment of the psychologist.

Chapter 8 is concerned with the gendered nature of the prison how this impacts upon the working environment and experiences of prison psychologists. This chapter aims to explore the form, function, and impact of the gendered environment on both those male and female psychology employees of HMPPS. This will include looking at both the gendered constraints and burdens that female psychologists experience at work, the sexism they encounter in the work place, and the sexualised gossiping and propositioning that they can be subjected to. This chapter will also discuss the coping strategies that female psychologists employ in order to navigate working in the prison. These are split into two distinct forms: armouring and avoidance both of which result in differing forms of both emotional and emotive labour.

The final chapter explores the both the central paradox of being vulnerable adjuncts of power and some of the implications of the core findings. This paradox reveals that the formulations, experience, and even awareness of power are often more multifaceted than we like to think. It is often the case in criminology, and wider discourses, that those who wield power within coercive environments are cast as uncomplicated, reductive, villains. However, what is clear from the experiences of the psychologists who appear in this book, this narrative of simple impositional power and coercion is much more complex than this. Many of those interviewed had never even considered that they themselves were powerful. This may be as a result of varying forms of denial or neutralisation but it nevertheless indicates a more confounded picture than we are often presented with.

In terms of the implications of this work I explore these in some depth. For instance, it was evident that the divergent practices of the differing types of psychologist meant there was not really a unified psychological practice. This presents a distinct set of consequences for the management of psychological services within the late-modern prison where the 'treatment industry', of which they are a significant component, has become increasingly politicised. A further issue that arises is from the identification of work place stress and the bullying and harassment that staff can experience and what this may mean for rates of attrition (Rayner, Hoel, & Cooper, 2001). Following on from this is what the reality of this experience tells us about the institution's duty of care towards their staff. Lastly, as all good academic texts tend to do (!!) I will recommend directions for further research. The research that underpins this book was largely generative in nature and as such suggests a number of further areas of research as well as a number of discrete hypotheses which could be explored. However, before we get to that, there is a story to be told …

Chapter 2

Disciplinary Capital: Forensic Psychology, Power, and Expertise

> Experts? I … erm, I don't really think of myself that way. No.
> Though, I suppose we … we are in a way.
> 　　　　　–Forensic Psychologist with many years of experience

Expertise is a complex issue. In their book *Rethinking Expertise*, Collins and Evans (2007) argue that there a great many facets and levels of knowledge attainment and performance which interact in order to produce what we think of as an 'expert'. Nevertheless, they point out that for an individual to be considered a specialist in a particular field (what we often think of as an expert), they must have attained a tacit interactional and contributory knowledge that goes beyond the ubiquitous knowledge of inductees within that field. More importantly, they then must be sought out, due to that interactional and contributory knowledge, in order to communicate that knowledge to expert others. They note that this communicative element is a fundamental aspect of how we consider, and confer, expert status. In this chapter I will set out the predicates of forensic psychological expertise, how this relates to the concept of disciplinary capital, and how this latter concept relates to the broader social and penal trends we see reflected within the late-modern prison.

In recent years it seems that we have once more become beset by distinct positivistic notions of human behaviour which have re-emerged into both the social and penal landscape. Something of a frustrating state for those of us that have spent years challenging and deconstructing Lombrosian legacies on the nature of man and 'criminal man'. However, from under their rocks such ideas have crept, crawling amongst us and infesting our societies once more. Here in the United Kingdom, we have seen those who believe in, and promote, racist Social Darwinism and Eugenics employed within the Prime Minister's office.[1] Here was an individual who was employed to advise on issues as diverse as immigration policy, the welfare system, and penal policy before being forced to resign (not before being backed by the Prime Minister's office it must be noted). Who would have thought that these legacies of the early 20th century which led to such misery

---

[1] See report here: https://time.com/5785400/boris-johnson-andrew-sabisky-race/.

Forensic Psychologists, 11–28
Copyright © 2021 Jason Warr
Published under exclusive licence by Emerald Publishing Limited
doi:10.1108/978-1-83909-960-120200003

and horror would, once more, gain a foothold in the popular, political, public, and penal imagination? Yet, here we are.

Whilst a seemingly extreme example it is nevertheless the end of a spectrum of thought that has, evidently, gained ground in our public discourses. These positivistic influences have shaped the evolution of a 'treatment' industry throughout the world which has, necessarily, infiltrated and influenced modes of penal policy. The idea that we can make 'criminals' better has, in the last 30 years, dominated. The concepts of rehabilitation, reform, deradicalisation, and a range of other 'correctional' signifiers abound within the dull, concrete walls of our prisons. More specifically, we see these ideations, delivered simply as if they are unproblematic, in the contemporary criminal justice system. This is because such conceptions have become inherently embedded by creating an entangled relationship between risk, the management of deviance, and specialised discourses. It is here we begin.

Medicalisation of Society and Deviance

The history of forensic psychology in the British penal context is closely tied to the wider processes of medicalisation of deviance in contemporary Western societies. Conrad (2007) notes that the processes of medicalisation within society were emergent in discussions on the conceptualisation and 'treatment' of deviance which arose in the 1960s (see also Pitts, 1968). However, these processes were far more prevalent in society than just in the realm of deviance and social control (Conrad, 2007). Quoting the work of Clarke, Shim, Mamo, Fosket, and Fishman (2003), he argues that the expansion of the sociomedical jurisdiction into areas of public/private life has been one of the most fundamental changes to Western life to occur in the last century. He argues that this expansion of jurisdiction has resulted in progressively more areas of social life and greater numbers of citizens coming under the purview of expert and professional medicalised discourse. Medicalisation processes, and indeed the development of a treatment industry, involve three fundamental practices: the first is when nonmedical problems are 'defined in medical terms' (Conrad, 2007, p. 5); the second is when they are 'understood through the adoption of a medical framework' or lens (p. 8); and the third is when these issues attract, or are treated with, a 'medical intervention' (p. 9).

Allied to these processes come associated forms of research and the evolution of treatments which only consolidate the pathologisation/medicalisation of the particular human problem (Gatens, 1996). For example, Bowles, Gintis, and Osbourne (2001) in their discussion of earnings and workplace productivity note that workplace behavioural dynamics are increasingly defined in terms of medicalised criteria, so a behavioural treatment/intervention industry now dominates in this sphere. In that field you hear talk of 'unhealthy' and 'toxic' working environments, which can be 'treated' with particular forms of managerial 'interventions'. It is the specialists and consultants who can advise and train staff and managers in these 'interventions' who charge premium fees in order to help a company have a more healthy (i.e., productive) workplace. See too the everyday management practices in the neoliberal university – mindfulness anyone?!

This new reality leads to Conrad's (2007) final point in that his identified tripartite process often results in both the dominance and the privileging of the medicalised discourse as it offers vested groups (companies, institutions, society, etc.) both a means of identifying and classifying the problem and then providing the means of treating it. These are the processes of discursive power discussed by Foucault in his seminal text *Madness and Civilisation* (1967). However, as with Foucault's discussion of madness and perceived deviancies, the processes of medicalisation are not always without controversies. For instance, as Bayer (1987) and then D'Emilio (2002) discuss, before an eventual divorce, the relationship between homosexuality and medicalisation (especially in relation to the American Psychiatric Society) has been long, bitter, and particularly controversial.

The entanglements of deviance with notions of medicalisation are far more dense, intricate, and compounded, especially with regard to criminality, than with most other social or human problems (Conrad & Schneider, 1992). They, along with Timmermans and Gabe (2002), note that the medicalisation of crime and deviance can be clearly linked to the growth of neopositivistic movements in the study of crime. Herein classification, aetiology, and treatment of criminality become the fundamental goals (Newburn, 2007) which further entrenches these medicalisation practices. This establishes 'regimes of truth' and significant modalities of power when it comes to who can, and who cannot, 'diagnose' deviancy and treatment (Foucault, 1994c). Whilst Conrad and Schneider (1992) give a number of examples in order to emphasise their point, including opiate addiction/treatment and delinquent hyperactivity and treatment, perhaps their most compelling account is the relationship between notions of the 'born' criminal and the control of crime through medicalised interventions.

The distinct shift from a classical ontology, the criminal as rational actor, to one where psychological, neurological, and even genetic processes are deemed the causes of crime allows for the medicalisation process (Conrad & Schneider, 1992). This is because these factors are, *a priori*, perceived as existing within a medical realm and therefore the solutions to these causes are to be found in the medical interventions that the related research fields can produce. It is here that we see the traces of Lombrosian (Lombroso, 1876) positivism as it permeates through into more modern and quasi-scientific ideations of what crime is, who the criminal is, and how we ought to treat them. Though early biological positivism has been largely discredited (Gibson, 2002), it has given rise to both the notions that the 'criminal' is an objective and distinctive 'type' as well as an entity that can be studied scientifically. We see this influence through from the early biological works of Dugdale (1877), who posited that crime was hereditary after his study of the Jukes family, to Lange's (1931) study on twins in *Crime as Destiny*, in the psychologically positivist work of Yochelson and Samenow's (1976) *The Criminal Personality*, and to the more contemporary Developmental Criminologies that we see today.

The defining characteristics of positivist criminology, whilst somewhat controversial and contested (Bottoms, 2000), have some overarching ontological and epistemological themes. These include the adoption of a purported scientific method, notionally drawn from the natural and physical sciences. Crime becomes a distinct and objective phenomenon that is 'capturable' via investigation. Crime is caused by some distinct factor, or set of factors, that lie beyond the mere rationality of the individual. Criminality is likely to be determined if these factors are present but not mitigated. The criminal is different from the noncriminal, and criminality can be reduced, or mitigated against, if the criminogenic factors which lead to it are treated by an appropriate intervention (Tierney, 2010). In this sense, the links between positivist criminology and the medicalisation of deviance become clear.

Sim (1990), drawing heavily on the historicism of Foucault, conducted an analysis of the advent, entrenchment, and promulgation of medicalised practices within British prisons from the late 18th century through to the late 20th century. Like Foucault (1979) and Ignatieff (1978), his choice of a historical method allowed him to challenge extant notions that the reforms that the prison had undergone (including the introduction of a prison medical service) in the period concerned were solely benevolent in nature or effect. He focussed particularly on the following themes: the notions of discipline, regulation, and exclusion, which are integral to 'medical' disciplines within carceral institutions, and the ways that these relate to the wider issues of regulation and struggle in society (Sim, 1990). He notes that medical practice within the penal setting evolved as a further means of achieving the control concerns of the establishment. He argues that, as with all professional groups who staff institutions, their presence is a direct consequence of a burgeoning structure of discipline. Such structures fragment and individualise the prisoner population into entities who are sorted, accounted for, and controlled. The introduction of medical staff to the prison further consolidates and entrenches extant processes of fragmentation because of the individuated documentation, personal focus, and penetrative surveillance on both body and mind. However, at the same time as individualising the prisoner through practice Sim notes that it also homogenises them into a single narrow 'offender' category (which includes subsets of 'offender' identities) which denies the reality of their individuality and subjective experiences.

Much of the 'discourse' that envelops medical practice in prisons is concerned with employing their specific advice and expertise in order to achieve the 'normalisation' of those confined (Sim, 1990). This trend is particularly true of forensic psychology where much of the practitioner literature, as well as formal discourse, is either predicated on practices and theories of change or evaluations of those practices (see Adler & Gray, 2010; Bartol & Bartol, 2015; The British Psychological Society, 2010; Gavin, 2014; Pakes & Winstone, 2007; Watkins, 1992 etc.) This 'normalisation' involves diverse practices geared towards creating or moulding, echoing Goffman (1961), the 'model individual' who will conduct themselves according to the prescribed precepts of the institution and medical discourse. Here Sim follows Foucault's (1975) reasoning that it is the 'professional expertise' of the medical practitioner upon which their power and authority is predicated and it is through the tools of examination, assessment, and treatment that the disciplinary and controlling aims of the prison can be achieved.

A further issue that both Sim (1990) and Foucault (1963, 1975), and to a lesser extent Conrad and Schneider (1992), discuss is concerned with the experience of those subject to the medical power in the contexts that they address. They conclude that these forms of power are experienced more keenly than straightforwardly physical forms of power because the process of examination, assessment, and treatment is far more individual, penetrating, intrusive, and psychologically controlling than what occurs with physical domination. Foucault (1963, 1975) argues that these types of discourse open up aspects of the incarcerated to forms of observation and regulation that were not previously known. In essence, they create or become involved in a form of 'panopticism', whereby not only is the body of the prisoner observed and controlled but so too is the psyche. The second reason is that it categorises and classifies the individual, affecting both the manner in which the individual behaves and the way that others act towards them. When people are assigned labels by accepted 'experts', this will inevitably affect the manner in which others perceive and engage with them, and eventually effect the way that the individual sees themselves and acts within the group (Lemert, 1972; Moncrieffe, 2007). However, these processes are not just limited to those who are subjected to the inspection of medical and psychiatric expertise. In the contemporary prison those who are subjected to discourses concerned with the double-headed Hydra of risk and rehabilitation also experience these intrusions of power.

Power, Knowledge, Expertise and the Prison

The very purpose of the prison, as well as the clinic and mental health institutions (Foucault, 1979, 1963 see also Foucault, 1994a), is engendering control and compliance in those captured within its stony embrace. Of course, this control and compliance has both intramural (within the wall) and extramural (without the wall) components. After all, the prison does serve the political economic interests of the State. Nevertheless, all entities that operate within the penal institution must, in some way, serve the interests of that institution. This means that those entities are all, in some way, engaged in processes that facilitate that control and compliance. Of course, these end states are predicated on a nexus of interconnected and intersupporting modalities of disciplinary governance. These differing modalities influence, coerce, manipulate, induce, and change the individual who is subject to the purview of the institution. Foucault notes (1979, p. 179) that the *'very rationale of a disciplinary system is that of correction'* – or indeed normalisation (see also Mathiesen, 1990). Professional, or expert, discourses are privileged within the institution because it is through these discourses that the interests of the institution are achieved and legitimated. Therefore, what occurs is an interdependent form of discursive power that is both privileged and self-perpetuating. Here, then is Foucault's main contribution to the analysis of power within both society and institutions. Utilising notions discussed by Rogow and Lasswell (1963) in their treatise on language, politics and corruption, Foucault argues that power is not just grounded in the merely physical and spatial but in the manner in which discourses are constructed, communicated, adopted, and adhered to. Power is inherent to systems of knowledge. In this sense, power is related to both 'knowing' and 'communicating' – those with power are those who know (or are able to know) and who are listened to because of their knowing – what Collins and Evans (2007) define as the basis for the formation of the expert or the authority. In terms of crime and the prison, Foucault locates the psychiatrist/psychologist as being the focal point of developing modalities of power in the carceral setting in the 19th century as they bought to bear their rationalities of knowing, as well as their preordained authority, on the issues of crime and deviance (Foucault, 1994c).

Systems of knowledge which permeate and influence the prison (security, risk, rehabilitation, education, offending behaviour, etc., see Ugelvik, 2014) are multifarious and conjoined to the physicality of coercion and force, as well as the manipulative influences of inducement and incentive (Mathiesen, 1965). Distinct systems of knowledge are all accompanied by corresponding specialists (experts) whose role is to both communicate and embed their particular disciplinary (corrective) discourse within the prison. Think for a moment of the role and status of Security officers within the prison and their role in centralising that securitised knowledge into the quotidian routines and rituals of the prison. This occurs because they occupy both a very powerful and a very privileged position due to their knowledge of the prison's security processes, weaknesses, and vulnerabilities which threaten the good order and discipline of the prison conjoined with their 'expertise' in intelligence work, surveillance, and investigation which mitigates those threats. The combination of these factors cements both their role and the importance with which that role is perceived within the lifeworld of the prison.

Yet securitised knowledge is not the only discourse which serves the interest of the prison. There is a confluence of other discourses operating within, and shaping, the institution. Thus, the prison itself then becomes a site constructed from, as well as one constantly constructing, these penal and disciplinary discourses in order to control those who are subject to its power. It is beholden on the institution, and thus the matrices of disciplinary discourses utilised within such spaces, to collapse the distance between the interests of the institution and the interests of those subject to it (Robert, 2009). This is how the notion of discipline is defined within carceral settings and how the functionality of systems of punishment become established. These discursive influences are not only designed to change/normalise the prisoner but also necessarily act as a means of imposing, or reinforcing, ideations of norms on those who are the arbiters of those matrices of power.

In prisons, these issues are starker and more visible than with other institutions. The modes of coercion and direct power within the institution become more evident (Sim, 1991). Yet these do not supplant the other forms of discursive power that exist within the carceral space, rather they bolster their influence and penetration (Crewe, 2009). An example of this is the growing acceptance of the practice of, or need for, coerced 'offender' rehabilitation in carceral locations (See Burdon & Gallagher, 2002; Day, Tucker, & Howells, 2004; Douglas, 2014; Goldsmith & Latessa, 2001; Murphy, 2000; etc.) and the role of treatment 'experts' (including psychologists) in the delivery of coerced offending behaviour interventions. This literature is concerned with utilising the more coercive elements of the carceral state in order to effect change in recalcitrant offending populations. The logic is predicated upon two core arguments: firstly, that disciplinary incarceration is both morally and legally justifiable; and secondly, that if correction via incarceration is justifiable, then so too are other forms of intervention designed to affect the same changes in the 'offender' population. The notion here is that disciplinary power, whether it be physically carceral or discursive in nature, is legitimately administered in achieving a normalising affect for those people perceived/defined as being deviant and offending. Here it becomes evident, via both the processes of medicalisation of deviance and the manner in which psychological discourses have become inherently subsumed into the disciplinary discourses of the prison, that the role of the contemporary forensic psychologist is one that is power-laden (Crewe, 2009). Theirs is a position that enables them to constrain or intervene, coercively or not, in the lives of prisoners to achieve some desired change.

Traditional commentators on power in penal settings often, and rightly, turn to descriptions of force as the underlying form of social power that is evident behind the wall. This tends to be the case because, as both Wrong (1995) and Clegg (1989) argue, force is typically characterised as the implementation of negative *physical* sanctions in order to prevent or constrain the action alternatives of a subaltern (see also Lukes, 1986). In any penal setting, the 'usual' subaltern in question is the prisoner and the 'usual' principle is any member of staff who necessarily wields some form of authority over that prisoner. As will be discussed, however, the loci of control within power relations are often transient and less dyadic than this. This simple binary notion of power is somewhat proscriptive, especially as those staff who are in the employ of the prison are also 'subject' to the power and authority of the institution itself. Yet previous accounts of power in prisons tilted heavily towards the force and coercion that uniformed staff could bring to bear (Dahl, 1957, 1968; Hepburn, 1985). Often this force and coercion was based around the conjunction of physical security and situational control measures employed within the particular prison (Carrabine, 2005). Nevertheless, as Carrabine (see also Sykes, 1958) argues, force as a means of control is both impractical and exponentially expensive. As such, the carceral institution must adopt or adhere to other forms of control (Scott, 2007).

Modes of control and discipline that focus on the psyche are less resource-intensive and thus become more attractive to the institution. Fiscal concerns aside, they also have greater efficacy in serving the interests of the prison (Foucault, 1979). Prison life in the 1970s and 1980s was characterised by a sense of heightened and enforced security where power relations became profoundly dominated by indices of both *physical* and *mental* discipline, surveillance, and control (Sim, 1991). Force was not solely viable and thus other forms of control emerged and eventually became entrenched. Hepburn (1985) notes that these forms of control are concentrated around six forms of power that are utilised by prison staff: coercive power, which is predicated on systems of force or punishment; reward, which utilises processes of inducement; legitimate power, which here relies on processes of signification; exchange, which involves appeals to utility; expertise, which relates to forms of professional authority; and respect, which is predicated on personal authority and emotional entanglement.

It is important to note here that systems of expertise are signifying formulations of dominance. Domination involving expertise occurs when specific cognitive symbols are organised into formal epistemes that give some party the ability to constrain the behaviour of some other party. This is similar to Gramscian processes of cultural hegemony (Gramsci, 2011), in which control works through cultural formulation. Within such formulations, designated individuals become experts because of the specialised knowledge (Stoddart, 2007) or skill, and others defer to them and their knowledge (Scott, 2001). The power relation here is determined not by the position that someone may hold within a command structure (signification), their personal authority (respect) or what processes of inducement (reward) can be brought to bear but by trust in the specific and specialised knowledge, or skills, that person has. The classic exemplar of this is the power relation that exists between a doctor and a patient. The authority of the doctor is based upon the trust that the patient has in the specific specialised medical knowledge that the doctor has. Any order is heeded not by any reasoned assessment of the order, or its normative content, or who the doctor is in a structure of authority, but because of a substantive trust that the subaltern has in the expertise of the principle (Scott, 1996; Wartenburg, 1990).

A consequence of this is that subalterns are rendered passive agents by their lack of the specific technical or specialised knowledge. In terms of this research then, the power associated with forensic psychology is predicated on the symbolic weight of the signifiers utilised within psychological discourse. This is the site of their expert power. Mann (1986), Wartenburg (1990), and Wrong (1995) note that discursive formations of expertise tend to result in formalised institutions that are organised around the particular specialised, or technical, knowledge. Institutions constructed around a specific episteme become monopoly holders of that knowledge, and the inculcated members of those institutions become both the expert purveyors and gatekeepers of that specialised knowledge (Foucault, 1963, see also Scott, 2001). It is thought that structures of domination based upon professional authority (expertise) are experienced far more positively by subalterns than in structures involving coercion and inducement (Etzioni, 1961; Giddens, 1982). However, as Beetham (1991) points out, whether or not a person experiences a structure of domination based on expertise positively or negatively depends largely on location, context, and the trust or investment that the subaltern has in the expertise of the principle. Furthermore, as Haugaard (1997) notes, if a subaltern is subject to a system of expertise where the 'professional' decisions made concerning them are overtly paternalistic, have negative effects, or where no effective recourse to those decisions exists, then even the system of expertise will largely be perceived and experienced in much the same manner as a coercive system – illegitimately.

Crewe (2009), investigating the contemporary prison and building upon themes discussed by Liebling (2004), found a very different penal landscape, characterised by very different power relations than traditionally described. Although 'hard' forms of power still existed within the prison he studied (inevitably so), they were no longer the prevalent factor in shaping staff–prisoner relationships. In fact, he found that in many ways the uniformed body felt powerless and enervated within their own establishment (2009). The type of collective power that characterised uniformed culture in the past (Crewe, 2009), and in some circumstances elsewhere, did not exist here. Crewe (2009) found that officers were 'sidestepping' their active duties by retreating to and depending upon formal bureaucratic means of control. This effectively meant that the responsibility for the control of inmate behaviours on the wing was diverted towards mid-level and senior management (Crewe, 2007). A compounding factor in this reality has been the imposition of neoliberal political economic policies of austerity that have impacted the contemporary prison, and the wider criminal justice system (Allen, 2013), in England and Wales in the last decade. The logics of economy of scale utilised, and the later benchmarking exercises undertaken, by the prison service's governing body in order to reduce costs led to a significant reduction in front-line staff. As I have discussed elsewhere (see Warr, 2014), such a situation led to an increase in staff diffidence. This created a vicious circle where, in a circumstance of heightened threat, staff began to retreat from the direct policing of the further reaches of the prison wing to 'safe' spaces (wing office or staff areas). This then resulted in a consequential vacuum of directed power in the front stage arena of the prison. That led to increases in prison violence and underlying threat, which then led to further staff diffidence, further retreat, further violence, and so on. This further entrenched the peculiar situation that the effective power relation that prisoners had was not really with the prison officer with whom they had daily, if sporadic, contact but with remote, powerful others that they had little or no contact with (Warr, 2008).

This introduces a new notion to carceral power relations. Ordinarily power in social interactions is theoretically characterised by a dyadic relationship – adjunct and subaltern (Wrong, 1995). However, as Castells (2013) points out rarely are social relationships this simple (also see Bachrach & Baratz, 1962). He argues that increasingly with the dominance of organised networks in societal construction, social relationships cannot be discussed in terms of dyadic relationships due to the inherent interaction of multiple actors. He further argues that, in any organised grouping, triadic power relations are much more likely because within networks discursive influences are not usually held directly by a principal actor – they are both more fluid and transitive. In contemporary organised networks discursive power is often passed through, or communicated by, intermediaries (see also Haugaard, 1997; Kasperson et al., 1998). Returning to Crewe's (2009) analysis, it is evident that he is describing a triadic power relationship occurring where the wing staff act as 'conduits', or 'transmitters', of the power held by the managers (principles) and deliver it to the prisoners (subalterns). Consequently, as wing staff were acting as 'conduits' and not principles, the harder forms of power that were usual to historical and traditional prisons now no longer existed in the same way. Crewe discovered that 'softer' forms of power were the most prevalent forms of power employed within the establishment and therefore underscored every power relation that prisoners had with staff (Crewe, 2007, 2009; Warr, 2014).

In geopolitics, soft power is defined as those forms of power which *can* constrain the actions of subaltern parties without resorting to the negative physical sanctions which hard forms of power rely upon (Nye, 2004). In penological terms, the importance and role of soft forms of power have been noted before. Mathiesen (1965), though not specifically using the term 'soft power', nevertheless discusses the importance, role, and impact of processes of power within prisons that do not rely upon coercion, manipulation, or inducement. As Dias and Vaughn (2006) note in criminal justice agencies, especially the prison, these processes of power are often bureaucratic in nature and as such are experienced indirectly and are not necessarily any more benign than harder forms. As Crewe (2009, 2011), echoing Sim's (1990, 2008) sentiments, highlights, often this 'soft' power had far-reaching consequences for prisoners, was more insidiously controlling, often inconsistent, confusing, bred a new range of frustrations and 'pains', and was incontestable.

A further pertinent aspect of contemporary penal power lies in the fact that the effects of power are often deferred with, potentially unanticipated, consequences of perceived rule infringement coming at much later points of the sentence. Prisoners in Crewe's (2009) study noted that being *'killed off on file'* (114), with the attendant negative impacts that this could have on their IEP status, job, home leave, parole, and carceral life represented a far more potent, constraining, and painful form of power than the more straightforwardly physical forms of the past (see also Crewe, Hulley, & Wright, 2020).[2] This notion of power being manifest through files and reports characterises a major penal and societal shift (see Cane, 2016) in the last 30 years. The bureaucratisation of authority within the modern prison, a direct consequence of neoliberal penality and New Public Management impositions on disciplinary governance (Carlen, 2005), is an example of the expansion and entrenchment of a Foucauldian-type discursive structure. This 'governmentality' (Foucault, 1978) enmeshes those within the prison (both prisoners and staff) within a wide-ranging, yet largely abstracted and hidden, penal reality that both governs and records the behaviours of those within the institution. Within such structures, power is both manifest and evidenced through the control of the processes by which information is transmitted, amplified, and disseminated (Habermas, 1981; Kasperson et al., 1998). Power in the context of this process is dependent on who is in control of the transmission acts and what they can achieve through the transmission/amplification process. It is evident, however, that the greater the symbolic connotation, and in this sense that means 'expertise', and interactivity, to the information being transmitted, the more probity and capital it has in terms of serving the interests of the prison.

Here we see the fundamental nature of *disciplinary capital* – the more a discursive structure serves the interests of the prison, the more disciplinary capital is attached to the product or outputs arising from that discourse. Here the notion

---

[2]The Incentives and Earned Privileges scheme is a mechanism of formal distribution of privileges based on wing behaviour and adherence to imposed sentence plans. There are three core levels: basic, standard, and enhanced. This model of prisoner governance was introduced in the mid-1990s and was given a more punitive overhaul in 2014. See Incentives and Earned Privileges (https://www.justice.gov.uk/prisoners/psis/prison-service-instructions-2013).

of disciplinary capital is adapted from Bourdieu's (1986) notion of symbolic capital – any nonembodied (or doxic) asset that transmits some quanta of authority (see also Chase, 1954). In the prison, disciplinary capital relates to those products or artefacts, of information and data, which communicate some symbolic connotation that achieves the disciplinary constraints the prison both seeks to impose and is constructed from. Returning to the point being made above, the greater the disciplinary capital of the information being produced, the more it becomes incontestable within the scriptural economy (de Certeau, 1988) of the institution, and the more likely to produce significant consequences. Here the scriptural economy is based in, and is perpetuated by, the bureaucratic mechanisms by which information is managed, stored, and transmitted. This is the dynamic process by which discursive power becomes implemented and disseminated within the contemporary prison. However, once expert discourse is disseminated throughout an institution, it does not dissipate, instead it becomes an embedded aspect of the lifeworld, the cognitive backdrop which informs the experiential reality (see Habermas, 1981, 1990), of those who inhabit the institution. Lukes (1974) notes that power, in any of its formulations, increases its potency when it is unobserved or undetected. The more expertise becomes embedded into the lifeworld of the prison, the greater its symbolic interactivity, the more hidden and abstracted the modalities of power become, resulting in a greater transitive affect and a deeper penetration in the mind of the individual. Here Foucault's (1979) *Panopticism* becomes a penal reality – the power of the institution and its various discursive modalities infuse, or colonise (Weaver, 2009), the lifeworld of the prison and become entrenched within the minds of prisoners. However, as Tait (2011) notes, these processes are not solely related to just the prisoner but also impact on the prison officer.

Here, then, we have wide-ranging and intangible indices of power, operating at the symbolic level, that are formulated from notions of medicalisation of deviance, the construction of bureaucratic control, the entrenched role of the expert, and a new understanding of power that moves beyond the traditional dyadic forms. These combine to create a situation whereby contemporary penal power is diffused throughout the lifeworld of the prison and is constantly being transmitted and communicated by those other than the principle adjunct. Disciplinary discourses, underpinning the bureaucratic mechanisms of the prison, trade in disciplinary capital and their power then becomes incontestable but can have both severe and deferred consequences for those who are subject to those varying modalities of power. It is now time to examine in a more explicit manner the relationship that psychologists in the prison have to power.

Psychology, Power and the Prison

It is evident when looking at the history of psychological services (see the next chapter) within the prison system of England and Wales that there has been an evolution of service and practitioner that mirrors that of the technologies they employ. Not only has penal ethos and psychological practice gone hand in hand but also has the enmeshing of the discursive structures of power that define them. Crewe (2009) reports that many prisoners in his study identified psychologists as a particularly powerful group within the prison setting. These prisoners expressed both suspicion and anger towards forensic psychologists due to the perceived role that they played in the parole/decategorisation process and thus the carceral lifecourse of many. However, Crewe's research reveals a number of deeper, though related, causes for the antipathy that prisoners hold towards their forensic assessors. The first of these is concerned with the discourse-laden labels, and their symbolic weight, given to prisoners and their behaviours. As was discussed by Sim (1990), Miller and Rose (1996) as well as Conrad and Schneider (1992) and Conrad (2007), medical, and other expert, discourses lead to more constraining forms of power because they categorise, label, and pathologise the individual via the symbolic language of their discourse. As classic labelling theory posits, this affects the manner in which the individual perceives themselves and is in turn perceived (Becker, 1963; Moncrieffe, 2007). Two factors that affect the perception of the 'labelled' are the symbolic connotation (in this sense the disciplinary capital) given to the labels they have attached to them and the level of dramatisation given to those labels when communicated (Ng & Bradac, 1993).

Pathologized 'offender' labels, as constructed categories of professional discourse, do not relate specifically to the substantive offender but are instead the basis of the prisoner simulacra, a constructed ideation of a prisoner, mentioned by Carlen (2008). Prisoners are categorised or 'imagined' in such a way that they become reified in terms of the categories they are assigned. This is particularly the case where the modalities in question are designed for actuarial and auditable purposes. Prisoners become defined in terms that are measurable as opposed to those which have subjective relevance. The more potently imposed identities, in terms of symbolic connotation and the penality-laden lifeworld of the prisoner (see Weaver, 2009), are those associated with the disciplinary discourses (or discursive penalities) of risk and rehabilitation. As Hannah-Moffat (2005) argues, prisoners in the modern penal era become transformed into individualised risk subjects, whereby their needs become both conflated and imbued with ideations of criminogenic risk. In effect, the identity of the prisoner becomes entwined with notions of risk and this carries a great deal of symbolic weight within the disciplinary-laden lifeworld in which prisoners are ensnared. In such a risk-infused lifeworld, the concept of rehabilitation becomes the mechanism by which that risk is shed (Warr, 2019). Here then, rehabilitation is not a process of positive change, what we tend to think of in our folk perception of the term, but rather a means of assuaging or even mitigating risk; and as such, it becomes a disciplinary lens of judgement.

Much of the anger towards psychologists that Crewe (2009) identified is due to the fact that it is they, more than any other reporting 'expert', who play the biggest role in both the official 'identity' construction of the prisoner and the communication of that identity to others. It is forensic psychologists and their specialist knowledge who create the most significant lens through which prisoners are viewed. For prisoners, psychology reports have the greatest disciplinary capital. This is due to the fact that the 'labels' (riskiness or rehabilitatedness) ascribed by psychologists, due to the symbolic connotation with which they are imbued, are both more 'adhesive' than those ascribed by other reporting members of staff and are designed to achieve the prisons disciplinary objectives. Also, as a communicative and discursive mode of power, their 'labels', or knowledge, have greater transitive impact as they are not constrained by the physical boundaries of the prison. In fact, the labels imposed by the psychologist render the wall of the prison semipermeable in that these can influence both parole and decategorisation decisions made by external others (see Bowers & Friendship, 2017) and can follow the prisoner out into the world beyond, impacting on their very future. Inevitably, this places some prisoners in conflict with the disciplinary discourses to which they are subject (even if they accept the veracity of them) because of the implications they carry (Sim, 1990).

Authoritative structures only adhere to risk-related modalities of power (Douglas & Wildavsky, 1982; Renn, 1992), when to do so directly furthers the interests of the controlling authority (Habermas, 1990). Resistance to these modalities will inevitably provoke reactions from the authoritative structure in order to counter, mitigate, or even subvert the resistance (Barnes, 1988). Even if negative physical sanctions are not bought to bear, other mechanisms of countering and subversion often are. Mathiesen (1991), highlighting how 'rehabilitation' is a further mechanism of control, shows how interconnecting modes of disciplinary power are used to constrain the prisoner – if he/she/they do not adhere to the normalisation process of one modality to which they are subject, then they become judged through the lens of another, and remain in moral abeyance. It then behoves the prisoner to navigate these labyrinthine discourses in order to find a way back to both institutional and societal acceptance. Each nonadherence results in different modalities of power being brought to bear on the prisoner (Foucault, 1979). In effect the more the prisoner resists the forms of power to which they are subjected, the more they challenge or reject the labels assigned to them, the more enmeshed within the structures of power they become, and the more disciplinary discourses are focussed upon them.

This is evidenced by the difficulty that prisoners face when trying to challenge or resist psychologically informed, and symbolically weighty, labels. As Crewe (2009, 2011) notes, though it is possible for prisoners to challenge the labels imposed upon them, it can be potentially hazardous to do so (even when commissioning external experts (see Forde, 2018)). If for no other reason, their lack of induction into the complexities of the discourses within which they are enmeshed can often result in them reaffirming the labels ascribed to them. This results in them becoming ever more deeply ensnared within the laminated disciplinary discourses of the prison. However, a further aspect of psychological power within the prison comes from the self-reinforcing nature of the symbolically laden labels that it utilises. Darley and Gross (1983), and later Kassin, Dror, and Kukucka (2013), discuss how confirmation bias can be endemic in forensic settings. Fundamentally, the process involves a circularity in applied logics so that once a label has been ascribed and recorded, then future analyses begin at the point of that label. For instance, if a prisoner is classified as being violent or having substance misuse issues, or something more symbolically potent such as scoring high on a psychopathy test, then this forms the basis and starting point of any future assessment. However, as these authors highlight, this process inherently biases towards confirmation (see also Martin, 1994 on the Rosenthal Effect).

However, Darley and Gross (1983) go further and also note that this confirming bias can be communicated to others – in this sense it is the weight or probity (disciplinary capital) of the label which then influences the manner in which others perceive the individual under assessment. With each iteration of the assessment, the greater the information becomes 'amplified' and the 'symbolic connotation' densifies resulting in the deepening of the confirmation bias (see also Neal & Grisso, 2014). This then is the mechanism by which diagnoses become inescapable – as Sim (1990) notes once the psychiatric/psychological gaze is focussed upon a prisoner its conclusions stick. A further issue of bias is with regard to the notion of objectivity and forensic psychological assessment. As was hinted above, forensic psychological practice has evolved significantly, even in the last 20 years. Assessments are now more rigorous than was once the case and individual clinical bias was, supposedly, written out of the tools utilised by the contemporary prison psychologist. However, as the experiments of Murrie, Boccaccini, Guarnera, and Rufino (2013) highlight, forensic psychologists and psychiatrists are potentially subject, when deploying 'objective' risk tools, to allegiance bias in adversarial settings. The authors found that forensic practitioners tailor their interpretations dependent upon the interests of those who commission their services. This is true whether it be for the court system or in custodial settings. A combination of these biases results in a situation where psychologists in the employ of the prison are, without intention, entangled in processes that serve the interest of the prison and reaffirm conclusions wrought by their own expertise.[3]

The 'adhesiveness' of the conclusions that prison psychologists can draw and the inability of the prisoner to effectively challenge them become a focal point of contention. Add to this the fact that those psychologists were likely to be located off-wing and therefore inaccessible, and that their power is also both indirect, with deferred long-term consequences, and being largely unknowable (see Atrill and Liell, 2006), all result in the anger discussed by Crewe (2009). As he argues what prisoners are responding to here is both the '*all-encompassing*' (p. 126) nature of the psychological gaze and the form and reach of the power attached to psychological expertise within the prison. As Foucault (1994a, 1994b) argues, medicalised knowledge, such as the discourse of forensic psychology, insists upon more and more of the prisoner being exposed to inspection, she/he/they become not an individual prisoner but a risk subject whose behaviours, interactions, and life need to be known, judged, and controlled. Resistance to psychological/psychiatric conclusions becomes counterproductive as it only reaffirms diagnoses and results in the prisoner needing further intervention (Foucault, 1979; Sim, 1990). Thus,

---

[3]For further criticisms that are specifically focussed on psychological services in prisons in England and Wales, see Forde's (2018) *Bad Psychology: How Forensic Psychology Left Science Behind.*

within extant penal hegemonies forensic psychology, risk and its related discourses (rehabilitation) are tools by which the perceived aberrant populations, with which they are concerned, are controlled (Hood, Rothstein, & Baldwin, 2001; Massumi, 1993).

One further source of resentment is the distinct lack of what Crewe (2009) refers to as neutral forms of intervention (see also Crewe et al., 2020). He points out that many of his prisoner participants expressed deep concerns with regard to mental health issues, personal traumas, and childhood events but yet had little opportunity to explore such issues outside of the formal structures, and the labelling/stigmatic disciplinary power to which they are subject. There is no confidentiality clause underlying the relationship between psychologist and prisoner – whatever is said by the prisoner is not only subject to reportage but also storage. This generates a fear of having information, in the form of a psychology report, which can be perceived as negative being placed within the prisoners 'file' (see also Towl & Walker, 2015; Warr, 2008). Crewe argues, in concurrence with Hannah-Moffat (2005), that the system, through such practice, removes any kind of benefit for the prisoner because whatever concerns were raised by them would quickly be 'subsumed into institutional discourse' and would then be 'transformed from needs to risks in the interests of public protection' (Crewe, 2009, p. 120).[4] This situation also creates a distinct trust gap at the heart of the relationship between psychologists working in prison and those people with whom they work – a trust gap that is defined by the power of the psychologist and the powerlessness of the prisoner and a trust gap that defines just how that relationship is perceived by the people confined to the prison.

The Keepers of the Gate

However, the resentment, and to some degree the trust gap, discussed above does not just originate from within the walls but also from without. Over the last two decades, it has been evident that the discourse of forensic psychology, with its particular and rather narrow quants based notions of methodological rigour, has been tasked with a 'gatekeeping' role. As Stevens (2019) discusses in her article exploring the political and ethical interference into research on sex in prisons in England and Wales, when it comes to the type, scope, and form of research that is undertaken within the contemporary prison estate, forensic psychologists have become established as agents of control. It has become standard protocol for research applications to be submitted to the National Research Committee

---

[4]To some degree this issue has been recognised, and an attempt to alleviate the problems associated with mentally disordered prisoners has been made with the advent of the prison 'in-reach' teams supplied by local health care authorities. These teams are designed to provide the type of care that those suffering with ill mental health, and who are not subject to sectioning, would receive in the community (OHRN, 2009). The recognition of this problem took place in the late 1990s and early 2000s (see HMPS/NHS Executive, 1999). However, widespread and affective in-reach services have been difficult to achieve and often they have been overwhelmed by demand.

(NRC) via the IRAS online system. The Committee is populated by forensic psychologists as well as analytical and business consultees. Even at local level, applications are passed from the NRC to the Area Psychologist and to an establishment's psychologist team for review.[5]

This has arisen partly because of the wide range, and sheer scale, of requests for research that every establishment receives. Due to this, the psychologists, rather than the governing Governor, are charged with filtering these requests and to judge the merits of the research, the suitability of the methodology, and the benefit of the proposed project to either the individual establishment or the wider prison service. As these psychologists note

> Psychologists are by most part the research access points to prisons and regions and I think it is about trying to manage that and not only demonstrate the importance of good research but also make people aware of the damage bad research can do as well

> We get a lot of research requests here at [omitted] ... a lot. It is our job to filter these and find those one or two which are well designed, ethical and will be of benefit to [HMPPS]

They are charged with this duty due to the position and disciplinary capital attached to their perceived expertise. Their very discourse, their positionality, their training, and their professional development means that they are the single body of staff within HMPPS who are suitably qualified to undertake this role of assessing the utility of research projects; if not necessarily the varied methodologies that such research frequently entails. However, it goes beyond that mechanical process of evaluation to one in which they are also those most able to protect the institution from 'troublesome' (Stevens, 2019) or challenging research. This is a flip side of the disciplinary capital produced from their 'expert' status. Ordinarily this is geared towards furthering the disciplinary interests of the institution, but in this regard, it is focussed upon protecting the institution from an external gaze that may be critical of, or which may represent a threat to, the interests of the institution.

Many of those interviewed noted that it was up to them to make sure that research conducted in their prison was '*up to standard*' and '*robust and ethical*'. One even went so far as to suggest that they were the only suitable people to judge research applications because '*as psychologists we have a comprehensive understanding of ethical research where others ... errrm where others don't*' – an interesting perspective. Others noted that it was their responsibility to ensure that the research that was approved, and those researchers granted access to the prisons they represented, '*served the interests of the prison and the governor*' or at the very least would not '*rock the boat too much*'. For many of those interviewed, these attitudes were extensions of, or were incorporated within, their wider ideology of public protection. For many, protecting the institution became conflated with

---

[5]See PSI (22/2014) for details on Research Applications.

protecting the public and was indicative of just how entangled their profession had become with the power inherent to their penal status. The motivations of others of having this institutional first ethos were less clear, unfortunately, the data gathered do not allow me to explore that in any more depth. Nevertheless, what is certain is that this institutional and professional role of judgement and barring does create a great deal of resentment and hostility towards forensic psychologists from beyond the prison wall.

A compounding issue, especially with regard to a trust gap, that became evident in discussion with the psychologists who participated in this study was that for many of them, though they were rigorous in employing their expertise in their gatekeeping role for those external to their field, they themselves had bypassed this scrutiny when it came to conducting research in prisons. Some had managed to conduct empirical research in prisons for their undergraduate degrees in psychology and a number specifically spoke about having done their masters degrees in prisons too without having gone through the NRC or IRAS application process (even though these processes had been in place at the time of their studies). A further two had spoken of allowing university psychology students in to do research under their gaze also without having gone through the normal protocols. For the individuals themselves, they described a situation whereby their supervisors, who had been prison-based forensic psychologists, secured them access to their prisons, as volunteers or assistants, in order to conduct research. These three psychologists explained

> ... so one of the lecturers was a psychologist in a prison, a local prison, so I went there one day a week pretty much for the whole time that I was there. Did a lot of the mundane data entry and the stuff that you do as a volunteer to benefit them but then the flip side was when I did my dissertation, I was able to access the prison population there to do my research

> My supervisor arranged access for me ... I got to work in the prison and then whilst there got to do my research ... [they] sorted everything. It meant I didn't have to go through the NOMS application process, I could just ... do the research

> Yeah my supervisor helped a lot. They got me into the prison they worked in, by the back door as a volunteer, so I could do my research on the sex offenders who were there ... I didn't have to do the application ... um the NOMS application ... and that made it much easier

One of the psychologists interviewed even noted that this backdoor access was an ongoing one when they stated that their department would always help psychology volunteers from a local university to do research in their institution in exchange for help with the mountains of administrative work that their department was being buried beneath. Here we see a seeming collusion between the psychology departments in question, and to some degree the hosting prisons involved, in facilitating this practice. However, the psychologists who spoke to this issue did not seem to perceive any double standards or hypocrisy in allowing this access to psychology undergraduates and MSc students but denying it to others. In fact, it was often these very psychologists who were most vociferous about the need for them to monitor, assess, and deny access to external others. There seemed to be a number of underlying, and not entirely justified, assumptions about forensic psychology, its methodological rigour, its ethical practice, and the research conducted by their brethren/sistren (home team) that made this okay. Correspondingly, there were a number of equally unjustified assumptions being made about the methodologies, methods, ethics, and research practices of those from other academic/practitioner disciplines. In many ways such assumptive positions seemed jarring considering their professional attitudes in other regards but, given the embattled and redoubted position that many expressed, perhaps such in-group subject bias dynamics are inevitable.

Chapter 3

Risk, Rehabilitation, and the Development of Forensic Psychological Services

> You've seen plate spinning, right? Often that's what its like being a psychologist here. Trying to keep lots of different plates spinning whilst each of the … errrm pole thingys are getting all tangled up! That's what I do on a day-to-day basis.
> –Psychologist with 7 years' experience

One thing that you may have noticed thus far is that a core theme of this book is entanglement. The fundamental discussion of this book involves an entanglement of experiences of individuals who inhabit our prisons. The influence that underpins the expertise and power of forensic psychologists is an entangled matrix of discourses and interests. Likewise, the development of forensic psychological services within the prisons of England and Wales is one of an entangled evolution. As the ideas of risk and rehabilitation steadily became defined in terms of each other in the wider criminal justice system (the latter has become very much the medium of mitigating the former (Warr, 2019)), so they became enmeshed with the professional discourse of psychology in the contemporary prison. The development of forensic psychological practice cannot be divorced from these two ideations – just as those ideations cannot now be disentangled from the practice of forensic psychology. As the quote above notes, the quotidian working life of forensic psychologists also involves an entangled mess of tasks and duties that are often being done against a backdrop of administrative and temporal pressure. Therefore, in order to understand the now of prison psychology, you need to understand how these varying entanglements arose.

Thus, the primary aim of this chapter is to explore the genesis of psychological services within the Prison Service since the Second World War and rise of what has become known as the 'treatment industry'. Secondly, it is important to have some understanding of what the 'industry' looks like in praxis. As such, there will be a brief overview of the day-to-day practices and roles of forensic psychological work in the contemporary prison. However, and this is because this becomes important in later discussions of how individual psychologists experience those practices and roles, there will be some exploration of other prison staff cultures

Forensic Psychologists, 29–53
Copyright © 2021 Jason Warr
Published under exclusive licence by Emerald Publishing Limited
doi:10.1108/978-1-83909-960-120200004

and the emotion work that the prison necessitates. Prisons are, if nothing else, emotionally laden environments (Crewe, Warr, Bennett, & Smith, 2014), which impact on the work and lives of all who exist within their asperous murality. If you are already familiar with much of this material, then please do feel free to skip ahead to the next chapters. Some of the detail here is essentially important to our tale but is, I admit, not the most thrilling of reads.

However, before beginning in earnest, it must be noted that at the time of the fieldwork, psychological services within the Prison Service were going through a structural reorganisation. This process involved moving from a localised to a regional model of service delivery, which impacted on the experiences of many of those interviewed and was a significant source of interest for some and worry for others. However, due to the vagaries of the structuring and management of the prison estate, this changed model of service was not implemented as fully as was originally planned. A familiar plot twist to those with any experience or knowledge of the prison estate in England and Wales. There have also been a number of subsequent changes that psychologists in the employ of the Prison Service have had to contend with. These have included changes to service delivery, operational requirements, the prison population (distinct changing cultures, age profile, substance misuse issues, violence, sentence lengths, etc.), governance structure of the institutions, technologies, crises (on top of crises on top of further crises), and parole diktats, serious case reviews, and a much politicised penal landscape. Whilst this upheaval does have some pertinence to some of the experiences outlined in the rest of this book, the majority are concerned with more general and lasting themes that relate to the lived experiences of prison psychologists that derive from that set out below.

The Development of Psychological Services

At present, and for much of the last three decades, the Prison Service, and what was the National Offender Management Service ((NOMS), now HMPPS) has overwhelmingly been the major employer of forensic psychology graduates in England and Wales (The British Psychological Society, 2010; Forde, 2018). Here they are employed, whilst working towards their Chartership (see below) and once qualified, within prisons, young offender institutes, Prison Service HQ, probation, HMPPS and the Ministry of Justice, fulfilling a number of roles that will be discussed below. There are currently, at the time of writing, just over 500 forensic psychologists employed to deliver services across the 117 public and private sector prisons of England and Wales (Ministry of Justice, 2018).

The role of forensic psychology in prisons in England and Wales and the entrenchment of risk discourses into the criminal justice setting are symbiotically conjoined. In fact, the expansion and solidification of contemporary psychological practice within prisons has the same genesis as that of risk discourse. However, the early history of psychology in prisons was, as noted by Gudjonsson (1991), based around the employment of psychologists, from the late 1940s onwards by the Prison Commission and later by Prison Service HQ after the commission's dissolution in April 1963, in mainly occupational or organisational roles (Crighton & Towl, 2008). For example, the majority of psychologists employed in this period were engaged in staff training/assessments and other forms of vocational assessment or analysis. The exceptions to this were the applied psychologists employed, across the estate and especially in Young Offender Institute (YOIs), to provide the extremely limited clinical and counselling services that existed then (Towl, 2004).[1]

This post-war period was also the era in which the mode of penality now known as penal welfarism came to the fore, despite a massive expansion in the number of people being committed to prisons and borstals. A defining characteristic of penal welfarism was the entrenchment of the belief that prisons should not merely punish prisoners but also rehabilitate them (Soothill, 2007). The concept of disciplinary change became formalised within this era, and many of the operational aims and expectations began to refocus on mechanisms of achieving this. As with many other changes that occurred to the penal landscape in this era, the fundamental role of the psychologist employed by the Prison Service also began to change. This was due to four interrelated forces. The first of these was the growth of what is often referred to as 'the risk society' (see Beck, 1992a, 1992b; Giddens, 1990, 1998; Luhmann, 1993; Massumi, 1993) and the impact this had on our criminal justice systems, the second was the advent of, and neoliberal obsession with, New Public Management (NPM) ideals (Clarke & Newman, 1997), the third was an emergent forensic and correctional psychological infatuation with the risk, needs responsivity model (and related assessment technologies) proposed by Andrews and Bonta (1994), and lastly, a more overt Public Protectionist agenda that evolved into a rallying point for the Blair, New Labour government (Garland, 2001). These forces coalesced to produce the fertile political and ideological earth from which the contemporary psychological service (industry) emerged.

We cannot underestimate the manner in which the fetish for 'risk' permeated and shaped both the civic and judicial landscape in the United Kingdom and elsewhere (Adams, 1995; Lupton, 1999). As Hudson (2003) argued what arose in this era was a risk orientated and 'justice-careless' ethos that carefully and insidiously moulded criminal justice practice. The concept of 'risk' became the paradigmatic focus for all public and criminal justice agencies. With regard to the prisons of England and Wales, this created a new awareness of, and the development of a subsequent need for, the Prison Service to be able to identify and manage risks as they presented within its systems of governance (Home Office, 1959). One of the first indicators of this shift and the envelopment of these risk

---

[1]It is interesting that though many of the psychologists employed within YOIs in this early period provided counselling services, this was not their main function. In fact as Towl (2004) points out, it is only in recent times that a dedicated counselling service has been operating within prisons; and even this is mainly focussed within the women's estate. The introduction of in-reach teams, which are based in the local Primary Care Trust, has redressed this issue somewhat – though it is still the case that demands far outweighs supply.

ideations was, after the key Mountbatten Report (Home Office, 1966) and the Advisory Council on the Penal System – chaired by Leon Radzinowicz (1968), the establishment of an estate-wide categorisation system. This led inevitably to the need for the adoption of processes in order that the dangerousness of prisoners could be accurately assessed and the appropriate categorisation assigned. It also, in the face of the growing 'nothing works' miasma (Cavadino et al., 2019), created a need for the service to provide accountable and efficacious 'rehabilitative' interventions for prisoners that could mitigate the 'risks' those people represented. This of course established the link between risk and rehabilitation which meant that within the criminal justice system, each concept necessarily became defined in terms of the other (more on this later).

In order to meet these varying disciplinary and risk-related needs, the Prison Service turned to those psychologists that were already based in their prisons (Pakes & Winstone, 2007). This is really the first instance, set against a background of concerns based upon public safety, whereby prisoners were being assessed by psychologists for risk so that they and their offending behaviour could be managed (Hudson, 2003). However, even though this had begun to occur throughout the penal estate, and especially in higher security establishments, the numbers of psychologists employed by the Prison Service were still fairly modest. By the early 1980s, there were fewer than 150 applied psychologists in the employ of the Prison Service (Towl, 2004). Not every prison had a psychologist to call upon in order to assess prisoners for security classification; and even where there were 'prison psychologists' to call upon, the risk assessment technologies available to those psychologists were limited (Andrews & Bonta, 1998).

In those early days, the risk technologies that were available to the prison psychologist were based upon clinical assessment/prediction and were dependent upon the individual knowledge, expertise, insights, experience, biases, and, if we're being honest, guesses of the psychologists concerned (Hurst, 1998). These (first generation) risk 'technologies' were largely inadequate, leading to inaccurate, misleading, and largely unsatisfactory results (Bartol & Bartol, 2015). Then came a second generation of risk technologies which were based upon simplistic actuarial tools designed to offer descriptions of the probability of future offending based upon known historical factors. Once again, these technologies proved to be problematic as they were underpinned by an ecological fallacy – whereby inferences about the nature of an individual's risk were abducted from inferences about the risks represented by the group to which the individual belonged. This ecological fallacy was inescapable and thus warped the assessments being made, often resulting in unsupported, rigid, and temporally, as well as geographically, specific results that were not designed for the type of extrapolations that the risk assessment of prisoners required (Clear & Cadora, 2001; Hannah-Moffat, 2005; Swets, 1988). There were also serious ethical and legal issues surrounding this burgeoning risk assessment process due to, in the early-to-mid 1990s, some psychologists being pressured, by their prison employers, into hastily providing assessments, utilising inadequate risk technologies, that would cover an unlimited time frame and hold across an unspecified range of penal and nonpenal environments (Crighton & Towl, 2008) – something that not even the most sophisticated contemporary risk assessment tool would be able to do. The requirements of the institution to measure and mitigate risk were then creating a coercive environment for psychologists where unethical practice was being imposed.

Throughout the 1980s, the numbers, as well as the role, of psychologists employed throughout the Prison Service had remained fairly static. However, this began to change during the early 1990s. In a wider societal context, NPM became a means of reformulating the capitalist state where welfare provisions could be modernised in line with the dominant neoliberal political ethos (Clarke & Newman, 1997). The ideology of NPM resulted in private and corporate management practices being introduced into public services, introducing and entrenching cultures of auditing and budget management and outsourcing of auxiliary services. To a degree, the implementation of these managerialist practices was the neoliberal response to the Adam Smith Institute's Omega Project from the 1980s which had posited the privatisation of all nonlegislative/executive government functions on fiscal grounds (ASI, 1983).

In terms of prisons, managerialism – as well as introducing the notions of opportunity and responsibilisation for prisoners – also inculcated an adherence to, and a belief in, strategic planning, budgetary obedience, target-setting, and performance measurement (Liebling, 2004). All of this resulted in a prison system obsessed with measurable processes and performance auditing. Such processes have led to an entrenchment of what de Certeau (1988) refers to as a 'scriptural economy', whereby written formats of communication become a defining element of an institution. These scriptural economies create systems of bureaucracy that fundamentally underpin the institutions operations and demand ever more specialised 'experts' to feed and manage that bureaucracy. With regard to psychological practice in British prisons, the dominance of NPM led to an explosion in the numbers of psychologists (somewhere in the region of 1000 at their peak) being employed within the Prison Service between the mid 1990s and the early 2000s, as well as a change in their working ethos and practice (for further discussion see Forde, 2018).

Primarily, this occurred for two reasons: the first was that as 'risk notions' became entrenched within the scriptural economy of the prison, and the prison population grew exponentially, there was ever greater need for an adequate number of forensic practitioners across the whole estate to provide auditable risk assessments. The second was the belief amongst the prison authorities that forensic psychologists were needed not only to monitor but also to deliver the psychologically designed/informed cognitive behaviour therapy (CBT) programmes that had begun to proliferate (Crighton & Towl, 2007). These programmes came about specifically as a result of the studies that came in the wake of the 'What Works' debate of the 1970/80s (Martinson, 1974) and the consequent commitment to evidence-based practice in forensic psychological services (Adler, 2004; McGuire & Priestly, 1995). In and of themselves they offered a tangible (auditable) mechanism for the mitigation of prisoner risk, and thus were attractive to institutions operating with a disciplinary infused scriptural economy.

Massumi (1993) argues that one characteristic of the modern risk society is the prevalence and promulgation of both promoted risks and risk reducing products, which is echoed in the notions of societal medicalisation already noted (Conrad, 2007). In this sense the risk technologies and subsequent psychologically informed interventions, which have a great deal of disciplinary capital, can be seen as risk assuaging consumables offered by a forensic psychological industry. Here the prisons, and by extension the government, create a market demand as they become the consumers of risk assessing and risk assuaging products (Stenson, 2001). A wide range of these 'interventions' were particularly attractive to the new Chancellors of the prison scriptural economy as they offered a quantifiable element to the previously unquantifiable practice of prisoner rehabilitation (Stenson, 2001). Thus, the criminologically/ psychologically positivistic 'treatment industry' was born, and a 'hooked' product needing/dependent institutional 'user' created. However, and rather ironically, this also led to the downfall of rehabilitation in prison as a process of self-recovery/change. Instead rehabilitation became, first and foremost, a means of mitigating risk within the scriptural economy of the prison/criminal justice system. This is most clearly evidenced by the fact that what was often being quantified was the number of intervention completions and not the effectiveness or suitability of the intervention for individual prisoners (Hannah-Moffat, 2005).

Many of those psychologists in this generation tended to be adherents to Andrews and Bonta's (1994) ideological 'risk/needs responsivity' approach to psychological practice, captured in their seminal work on *The Psychology of Criminal Conduct*. They were also largely influenced by the dominant just deserts/ rehabilitation penalities that characterised the period (Garland, 2001). This ideological approach lay at the heart of this generation's psychological approach and as such they became both the progenitors of, and the public advocates for, their discipline developed CBT, and cognisant, based interventions in the treatment of prisoners (Towl, 2004). It is also this generation of psychologists who were responsible for the rapid expansion as well as professionalisation of psychological services within the Prison Service of England and Wales. However, one of the unforeseen consequences of this rapid expansion of psychologists in the 1990s was that the service became swollen with trainees as opposed to Chartered psychologists as one long serving psychologist interviewed for historical context noted:

> … massive recruitment over a very short period of time of lots of trainee psychologists who we then could not cope with, could not train properly. That probably was about the mid-90s too. Even since that has happened, we have had this imbalance with far more trainee psychologists than qualified psychologists.

This imbalance has been maintained, though an equilibrium is slowly beginning to emerge. However, this generation though creating this problem also pushed for and set up the forensic division within the British Psychological

Society (BPS, 2010) and moved to influence the managerial structure of psychological services within the prison estate as a whole, developing the Area Psychologist position and entrenching evidence-based practice to their profession. It is also with this generation that we moved away from the old 'prison psychologist' label, which by the mid 1990s had become something of a pejorative to the more accurate and professionally sounding forensic psychologist (Crighton & Towl, 2008).

A further contributing factor was the development of third-generation risk technologies by these nascent forensic psychologists. As was noted previously, the first and second generations of risk technologies, though greedily consumed by penal institutions, were largely inadequate for purpose (Bartol & Bartol, 1999, 2015). As such, improvements and developments in risk assessment technologies were the subject of much psychological research throughout this period. These third-generation assessment tools involved multilayered procedures and considerations which overcame some of the problems that had beset the previous technologies. Of course, the ecological fallacy which haunts their utility remains. As Forde (2018) highlights, even the best of these risk technologies has a 70% accuracy rate at the population level and even lower success rates at the individual level. However, what underpins, and thus separates them out from previous technologies, is that they involve separate yet interrelated stages that demand that the practitioner be specific in defining the variables related to each stage of the process (Crighton & Towl, 2008). This process enabled forensic psychology practitioners to conduct more thorough, penetrating and (to some degree) reliable risk assessments which have a higher chance of holding true across varying circumstances, geographies, and times. Regardless of efficacy, what is important in noting is that the contemporary penal system has become not only dependent upon these technologies but also enmeshed in their utilisation. They have such disciplinary capital, and have become so entrenched in the disciplinary logics of the prison, that they are now a central facet of prisoner management. These factors have resulted in an overreliance on behalf of the prison authorities in their psychological staff that almost guarantees that the historical trend of recruitment will continue (Towl, 2004).

Lastly, one factor that has undoubtedly impacted on this entrenchment of psychology services is the increased workload that came with the overt emphasis on public protection that occurred with the introduction of the Criminal Justice Act 2003. As Garland (2001) notes, the principle of public protection is nothing new to criminal justice policy and legislation more broadly. In many ways, public protection is their raison d'être. Nevertheless, the advent of the Criminal Justice Act (2003) represented a more overt centralising of public protection ideals, not just in the intent of the legislation, but as a goal in and of itself. This has, of course, been subsequently amended and replaced in certain regards by later legislation, especially the Criminal Justice Act of 2010 and the Legal Aid, Sentencing and Punishment of Prisoners Act (LASPO) of 2012, but nevertheless it was the provisions under the 2003 Act that influenced the working reality of the forensic practitioners interviewed for this study. However, each of the Acts has added to the burdens/workloads of forensic psychologists. The major consequences for the forensic psychologists in this era were in the types of sentence that came under their remit. The 2003 Act introduced a specific, and immensely problematic, indeterminate sentence entitled: Indeterminate Sentences for Public Protection (IPP). Those with IPP sentences, and those given either life or Her Majesty's Pleasure sentences, come under the remit of the Parole Board. However, they will be given what is essentially a 'tariff', a minimum period of incarceration, which they will have to complete before becoming eligible for release. These IPP sentences created a population overload for the Parole Board (2013), for psychologists, and probation working within prisons and the community. There are still many thousands of people serving an IPP sentence, most of whom are well beyond tariff (Ministry of Justice, 2020). LASPO (2012) largely abolished the IPP sentence and replaced it with an automatic two strike life sentence. As a result of these political and legislative machinations, the prison estate now has just under 10,000 prisoners serving some form of indeterminate sentence, compared to less than 3,000 in 1992 (MoJ, 2020). This then means that not only has the workload increased for the Parole Board but also for those who are tasked with advising or guiding the Board – a role which particularly falls on the shoulders of forensic psychologists.

Finally, the 2003 Act introduced, and subsequently reinforced in later legislation (see Easton & Piper, 2016), reforms whereby decisions relating to both the sentencing and release of those prisoners either on, or likely to get, parole-eligible sentences will be, for the first time, subject 'to the same risk-based criterion' (Shute, 2007). The uniform risk-based criterion that is referred to in the 2003 Act was the Offender Assessment System (OASys). This is important to note, for it impacts upon the role and duties of those forensic practitioners employed not just within the Prison Service but the whole of HMPPS. There is, however, something of a bifurcation in the role of assessment here entailed. At the presentence stage, the OASys assessments largely fall within the remit of the probation officer who is assigned the case whilst it still sits with the court. However, at the point whereby an offender comes before the Parole Board, both seconded and home probation officers as well as the forensic psychologist will complete aspects of the OASys report.[2] Of course, OASys is just one of the risk tools that are employed by forensic psychologists. There are, in fact, a great number of differing tools employed (more on this below). However, the point really is that the varying Criminal Justice Acts described here then have had three consequences that must be taken into consideration. These are the types and increasing numbers of sentenced person that are required to be subjected to varying risk assessments; the presumption of dangerousness already attached to those prisoners, and the need for this to be assessed, managed, and mitigated; and the format of the assessments that are now required by the Parole Board.

---

[2]Field Notes – direct information from a senior HMPPS psychologist.

Historical Structure[3]

Traditionally forensic psychologists were recruited and employed by individual establishments in order to fulfil, or provide, those psychological services which those establishments required. Whilst it may be true that not every prison had, under this traditional format, a psychological team in residence, it was the norm, for most prisons at least, to have a forensic psychologist on their books. In prisons, and young offender institutes, classified as training establishments, for instance, it would usually have been the case for there to be a small team consisting of a Principle psychologist, a Senior psychologist, and a number of psychological trainees and/or assistants. Here the Principle psychologist who would be qualified, or chartered, would often be the head of the department. These titles changed over time as it was recognised that historically many of those referred to as 'Senior', whilst may have had extensive experience would not necessarily have been fully qualified and were thus somewhat misrepresented (Towl, 2004; see also Forde, 2018). The Principle psychologist would manage the day-to-day running of the unit, oversee the work and training of the trainees, ensure the effective implementation and delivery of services, and ensure that the prison's psychological key performance targets were being met. The trainees, those working towards their Chartership, would be involved in providing the psychological work of the department such as the delivery of programmes and conducting various forms of risk assessment. The psychological assistants would be employed to aid in the running of the department as well as facilitating on programmes.

The department in each establishment would then be subject to the authority of the psychological services team based at the regional head office, under the auspices of the Area Psychologist. These regional offices are largely determined by geographical location and in most circumstances accord with the governmental structures, or offices, in those areas. However, Crighton and Towl (2008, pp. 21–22) note that the offices of the Area Psychologists were created in order to provide 'a national network of senior and experienced practitioners' who would fundamentally be responsible for providing both the prison and, later, probation services with '… leadership in the strategic organisation and delivery of psychological services'. The office of the Area Psychologist performs a number of roles such as ensuring the implementation of policy handed down from head office, providing an advisory role on local policy decisions, and an 'on-call' service for the management of serious incidents (hostage situations, mutinies, etc.) within prisons in their region. However, perhaps their most important role, within the traditional model of day-to-day psychological service delivery, was their role in ensuring both that psychological staff are utilised appropriately within the region and that appropriate supervision, training, and support exist for trainees.

One further role that the Area Psychologists perform is that of acting as both a bridge and a filter between psychological services, the Prison Service, and the research community. It was recognised that the professional and academic

---

[3]Much of this following description was communicated to me via those nine individuals responsible for the development of psychological services in this period.

expertise that was held at the regional offices, and indeed within the applied unit's themselves, could provide an invaluable resource for the Prison Service at all levels. This acknowledgement of the expertise held within regions, which could provide a wide range of expertise and skill sets, would prove an important factor for the intention to move towards a stricter regional model of service delivery. In this regard the Area Psychologists also became the primary contact points for all research matters relating to the establishments within their purview, whether they be internally commissioned or external requests. This 'gatekeeping' role was an important development for the Prison Service as it enabled them to not only keep a track on what research was being conducted nationally but also allowed them to introduce a national approach to external research requests. This gatekeeping role also cemented the disciplinary capital of these psychologists. Not only did their assessments and pronouncements confer symbolic potency to the interests of the prison but also their monitoring and evaluation of external research protected the institution to any academic/discursive challenge to those interests. In many ways this both cemented the discursive power of psychology in terms of the contemporary prison estate and also provides the evidence for the disciplinary capital of forensic psychology.

The authority structure of psychological services was thus pyramidic in nature. As the Area Psychologists governed over those employed within the establishments in their regions so too were they answerable to a narrowing authority structure above them. This was fundamentally, from 2000 onwards at least, the office of the head of psychological services for prison and probation based, initially as part of HMPS within the Home Office, and then, after the establishment of NOMS, and from 2017 HMPPS, within the Ministry of Justice. This office, and indeed this position, was created in the wake of the organisational and professional changes that were taking place within the prison and probation services throughout this period. However, the role and purpose of this office was, as instructed by the Prison Service's senior management team of the time, to enforce a more cohesive approach to the design, development, and delivery of psychological services across the penal estate. A further concern was to ensure that such services were 'in line' with the broader penal policy dictated by the Minister for Justice and the head of the Prison Service/NOMS/HMPPS.

Staff Cultures and the Experience of the Prison

Culture can be defined as the coalescence of a number of particular commonalties that bind humans together in the creation of distinct forms of sociality (Carrithers, 1992; Godelier, 1986). These can include specific beliefs, rituals, and practices, where these are located, who is inculcated and included, who is rejected and distanced, language and vernacular, shared symbolic understanding, mores and values, etc. (Boyd & Richerson, 2005). Fundamentally, culture is what arises from the production of, and informs the maintenance of, the behaviour and thinking of distinct groups. As Crawley (2004) notes, there had been an increase in focus on culture in both occupational and managerial literature throughout the

1980s and 1990s as profit generating institutions had sought first to understand the staff they employed and change the cultures they produced (for instance, see Deshpande & Webster jr, 1989; Dellana & Hauser, 1999; O'Reilly III et al., 1991). As a result, research on the nature and form of staff culture has become a mainstay of contemporary organisational literature. However, despite this widening inspection of staff cultures more generally, it is still relatively novel for prison staff cultures, which are often of 'low visibility' (Liebling et al., 2011, p. 2), to benefit from the sociological gaze.

Nevertheless, there has been consistent progress in the study of certain staff cultures within carceral settings. Perhaps the most studied staff group is, understandably, the prison officer (for instance, see Arnold, 2016, 2005; Crawley, 2004; Liebling et al., 2011; Tait, 2011; Nylander, Lindberg, & Bruhn, 2011). The reason for this degree of inspection is the centrality of the prison officer to the social and institutional world of the prison. They play multiple roles and perform multiple functions within the prison – from guardians of the peace (Liebling, 2000), enforcers of regulatory order (Robert, 2009) through to bureaucratic negotiators (Crewe, Liebling, & Hulley, 2011) and much more. However, other staff cultures have also been subject to investigation: prison governors/managers (Bennett, 2016; Bryons, 2008; Liebling & Crewe, 2013) and even prison health and drug workers (Kolind, Frank, Lindberg, & Tourunen, 2015; McDonald & Fallon, 2008; Walsh, 2009). However, what makes the study of prison staff unique in terms of researching staff cultures is the peculiarity of the setting – the prison. As Crawley (2004) notes prison work takes place in what is largely a domestic setting; just one that is infused with the power of the state. It is then the very nature of this intimate but yet formal, domestic but yet civic, site that both shapes the creation of staff cultures and how the prison is experienced by those staff.

Lambert et al. (2009) argue that in organisational contexts it is not only the institutional which impacts on stuff cultural development but also the materiality of the work experience. The *where* is as important as the *what* in terms of the forms of sociality open to staff. In some ways, this follows the logic presented by Bourdieu (1990) in his presentation of the habitus – the sociocultural habitat that a person occupies which shapes the manner in which they think, act, and behave. Fundamentally, the individual and the forms of sociality open to them are shaped by their habitus. Toch (1992) makes a similar point with his ecological analysis where he notes that there are environmental concerns that combine to create the climate of a prison which can govern the experience of prisoners. The same is true of staff – habitus/environment/ecology is central to the manner in which they experience the prison, the timbre of what cultures they produce, and the specifics of the sociality that they can and do engage in.

To return to the point made by Crawley (2004), the habitus of prison staff is one of symbolically laden and power infused constrained domesticity and therefore becomes one that is necessarily intimate, personal, and relational in nature and this means that prisons are 'emotional work environments' (Nylander et al., 2011, p. 470). As is argued elsewhere (see Crewe et al., 2014; Warr, 2014) what shapes or informs prison experience and cultures is the emotional geographies with which the carceral space is comprised. The prison is not a homogenous social space; different areas of the prison are designed for different purposes and activities, and as such each different part of the prison evokes different interactions and is thus experienced differently. Lefebvre (1991) notes that social spaces are produced by the interaction between people, the physicality and artifice of the space, and the environment evinced therein. The specificities of designed space (for example, a segregation unit of a prison) and the directed interactions that can occur within them necessarily produce particular emotional (and sensorial (Herrity et al., 2020)) contours which shape the emotional experiences that take place. Emotions are then a fundamental aspect of the penal environment as they not only shape the social and interactive geographies of the prison but also inform the relational timbre in any given penal space. These emotion zones are navigated continuously. Therefore, both staff and prisoners must engage in varying forms of emotion management in order to successfully exist, navigate, and operate within the constrained domesticity of the contemporary prison.

Emotional management is labour which '… requires one to induce or suppress emotions in order to sustain the outward countenance that produces the proper state of mind in others' (Hochschild, 1983, p. 7). Walsh (2009), following on from Mann and Cowburn's (2005) studies of nursing, in her study on forensic nurses working within prisons, utilises this concept of emotional labour in order to describe much of the emotion work that staff must undertake in order to successfully navigate the working environment. She describes emotional labour as involving one, any, or all of the following three behaviours: the faking of emotions that are not felt, the hiding of emotions that are felt, and the 'performance of emotion management in order to meet expectations within the workplace' (Walsh, 2009, p. 145). She argues that emotional labour is important to understand as it impacts on the ability of forensic nurses to provide care effectively in the penal context, their ability to engage in their professional practice, the coping strategies that they are able to develop and their subjective emotional wellbeing. She notes that there are four key factors that contribute to the emotional labour experienced by forensic nurses: firstly, the relationship that they had with the prisoner patient; secondly, their relationships with their co-workers; thirdly, their relationships to and with their host institution; and lastly, the internal conflict that arises due to the divaricated discourses of care and custody that they must engage in (Dale & Woods, 2001) – what in the psychological field is referred to as the 'dual-relationship' problem (Greenberg & Shuman, 1997).

Before moving on to discuss emotional labour more widely, it is important to discuss in greater depth the issue of dual relationships as it is a core element to all psychological work in prisons and other places of confinement. Greenberg and Shuman (1997) explain that this issue arises due to the conflict of roles that forensic psychologists and psychiatrists can experience when undertaking competing roles in adversarial or correctional settings. They argue that there is an inherent conflict when 'conducting client-focussed therapeutic psychological work' (p. 50) whilst at the same time 'detecting risk and upholding security principles as prioritised within highly politicised correctional settings' (p. 51). There are a number of potential consequences to this conflict from professional and emotional dissonance (derived from irreconcilable therapeutic aims and carceral practices) to diminished therapeutic outcomes and, of particular concern, ethical blindness.[4] Trotter and Ward (2013), and previously Ward and Syverson (2009), define ethical blindness as when practitioners become blind to the consequences of their actions due to the particular professional lens through which they perceive their practice. In this sense, forensic practitioners can cause the individual with whom they work great harm because the institutional lens (clouded as it is with disciplinary interests) through which they perceive the prisoner 'blinds' them to the negative consequences of their actions. They argue that this is a particular problem where there are involuntary clients, where power differentials are significant, and when the profession is uncritical of its own practice. It must be noted that this 'blindness' is distinct from Bauman and Donskis (2013) notion of moral blindness which arises from the technologies of knowing employed by the powerful in the liquid modern society. For Bauman and Donskis, moral blindness arises where these technologies of knowing result in an insensitivity to the very human which is to be understood. This blindness occurs because of the conceit of those who profess to know and their assumptions with regard to the probity and incisiveness of the technologies they employ. This goes beyond just not seeing the consequences of one's profession to not seeing the person with which that profession is concerned. Thus, we have two forms of blindness, one concerned with ethical implications of practice and the other of an insensitivity to the very people subject to the professional's gaze.

A significant example of this is the role that forensic members of the American Psychological Association played in the development, execution, and monitoring of the torturous Enhanced Interrogation Techniques used by the United States and allies in various military theatres in the wake of the 9/11 attacks (see Hoffman et al., 2015). Fundamentally, the psychologists were performing two functions here: developing and monitoring the use of techniques in live interrogations as well as monitoring the 'well-being' of those being tortured. It is clear from this report that notions of national security and the supposed risks of individuals had so ethically and morally blinded the APA and allied psychologists that they perceived no wrongdoing. Despite the core principles of their professional practice, they were uncritical of, and in many instances complicit, in torturing and harming individuals perceived as a national threat. Here then the dominating discourses that the psychologists were serving also acted to blind them to their ethical duties of care in these instances. This is an extreme example. However, as is evident in the report, this ethical blindness and the dual-relationship issue described by Hoffman et al. have their roots much more in forensic psychological discourse and practice *per se* rather than the vagaries of an extreme setting – a fact that should ring alarm bells for any psychologist operating in any carceral or disciplinary setting.

Gannon and Ward (2014) note that for psychologists working in the prison, the risk/needs model of service delivery can greatly exacerbate the problems of the dual relationship – in particular the issue of ethical blindness. They argue that the

---

[4]See Hothschild (1983) for a further discussion of emotional or emotive dissonance.

risk-needs-responsivity model (Andrews & Bonta, 2010), which has come to dominate correctional and forensic psychological practices, results in exactly the kind of ethical blindness discussed above because it prioritises risk, security, and disciplinary concerns as if they were therapeutic concerns (see also Haag, 2006). The conflation of these issues means the interests of the prison, and the criminal justice system more widely, are put above that of the prisoner with whom they work (see also Greenburg and Shuman (1997)). The forensic practitioner then becomes 'blind' to the actual therapeutic needs of the prisoner because they are unable to serve both masters as it were and therefore privilege the interests that most closely resemble their own – even at the expense of best practice. However, for Gannon and Ward (2014) and Ward (2014), what is of greater importance is that there is an acquiescence to the dual-relationship problem which constitutes a crisis because it erodes both the integrity of the professionals in the field and damages the efficacy of the discipline. The dual-relationship issue thus creates a number of distinct, and potentially severe, problems for forensic psychologists working in prison.

Returning to the notion of emotional labour more generally, Nylander et al. (2011), in their study of prison officers in Sweden, note that just as the prison is not a homogenous space, prison officers cannot be thought of as a homogenous collective. It seems an obvious point but people do seem to have a tendency for committing such compositional and/or divisional fallacies (Broyles, 1975). Anyway, as the authors note individually officers will interact with, and experience, the prison in different ways. Therefore, the emotions experienced and emotional labours engaged in are somewhat subjective despite there being both formal (organisational) and informal (cultural) feeling rules for prison staff to regulate emotion. They also note that prison officers do not always perform the same tasks and roles as their peers and as such differential practice in different institutions and carceral spaces can lead to different emotion responses and thus differing forms of emotional labour. Utilising Hochschild's (1983) notions of surface and deep acting, they also describe the differing levels of emotional labour that may be engendered by prison work when practice in these carceral spaces either adheres to or conflicts with the feelings and mores held by the individual prison officer. These varying types of emotion zone then required different types of emotion regulation (surface or deep acting) and therefore differential formulations of emotional labour by prison officers.

Rupert and Morgan (2005), following the work of Farbar (1990), in their study on work setting and burnout amongst psychological professionals, discuss the manner in which psychological work, which they argue is high emotion intensity work, can engender the need for emotion regulation strategies. They found a number of factors that correlated with the 'burnout' of psychologists. These included having a lack of control of work activities and workload, high-intensity work conducted over long periods, having to deal with negative client behaviour, emotions or experiences, as well as high levels of administrative work and management interference. Mann (2004) notes that undertaking people work, of the sort that psychologists and counsellors are tasked with, causes a great deal of stress due to the degree of emotion management and performance necessary (see also Mann & Cowburn, 2005). The example she gives is the harms that can be evoked if sympathy is not portrayed at an appropriate time, or if boredom (or some other negative emotion) is leaked at an inappropriate time. In order to avoid these harms, the psychologist/counsellor must constantly manage their emotional performances, increasing both the emotional labour and the levels of stress that they are subjected to by the quotidian administrative and managerial pressures of the workplace. Brown, Shell, and Cole (2015) further note that differential settings and roles can evince very different emotion needs in forensic psychological practitioners – for instance, for those engaged in work with prisoners convicted of sex offences the emotional toll can be much greater than for those conducting other forms of forensic work with less challenging populations.

In her discussion of prison officers Arnold (2016) extends this point and argues that a conjunction of these differing roles and the occupational motives of individual officers can affect wider aspects of the prison officer's professional and emotional life. This can range from degrees of acculturation to the internalisation of solidarity norms, degrees of empathy for the prisoner situation, and the level of negative emotions engendered which need 'labouring'. Tait (2011) confirms these connections in her analysis of how prison officers approach the topic of care. She found that though all staff members contend with the issue of care, their varying care approaches dictated not only the manner in which they viewed and interacted with prisoners but also their occupational and cultural realities or habitus. The habitus then could affect the manner in which they emotionally experienced their role as prison officer, which would then also influence the manner in which they experience the prison, what forms of sociality is open to them, and what form of emotional labour they engage in.

One facet of the emotional lives of prison officers noted by all authors mentioned above was that the emotional labour that they must engage in does not cease at the prison wall. Emotions are not only mutable but transitive in that they render the prison wall a permeable barrier. Thus, emotion work often followed the prison officer outside, away from the constrained domesticity of the prison, into their wider lifeworld. Crawley (2004) recognised and described this phenomenon of emotion 'spillage' as it related to prison officers working within England and Wales. Drawing upon Kauffman's (1988) work in the United States on corrections officers and their professional and private worlds she notes that that the nature of doing prison work can have a significant effect on the home life of prison officers. She identifies five fundamental areas of 'spillover': personality change, where doing prison work leads to key changes in personality and character; institutionalisation, whereby the prison officer becomes reliant on routines, procedures and systems of control; material and symbolic contamination (vicarious contamination for loved ones), whereby either the 'filth' (in any of its meanings) or the stigma of the prison impacts on the home life of the officer and their families; the inclusion of punitive practices in home life, where the officers bring home the punitive behaviours and attitudes that mark their working practice (the example given is that of given a rub down search to a child or doing a 'spin' on their child's room); and lastly what could be called dramaturgical conflation, where the adopted professional persona begins to be indistinct from that of their private persona.[5] All of these facets of 'spillage' highlight just how much emotional labour is required not just to operate within the occupational space but also the personal (home) space.

It is clear here that the transitively emotive nature of the prison not only infests the occupational habitus of those who work in the prison but also their wider lifeworld. However, the psychologist, who is often located away from the prison wing, has a more episodic and nondomestic relationship to the prison than other prison staff. Nevertheless, as with other prison staff who experience a more remote yet deeply personalised interaction with prisoners, such as both drug workers (Kolind et al., 2015) and nurses (Walsh, 2009), their habitus and lifeworld too is one of emotion and emotional labour. Put simply, all prison staff carry the prison home in some way. However, these staff populations are engaged in what Rupert and Morgan (2005) describe as deep and high impact emotion work (given nature of interactions) and also have a more explicit form of the dual-relationship phenomena to contend with than prison officers and prison managers. For forensic psychologists, employed in the prison then this situation can deepen both the nature of emotional labour necessary to perform successfully and the degree of spillage likely to be experienced.

Further to this point, the nature of the wider occupational stresses experienced by psychologists working in correctional and penal contexts can too be very different from other prison staff. Garland, McCarty, and Zhao (2009), in their 2005 US-based Prison Social Climate Survey, of whom correctional psychologists were a part, found that workplace stresses for this particular group come from multiple sources, not all of which were shared by their educational and unit management colleagues. Those that were shared can be categorised as client trauma: negative experiences whilst working with prisoners, and occupational pressures (training, case load, management, etc.). However, the specific (or subjective) workplace issues related to the issues of case trauma, the vicarious trauma experienced from listening to and working with very troubled and damaged prisoners, differing iterations of the dual-relationship issue (dependent on role at time of survey), and the degree of emotion performance/labour that was needed to operate in US corrections. These last two issues were correlated with negative workplace experiences that then had an influence in the social climate in which their occupational cultures existed. They also found that there were significant areas of work that were more positively correlated with occupational culture and institutional loyalty. These included good supervision from management where value was communicated for the work done by individuals. As equally important was a perceived effectiveness with 'inmates' – where the psychologists could see the positive fruits of their labour. The researchers also found that the amount of time psychologists had spent working in a prison was also a common predictor of institutional commitment.

A further study by Mackain, Myers, Ostapiej, and Newman (2010) on correctional psychologists in the United States, extending the work of Boothby

---

[5]Colloquial prison term for an in-depth cell search.

and Clements (2002), found that there were three core areas which could impact on the stress levels and occupational satisfaction of psychological staff. These were listed as economic factors, perceived organisational support, and interpersonal relationships. The first of these factors was based upon the economic situation of the participants and relates to the job satisfaction that they associated with their remuneration. Of all the factors that affected job satisfaction, those most closely correlated with negative work experiences related to a perceived poor level of organisational support. The competency of supervision, training, recognition of work success and job security all directly affected perceived job satisfaction. Notably, given the context of the research and in contradiction to the findings of Garland et al. (2009), two factors that were not significantly correlated with job satisfaction were relationships with inmates and safety. Here it was much more organisational and institutional factors, the prison and its management, that were likely to lead to negative work experience.

Although there are some fundamental differences in practice between British prison psychologists and their US correctional counterparts, there are necessarily points of comparison. This is especially true when the traditional welfare-oriented role of the 'correctional' psychologist is being supplemented by practices of crisis intervention, inmate classification, delivering community risk assessments, developing behavioural management programmes, and the development of release plans (MacKain et al., 2010). These points of comparison highlight the importance in understanding both the institutional and occupational role of the psychologist in the prison and the impact of both those factors on the psychologist themselves. It is necessary, if we are to treat those psychologists employed within the prisons of England and Wales as a distinct population worthy of study, to understand how their occupational habitus is constructed and how their wider lifeworld is shaped and formulated by the prison, the power they wield and the power they are subjected to.

Current Roles

The role of the contemporary forensic practitioner is much changed from what it was in the early days of the Prison Commission (Crighton & Towl, 2008). No longer is the primary role of the 'prison psychologist' one of occupational or organisational planning and assessment, though those duties have not been relinquished. Neither is it as narrowly focussed nor as peripheral as it once was. Instead, the role of the contemporary psychologist is many and varied and intrinsic to the running of the modern prison.

Crighton (2004) argues that in the modern penal era, risk assessments and management are fundamental aspects to the forensic work undertaken by psychologists based in prisons. Though undoubtedly true it is far from being the complete picture. There are also an extensive range of operational, managerial, developmental and analytical activities that can come under the remit of the contemporary forensic psychologist that are not strictly based in risk assessment/management (Towl & McDougall, 1999; Crighton & Towl, 2008). For instance,

Ireland (2002) points out that one of the most important aspects of the work that forensic psychologists currently undertake within the contemporary prison is in investigating the impact of bullying within the prison environment and developing and evaluating, both locally and nationally, strategies for combating it. Related to this is that work which involves creating and implementing strategies to reduce, as well as aid staff in coping with, instances of suicide and self-harm (Bailey et al., 2002). Often this work falls within the wider efforts of violence reduction which has increasingly been a significant facet of their work. Since 2012, and in the wake of the benchmarking fiasco, violence in prisons in England and Wales has grown exponentially. As a consequence, violence reduction has been reviewed, reformulated, and redelivered throughout the estate. On top of their other duties and responsibilities, many forensic psychologists have been at the forefront of these efforts.

A further aspect of their modern role is in both the delivery and management of nationally recognised interventions and sex offender treatment programmes that have been run-out over the last three decades (Mann & Riches, 1999). In addition to the delivery and management of these programmes, part of the forensic psychologist role can also include overseeing the training of prison/probation service staff in the delivery of these courses as well as the monitoring of treatment groups to ensure the auditable targets of standards and quality are met (Friendship, Blud, Erikson, & Travers, 2002). A different aspect of the contemporary role of the forensic practitioner is in advising senior prison management, as well as providing expert assessments and overseeing the provision of support during serious incidents or disturbances (Home Office, 2003). This can include developing techniques of threat analysis, coordinating the initial strategic response to hostage situations, active hostage negotiation as well as the support and relief of victims and staff after the conclusion of the incident/disturbance (Evans & Henson, 1999).

There is also a consultancy aspect to their role in the modern prison which is based upon the 'expert' nature of their particular discourse. It often falls to the Principle psychologist in, or associated with, a prison to liaise with and provide consultancy to the medical staff both within the host prison and those in external organisations, the uniformed staff, probation officers (both seconded and external), representatives of the judicial and legal systems including the police, and, in some circumstances, social workers and counsellors (BPS, 2010). All of this on top of their gatekeeping role (Clark, 1999) discussed previously. What was interesting in terms of the psychologists who were interviewed for this study was that very few had experienced the opportunity to exercise this aspect of their role. This hampered their chances of gaining Chartership (see Chapter 5) but really derived from the manner in which they and their profession were viewed by the prisons they worked in.

The Treatment Industry

When Sir Martin Narey, in his Forget Rehabilitation speech at the International Corrections and Prisons Association annual conference in October 2019, rather disparagingly spoke of 'treatments' in prisons, he was echoing an accumulated sentiment within the penal commentariat. Sir Martin, like many others before and since, focussed on the falsity of promise made by an 'industry' in selling individuated 'treatments' as if they could possibly undo lifetimes of structural disadvantage.[6] This notion of a 'treatment industry' has haunted forensic psychological practice in prisons as it speaks to the very heart of what many of them are engaged to do. As we have seen, the role of the modern prison psychologist is multivaried. However, it must be acknowledged that though the job is now much changed, there are still two core roles which predominate. These are the roles of risk assessment and offending behaviour programme delivery.

Fundamentally, there are two forms of assessment that forensic psychologists engage in within the prison. The first is concerned with 'in-house' security and therefore focusses upon the assessment and monitoring of various high-risk behaviours within the prison. This can include actuarial assessments of such varied behaviours as self-harming and attempts at suicide, bullying and victimisation, sexual promiscuity or predation, terrorism or radicalisation type activity, and a wide range of (institutionally defined) 'seditious' behaviours. Often these varying assessments become subsumed under the title of safer custody practice. The second form is concerned with assessments that focus upon dangerousness, a prisoner's likelihood of re-offending, and public protection criterion and that are designed to supply focussed assessments to third-party decision-makers such as the Parole Board (Towl, 2007).

OASys came about as a collaboration between the National Probation Service and the Prison Service and was introduced as the standard assessment tool for the criminal justice agencies of England and Wales after the 2003 Criminal Justice Act. The intention behind OASys was to provide a measurable improvement to the business of risk assessment and as such was designed to implement a more dynamic mode of gathering and assessing information about the criminal and carceral past, the criminogenic factors that are believed to be associated with offending, and the risk of harm that the person being assessed represents. It operates on the presumption that the conjunction of offending history with varying individuated traits is significantly correlated with, and therefore can act as predictors of, the likelihood of reoffending (Morton, 2009). These varying factors include social and economic variables such as access to accommodation, employability, lifestyle and relationships, and personal factors such as cognition deficiency, attitudes to offending, substance misuse problems, and emotional well-being. The assessor completes all aspects of the OASys documentation after having read the relevant file material, the offender's self-assessment questionnaire (which the prisoner is now required to complete in order to be in adherence to their sentence plan (Hughes, 2012)) and interviewed the offender in person. The documentation is completed through 'ticked yes/no, scored or free text responses to questions' based on elements relating to the criminogenic factors mentioned

---

[6]See full speech here: https://www.slideshare.net/martinnarey/forget-about-rehabilitation-concentrate-on-making-prisons-decent.

above (Howard & Dixon, 2012). Once completed, the system numerically highlights the impact of each of these factors on the likelihood of reoffending and of causing serious harm to either themselves or others and a composite score is obtained. A high score equates with a high risk of reoffending and correspondingly a low score equates to a low risk of reoffending or of causing serious harm to others or themselves. In terms of the generational view on risk technologies mentioned earlier, this model is essentially a fourth-generation risk assessment tool (Fitzgibbon, 2008) and it remains the standard assessment protocol for the Prison Service (Moore, 2009).

Nevertheless, all those interviewed for this study identified a wider range of psychologically informed risk assessment tools that they would utilise in order to inform their responses to requests for risk assessment. Each of these assessments required expensive training, review, and oversight. What was evident is that many of these core assessment tools were predicated on, and utilised because of their, psychologically positivistic ideations of antisocial behaviour (which was conflated with criminal conduct in this context), violence, sexual violence, and personality disorder. The common belief was that these assessments would allow the psychologists to offer more dynamic and probative risk assessments than could be offered by OASys. Here is a list of just some of those mentioned:

- Domestic Violence Inventory
- Historical, Clinical and Risk Management-20 (HCR-20)
- International Personality Disorder Examination (IPDE)
- Juvenile Risk Assessment Scale (J-RAS)
- Level of Service Inventory – Revised (LSI-R)
- Level of Service/Case Management Inventory (LS/CMI)
- Offender Group Re-Conviction Scale (OGRS)
- Psychopathy Checklist Revised (PCL-R)
- Risk Matrix 2000 (rm2000) both versions for sexual and non-sexual violence
- Risk of Serious Recidivism (RSR-tool)
- Sexual Violence Risk-20 (SVR-20)
- Structured Assessment of Risk & Need (SARN)
- Violent Extremist Risk Assessment v2 (VERA-2)
- Violence Risk Scale (VRS) including the juvenile version
- Women's Risk/Needs Assessment (WRNA)

Though each of these were mentioned, the four most commonly referred to assessment tools were the HCR-20 violence risk assessment scheme, the Psychopathy Checklist Revised (PCL-R) for personality disordered prisoners, the Violence-Risk Scale (VRS), and SARN for those convicted of sexual offences. This latter risk tool was first introduced in 2000 and has been continuously developed in order to match, and keep up with, the requirements and demands of the Prison Service. This particular tool, derived from the Andrews/Bonta conceptions of offending, was noted as being of particular use as it distinguishes between static risks and treatment needs and deals with them as separate concepts

(Mann & Atrill, 2007; Webster et al., 2006). The HCR-20 is designed to blend both the theoretical and professional realms of risk practice and be employed across a number of forensic settings. Also, like SARN, it is comprised of both static and dynamic elements and is utilised in the formulation of treatment plans for people convicted of violent offences. The HCR-20 has become popular in forensic settings and with forensic practitioners primarily because it is easy to administer, understand, and score and can therefore facilitate quick and practical deliverability.

The revised Psychopathy Checklist (PCL-R), a tool developed by Hare (1980; Hare, Harpur, Hakstian, Forth, & Hart, 1990), has particular importance to the psychologists of this study as it has become a prevalent tool in contemporary penalities and has specific symbolic weight in terms of its labelling power. Here we see the interesting overlap of three forms of symbolic communication and inter-activity. Though the tool is fundamentally a clinical tool and thus confers a problematic and 'medicalised' concept of an individual's potential psychopathology, that concept also involves a communication laden in both moral and disciplinary abjection. Scoring high on the psychopathy checklist, especially in an environment that fetishises the concept of dangerousness and risk, communicates a wide range of extremely negative ideations by which that person becomes viewed and judged. Negative ideations become laminated on to the already criminalised identity of the individual and create a lens through which that individual is perceived. This lens, and the subsequent judgement that it evokes, cannot be escaped. As we saw before, all criminal justice labels are particularly adhesive and damaging and can have long-term consequences for prisoners – especially indeterminately sentenced prisoners. However, of all the labels that exist within the criminal justice system, none are as sticky as being a 'psychopath'.

Yet, this labelling element was something that many psychologists were just not aware of in terms of the PCL-R. For them, and the reports they prepared for the parole board, the tool just had a great deal of utility as a future predictor of a person's behaviour. As Serin and Amos (1995) argued, the checklist was noted as being an effective predictor of both general and violent recidivism as, when using the screening version, it was found that there was an above chance level of association between scoring highly and later violent offending. As such the model, though problematic as a risk identifier (see Toch, 1998), has also become a widespread tool for risk prediction in both forensic and nonforensic populations. As such, the PCL-R had become a popular tool for risk assessment in prisons in England and Wales. Part of the reason for this was the growing concern and focus levelled at personality disordered prisoners that began in the mid to late 1990s and, to a certain degree, continues to this day. With the advent of SDPD (Severe and Dangerous Personality Disorder) unit's and the consequent response of the Parole Board to the risk levels of those prisoners, it became common practice for the Parole Board to request PCL-R assessments in the case of indeterminate prisoners – even when this was not the appropriate method of assessment (see Towl, 2007).

This risk work is, nevertheless, one flip side of the 'treatment industry' coin. Once the assessments have been made, there is necessarily a need for risk mitigants. As was argued previously, there has been an influx of medicalised processes both in society and, in particular, within the criminal justice system, whereby those considered deviant/criminal are subjected to medicalised processes of intervention (Conrad, 2007; Conrad & Schneider, 1992). Nowhere are these processes more evident than in a further role of the contemporary prison psychologist – the development, delivery and assessment of a number of offender treatment programmes or 'interventions'. At the commencement of the research, the Prison Service, through the Offending Behaviour Programmes Unit (OBPU), delivered 13 programmes, either accredited or awaiting accreditation, throughout the estate.[7] However, this list grew throughout the project and has carried on apace since. These interventions are aimed at a range of 'offender' types including those who have been sentenced over sexual and nonsexual violence, those with learning difficulties, and those who have been assessed as having personality disorders. Excluding those that are delivered by community partners, the list of accredited interventions currently delivered directly by HMPPS Interventions, or Personality Disorder, Teams (MoJ, 2020a) are

- Alcohol Related Violence (ARV)
- Becoming New Me + (BNM+)
- Building Better Relationships (BBR)
- Building Skills for Recovery (BSR)
- Choices, Actions, Relationships, Emotions (CARE)
- Democratic Therapeutic Community Model (DTC)
- Democratic Therapeutic Community Model Plus (TC+)
- Healthy Identity Intervention (HII)
- Healthy Sex Programme (HSP)
- Horizon
- Identity Matters (IM)
- Kaizen
- Living as New Me
- New Me Strengths
- Resolve
- Thinking Skills Programme (TSP)

By far the most significant of these was the Thinking Skills Programme (formerly the Enhanced Thinking Skills (ETS) programme). It is a relatively short programme based upon cognitive behaviour modification therapy which addresses the thinking and behaviour associated with offending. This includes impulse control, flexible thinking, social perspective taking, values/moral reasoning, reasoning, and interpersonal problem solving (Clarke, Simmonds, & Wydall, 2004). It is the programme most frequently delivered; by 2010, over 40,000 prisoners had completed this course within HMPS (Sadlier, 2010). In the

---

[7]These do not include drug addiction treatment programmes as these are often outsourced and based on nonpsychological treatment courses offered in wider society.

period since, tens of thousands of further prisoners have been put through this form of intervention.

Giving the growing number of people in our prisons who have been convicted of sex offences (Mann, 2016), there has been an inevitable meeting of the need for interventions with this population. Those convicted of sex offences represent a diverse group with varying 'needs' and 'risks' and as such there was catalogue of accredited offending behaviour courses that were known jointly as Sex Offender Treatment Programmes (SOTP) (Mann & Atrill, 2007). These courses came in for a great deal of criticism but were nevertheless the go-to 'interventions' for this population. However, it must be noted that since the cessation of field work, there has been a fundamental change to these courses and their delivery. These changes came about in the wake of research that found that the extant suite of programmes, which had been delivered for 20 years, had either minimal effect on recidivism rates for many in this population or that, in some instances, undergoing treatment increased the risk of future offending (see Henry, 2017). This meant both a cessation of delivery for the core programmes and the rapid replacement of these with other programmes. These new programmes (Kaizen, Horizon, HSP) are designed to focus on future thinking and gradual self-improvement and have been the basis of sex offence intervention delivery since 2017. The efficacy of these programmes is unknown.

PIPES and Therapeutic Communities

There are two further current roles that forensic psychologists may be engaged with in terms of their working practices. These relate to Therapeutic Communities and Psychologically Informed Planned Environments (PIPEs). I include these here for completeness rather than context. Of all those who participated in this study, only one had worked in a therapeutic community and none had worked in a PIPE. I shall begin with a brief description of the former here. During the latter stages of the twentieth century, a number of quasi-democratic therapeutic communities arose within a number of prisons (i.e., HMP Grendon, HMP Gartree and HMP Dovegate) and which have been maintained within the contemporary estate (Woodward, 2007). These communities are designed to offer a more intensive and sustained system of rehabilitation and personal development for prisoners within a specifically designed and conducive setting. Lots of very good trauma-related work is often done in these units in recognition that many people in prison have been subjected to long histories of complex trauma (Bennett & Shuker, 2017). Much of the work which is undertaken within those sites is underscored by the same cognitive behavioural modification principles that have already been described. Such units have also come in for some criticism for the manner in which they shape the identities of those people who go through them. Often that identity becomes fundamentally fused with the moral ideations of them as 'offenders'. Many of those who go through such units are acculturated into reshaping their identities in terms of a pathologised, and flagellant, narrative as a means of demonstrating their rehabilitation and a reduction in their 'risk' status (see Warr, 2019). More widely in the prison system such prisoners are often referred to in the pejorative as 'therapeutons' as they struggle to reacclimate to 'normal' prison wings. Even after release many struggle to acclimate to the 'outside' world where their imposed flagellant narrative, which was a signifier of their reduced risk, has little social cachet. They are often left ontologically adrift, with what is rather disparagingly called the 'Grendon bends', as society demands a very different identity and societal performance from them. This would make a good research project for any aspiring doctoral candidate. Nevertheless, these Therapeutic Communities remain popular amongst prison reformers and 'rehabilitation' devotees.

PIPEs were developed in response to the joint venture between the Ministry of Justice and the Department of Health in order to provide a pathway for offenders with personality disorders (NOMS, 2015). PIPEs are not, in and of themselves, designed to be a specific treatment or therapeutic environment. Instead they are psychologically designed to support prisoners as they transition or navigate through the various significant stages of the Offender Personality Disorder Pathway. People will only be assigned to such units if they are 'successful' in completing an OPDP assessment and are deemed suitable for the PIPE. The environments themselves are predicated on the Enabling Environments designed by the Royal College of Psychiatrists in which spaces utilise the principles of therapeutic units to create supportive and positive living and working environments. Staff working on these units are specifically trained in the OPDP ethos and effective practices. There is a heavy emphasis within PIPEs on developing supportive staff/prisoner relationships and often psychologists work alongside prison officers in order to embed clinical practices into the carceral space.

There are three forms of PIPE which prisoners may access as they traverse the OPDP (NOMS, 2015):

(1) **Preparation PIPE** – These units are designed to help prisoners prepare for treatment or therapeutic environments which they will go on to access.
(2) **Provision PIPE** – These units are designed for those prisoners who need or will benefit from PIPE provision as they participate in treatment or offending behaviour programmes elsewhere in the prison.
(3) **Progression PIPE** – These units are utilised to offer support following the successful completion of an OPD treatment or OBP. The aim is here is to give these prisoners access to an environment that allows them to reflect and put into practice lessons learnt.

There are further provisions in the community which are sited in Approved Premises, but these lie beyond the scope of this book. PIPEs are arranged around six core guiding principles and are led by a Clinical Lead, who is usually a qualified clinical psychologist. Forensic psychologists, as well as mental health practitioners, can be Clinical Leads if they have the appropriate forensic, clinical, and analytic experience and training. This is significant as only a few of those interviewed would have had sufficient experience to qualify. However, PIPE units represent a very different working environment and practice to what the majority of forensic psychologists will experience. Here the focus is on the day-to-day living conditions and interactions which are designed to embed more prosocial ideas of living. Community here is the key and the focus and this is achieved by emphasising the clinical work that can take place in such environments. This is very different from the OBPs and risk assessment/management practice that dominates the occupational lives of most forensic psychologists in prisons in England and Wales.

Thus far we have seen how, through processes of medicalisation in wider society and the advent of increased modalities of power within the contemporary prison, prison psychologists are active agents in wide ranging matrices of disciplinary power whose outputs are laden with disciplinary capital. However, psychologists who inhabit the carceral estate are also members of staff, and they are employed by the Prison Service and HMPPS. As members of staff they are too subject to the authority and power of the institution just as is any other member of staff. Their experience of the prison, their interactions within it, their occupational development, their professional ethos and culture, their working life, their emotional well-being and mental health are all influenced and shaped by the prison. It is to this element of the prison world that I now turn.

Chapter 4

The Values and Perspectives of Forensic Psychologists

> I imagine most of the staff you speak to will be much the muchness
> in their outlook on the job. Ha! Actually, now I think about it, that
> might not be true at all …
> —Senior Psychologist prior to research beginning

When beginning this project my aim was to get a better understanding of those
forensic psychologists who worked in our prisons. There was no intent to
construct a typology of staff. Partly this is because typologies are inherently
problematic. They falsely and misleadingly collapse the complexity of individuals
into neat categories. Categories rarely if ever capture the wonderfully (infuriat-
ingly) entangled selves that we all are. Partly, it was because I had not thought to
do so. I had not, with any aforethought, designed my research materials/questions
in a way that set out the parameters or dimensions by which you may construct a
typology. Nevertheless, what became evident in the analysis of my data was that
there were quite clear dimensions and deviations in professional and moral attitudes towards the job of being a forensic psychologist. This unexpected emergence
almost forced a typology on me. Not one of the individuals themselves but more
of their approach to their work. This was also a typology that seems to have held
some validity for those many forensic psychologists who I have spoken to since
the end of the research. Many have told me that they recognise these 'types' either
from their own practice or from observing their colleagues. However, of course,
this perspective may be a result of those psychologists having been schooled in a
field that inherently classifies and characterises individuals into distinct groups!
Nevertheless, this chapter looks at, and proposes, a typology that allows for an
analysis of the varying moral and professional approaches to forensic psychology,
which shape the experience, methods of coping with, and reactions to the prison
environment.

However, before beginning that discussion in earnest, it is necessary to explicate a few points with regard to a 'typology'. Fundamentally, it is important to
note that there are differences between a basic form of classification and a
typology. Classification relates to the process whereby entities are grouped by
similarity in a manner that signifies both in-group homogeneity and between-

Forensic Psychologists, 55–89
Copyright © 2021 Jason Warr
Published under exclusive licence by Emerald Publishing Limited
doi:10.1108/978-1-83909-960-120200005

group heterogeneity (Bailey, 1994). For example, humans can, in one rather simplistic sense, be classified as either male, female or nonbinary – the classification criteria in this sense is gender. However, there are a number of problems with this quite basic system of differentiation, the most pertinent of which is that they tend to be rather limited in terms of their explanatory power. In essence, such classification can only inform us of how entities are similar or different. What is required for robust and satisfactory classification in social sciences is not only the identification of the fundamental variables which underpin the differentiations but also a tool which allows the wider relationships between the entities being classified to be captured and explored (Coxon, 1999).

Typologies are multidimensional and conceptually based rather than just binary formulations of difference. However, as Bailey (1994) argues, it is necessary that typologies be constructed from multiple dual criteria to maintain dimensional exclusivity. Without this an entity may fall between two categorical dimensions, introducing conceptual ambiguity which necessarily undermines any explanatory power. Collier, Laporte, and Seawright (2008) note that there are essentially two types of typology: those that are descriptive in nature, whereby the dimensions of the typology relate to specific conceptual forms, and those that are explanatory in nature, whereby the dimensions of the typology relate to 'hypothesised outcomes' (p. 153). Regarding that utilised here, the form of typology under discussion is necessarily descriptive. Given the emerging data, I was concerned with constructing an initial descriptive tool to communicate the occupational differences that were becoming evident. In this sense, each dimension of the typology relates to an exclusive occupational, or even ontological/positional, concept which fits the ethos which governed individual outlook and practice.

The first principle of creating a typology involves defining the conceptual variables that will form its basis (Collier et al., 2008). Black (1963) notes that when partitioning (in the sense of differentiating between types), the method of 'free sorting' is the only justifiable method. This is the process whereby 'native' partitions, those grounded in the data, are discovered by the researcher instead of being imposed by them. Both Black (1963) and Bailey (1994) note that there are two forms of free sorting: first, the quantitative method, which is based upon statistical adherence/deviance to a group's particular set of variables; second, the qualitative method which is based upon conceptual categorisation. Conceptual categorisation, in this sense, relies upon there being distinct and polarised concepts which capture the range of qualitative elements in the data. It is these polarised concepts that form the cells of the typology. An element is assigned to a particular cell due to the level of their deviation from or adherence to one of the poles (Bailey, 1994). As already noted, at the outset of this research, there was no intention to develop a typology, and therefore none of the formal techniques for delineating character or moral perspective were employed in the development of the interview schedule. There was no hypothesised outcome imposed in the research design and as such no hypothetico-deductive testing (Føllesdal, 1994). Yet clear, polarised, concepts emerged from the data which produced the necessary exclusive dimensions.

Human Resource literature describes five forms of occupational motivators: physiological, egocentric, belief-based, social needs, and goal achievement (Belilos, 1997).[1] Physiological motivators relate to the base needs of having to earn in order to live; egocentric motivators relate to pay, rewards and occupational self-worth; social needs relate to work place relationships as well as organisational placement; goal achievement relates to the realisation of one's aims and potential; and belief-based motivators (both internal drives and external motivations) are those subjective factors that impel a person to work in their field once their other 'needs' have been met (Mumford, 2011). Inner drives are the beliefs/mores which shape the way an individual will approach their role or occupation. External motivations are those attitudinal factors that mirror larger narratives which underpin the professional/organisational role (Belilos, 1997). It is from these belief-based motivators that personal satisfactions and ontological security can be derived (Ashman & Gibson, 2010).

Day and Casey (2009) note that in the field of forensic and correctional psychology the values held by practitioners are predicated on the values formulated and espoused in their various codes of professional practice. However, it was clear from this research that the values held by the psychologists interviewed in this study went beyond the occupational narratives of the 'role' and involved a blend of the often-competing official ideations of professional penal practice, as well as personal and political moralities. In forming the typology, it was necessary for there to be a number of polarised concepts which would adequately capture this range of values. Four polarised attitudinal concepts were displayed by the participants: rehabilitation, welfare, public protection, and punitivity. These partitions attached to both occupational narratives and personal motives and as such were both significant and broad enough to encompass the wide range of values discussed by the participants of the study.

It should be noted that none described their own views solely in terms of one position or another. Participants would make a series of statements over the course of their interviews which often highlighted points of deviation from one particular concept or another. These affirmations and deviations then indicated which position they were prone to lean towards and thus to which cell they belonged. For example, those that saw their role primarily in terms of public protection often saw rehabilitation as a distinct but related facet of their role. However, those who were more welfare-orientated often saw rehabilitation as being an indistinguishable part of their role. Due to this conjoining of dyadic motivations, a simple quadratic axis was sufficient to capture these attitudinal and motivational spectra (see Fig. 4.1).

Once these spectra had been established, a simple typological analysis, establishing each interviewee's expressed set of attitudes and beliefs, showed that each respondent could be mapped somewhere within these quadrants (see Fig. 4.2). The position of any dot within the quadrants indicates the extent to which that

---

[1]These motivators are often derived from, or perceived in terms of, Maslow's Hierarchy of Needs.

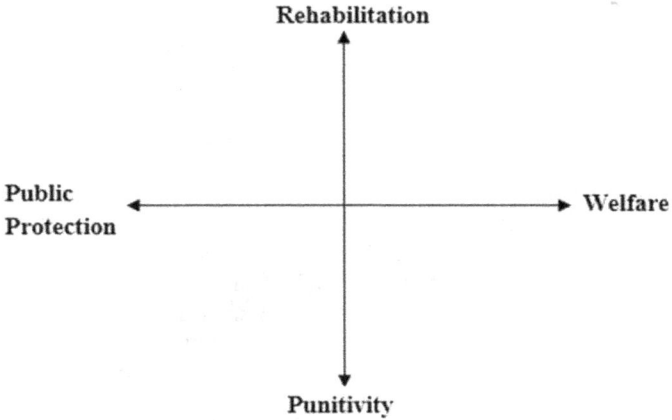

Fig. 4.1

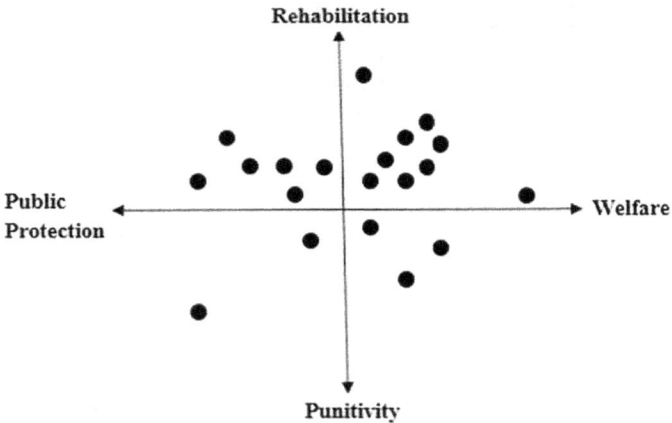

Fig. 4.2

individual portrays a particular attitude or motivation and the extent to which they deviate from the polarised position. For example, the dot nearest to the welfare marker indicates an individual who primarily saw their role, and that of all psychologists, in terms of the welfare of the people they worked with (be that staff or prisoner) yet also privileged the notion of rehabilitation over that of punitivity. Likewise, the individual closest to the rehabilitation marker was an individual who perceived psychological services in terms of rehabilitation and aiding prisoners in their desistence yet also saw welfare as a more guiding principle than public protection. Those whose dots fell between these two displayed attitudes/motivations that shared both perspectives, i.e., they saw their role as aiding the individual personally/emotionally as well as helping them in getting away from their offending lifestyles yet rejected or gave less credence to issues of public protection or punitivity as being driving factors of their occupational positionality.

The mapping exercise revealed four base groups of psychologists within the sample: Humanists, Functionalists, Utilitarians, and Retributivists (see Fig. 4.3). Each of these groups shall be discussed in full below. It must be noted that the last grouping was somewhat problematic as only two psychologists could be said to fall into this quadrant and those who did were very different from each other. This resulted in the quadrant having to be split between a Retributive Idealist and Cynical Retributivist. Nevertheless, these two individuals were really distinct from the rest of the sample yet shared some commonalities with each other. Mostly they saw their role in terms of public protection and as an essential aspect of the punishment of prisoners. The justification of their inclusion as separate categories will be explained below.

Before that, it is important to discuss emotion work. The literature on this topic discusses the internal process of emotional labour that is undertaken by staff in order to manage their own emotional selves (see Nylander, Lindberg, & Bruhn, 2011; Walsh, 2009). However, as Gray and Smith (2009) note in passing, whilst discussing emotional labour and nursing, there is also a need to work with the emotions of others. Hochschild (1983) argues that the purpose of emotional labour is to induce a proper, or correct, state of mind in a target population. It is occasionally necessary to alter the emotional states of those being worked with in order to achieve occupational/treatment success. For the purposes of this book it became necessary to make a distinction between *emotional labour*, that toil undertaken by the individual to manage their own emotion states, and what I shall refer to as *emotive labour*, that toil undertaken to induce, change, or control the emotion states of others.

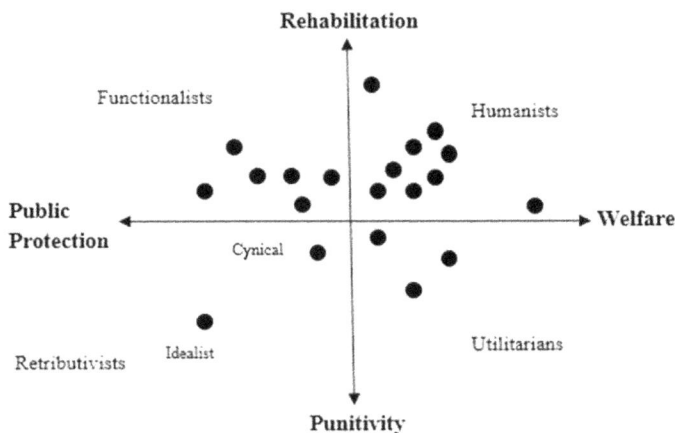

Fig. 4.3

The literature on managing the emotions of others in such settings is far less prevalent because it is generally perceived that such processes involve unethical elements of power such as manipulation or inducement (Thoits, 1996). Rosete and Ciarrochi (2005) highlight that in much of the organisational/management literature, the management of other's emotions is reframed as performance management – yet involves the same processes of provocation, comfort, and easing discussed by Thoits (1996). However, the management of other people's emotions is a necessary aspect of every form of human sociality (Clark, 1990). She argues, utilising Collins' (1975) notion of the 'emotional interactional substrate', that everyday interactions are dominated by emotional micropolitics where emotions are triggered, evinced, elicited, utilised, and managed. To deny this, she argues, is to fail to fully capture the nature of human interactions – something emotions scholars can often be guilty of. Even in therapeutic settings, the need to work with the emotions of others is recognised as being a central facet of practice. D'Zurilla and Nezu (2010), when speaking about problem solving therapy and wider CBT practices, note that there is a long-standing acknowledgement that controlling/managing disruptive emotion and behaviours as well as encouraging reflective emotion/behaviours is a core element of the therapist's role.

All of those interviewed spoke, to some degree, about these elements of managing the emotions of others. Therefore, in order to fully explain the nature of, and the distinctions between, *emotional* and *emotive labour* in this and the following chapters, it is necessary to add to the definition of emotive labour given above. Fundamentally, the forms of emotive labour described by the psychologists interviewed in this study can be thought of as involving the three following processes: evocation – the process of inciting emotion responses in others; deflection – the processes of altering the nature and course of emotion responses in others; and inversion – the processes of changing negative emotion responses in others to ones that are positive or meet the needs of the individual engaging in the emotive labour.

Humanists

A Humanist is someone that has a pervasive concern for human welfare, values, and dignity. As such, this was the ideal signifier for this group. All those who fell within this group, whether they were more rehabilitation or welfare-focussed, had the interests of the people they worked with at the forefront of their thinking:

> You become a psychologist because you are interested in human beings and so dehumanising people should be at odds with the psychologist.

> I felt, like [my] supervisor, that one of my roles in the prison was to remind everybody that the people in [the] prison are human. There is a really offensive thing going on at the moment where people in

some parts of the Ministry of Justice have started referring to prisoners as 'stock' which is awful isn't it? Here at [name of prison] I see it as my role to make sure those we work with are seen as people ...

It also meant that many derived enjoyment from the day-to-day contact that they had with prisoners:

I honestly just enjoy working with people ... a lot of my early work was with the enhancing skills programme which is all about, or certainly should be in my view, working with people, motivating people, listening to them ... I really enjoyed that.

The best thing? Err ... it's probably ... the best thing is working with people. I get to see so many and helping them ... that's what's good, you know?

I think that I take a lot pride and I take a lot of personal satisfaction from thinking that I do a job that makes a difference to other people.

This people-centricism had three further facets that distinguish the Humanists from other categories. These are the manner in which they both perceive and approach the prisoners and other staff members with whom they work; their interest in the welfare of those with whom they work; and, their attitude to, and the practice of, their rehabilitative role. In terms of this first facet, all the Humanists portrayed a highly optimistic and humane opinion of people in general and in particular those that they worked with. For example, one psychologist expressed amazement at the cynicism that many of the uniformed body displayed towards prisoners as they were personally of the opinion that there '*was more good to people than bad*'. This led them to question the motivations of other staff if they did not believe in the inherent goodness of people:

I get frustrated by staff who have a negative view ... why are you in this job if that is your view, what are you doing here?

Humanists displayed a strong moral sense of how people should act towards each other and consequently how they should be treated. The individual that made the above claim stated that they had been bought up to believe that

...you treat people with fairness and with decency, and things like trust and honesty are important and taking responsibility for yourself but also for others. And I think quite a strong sense of the fact that life is not just about looking after yourself and taking what you can from it, but actually helping other people as well.

This moral sentiment was echoed by many of those who have been classified as Humanists. They often couched their responses in terms of fair treatment of prisoners, respect, and empathy. As one noted when speaking about their style of engaging recalcitrant prisoners:

> ...being very clear about the purpose of your role, what you are there to do. But I think a lot of empathy, respect ... acknowledging those things, treating them as people ... it is quite powerful.

Whilst others noted that

> ... empathic, supportive, trusting relationships are some of the things that you need in order to assist people and to do this properly.

> ...and that is what I find hardest is... I don't mean feeling sorry for them because I think that is a little bit condescending...but I think empathy comes into it and I think although some people have done some quite terrible things, and I always say people have to take responsibility for that, but just because they have done that does not mean you can't feel empathy for what they have suffered.

> Well you try to be a person to them as well as a professional and that is probably a big negative on my career or whatever, but I don't believe you can just be professional. You have to know your boundaries and I think you can say to somebody, I like you as a person, don't like what you did, this is my role as a psychologist but you can still relate to them in a way. And I find that is one of the major humanities if you like that is missing.

Humanists shared a view that prisoners are people first and foremost and need to be treated in a manner that is appropriate for people. These moral sentiments bought to mind the classical Kantian approach, the second formulation of the Categorical Imperative (Kant, 1785), whereby people are 'an end in and of themselves' and as such shall not be treated as a means to some other end – i.e., achieving performance targets or abstractly protecting the public. This is not to suggest that the Humanists were the only grouping to cast their profession in terms of deontology – nevertheless they clearly viewed their 'duty' in terms other than a general utility. Holding this position also meant that they saw prisoners as individuals rather than an homogenous deviant grouping:

> Prisoners have their own individual needs ... which we need to understand so that we can help them to understand ... [their offending behaviour].

Humanists were more acutely aware of, and uneasy about, the power dynamic that underpinned their relationships with prisoners:

> I know it is a position of authority but I suppose I don't feel like ... that is my role. I am not thinking... I think maybe I am saying there are some people who thrive off that and that is not something I am particularly...I don't... I hope that I would not present in that way because of the fact like I said anyone can end up [here].

Another noted that

> Obviously as a member of staff and as a person conducting an assessment we are in a position of ... authority, but ... but you have to mitigate that as best you can. You have to be careful ... even in what and how you say things ... they can have a negative impact.

In this regard, the Humanists were far more aware and careful with the manner in which they engaged in *emotive labour*. There was an acknowledgement of the need to be careful with prisoners' emotions. Careless phrasing was to be avoided so as not to cause harm or even unintended harm. A number of the Humanists had noted early experiences in their careers where something that they had said to a prisoner had caused some offence or had evoked negative emotions in those who they were working with. For example, one psychologist relayed a story from when they were working on an anger management course and had made a flippant, throw away, and what they thought was an amusing comment, only to be met with offended silence from the men in the group and in particular the person they had been speaking to:

> To this day I can't remember what I had said. But, you know, I know whatever it were it were not appropriate. It caused ... pain. It changed everything in the group. From that minute on the group was a slog and the man I had been speaking to just withdrew and clammed up. I thought it were innocuous but it clearly weren't. I felt like I had failed not just him but everyone. Since then I am very careful with what I say ...

It was this aspect of *emotive labour* that was peculiar to the Humanist – it was that the wrong word or phrase or any behaviour that seemed thoughtless or careless had to be avoided not because it might impact on outcomes but because it might evoke negative emotions in the prisoner:

> ... you have to be so careful with what you say. You don't always know what the person has been through, what traumas lie in their childhood, what sensitivities they have ... you know? You don't want to, and I hate the term, but you don't want to trigger some

> past trauma and make things worse for the person. It's the last thing we should be doing.

> I was interviewing somebody who had got awful kind of marks round his neck where he had tried to hang himself and feeling really quite ... I wouldn't say uncomfortable about it but just ... I knew I had to be really careful.

Humanists' optimism also infected the manner in which they considered, and in no way questioned, the notion of rehabilitation. They often just accepted the probity of the concept – despite the problems the concept is laden with. Many felt that real change could be attained by prisoners if only the opportunities were made available to them. As one summed up '*You have to give people an opportunity and believe in their capacity to change I guess*'. Many of those who fell into this category believed in this aspect of rehabilitation. An inherent perspective, or ontology, to all psychological approaches is that there is something either fundamentally wrong or missing in the psychopathology of an 'offender' which causes their offending (Samenow, 2004). This positivistic approach to forensic and criminological discourse dictates that whatever this malignant or absent element is, it is both necessary and sufficient to cause an individual to offend (Day, Tucker, & Howells, 2004). Therefore, addressing this internal malignancy, or incepting that which is missing, will remove the causal factor in the individual's offending, and result in their desistance from crime. In the parlance of the contemporary prison, this 'deficiency' is often thought to be either cognitive impairment, which is 'treatable', or personality disorder, which is only manageable. Though still positivistic in their approach (I shall return to this point below), Humanists were far more likely to be both understanding of the external and structural factors that led people to offend and yet optimistic about the rehabilitation that prisoners could achieve. For example, one psychologist explained that they were always taken aback by just how little had to go wrong in someone's life for them to end up in prison:

> It is quite humbling when you think I could be there, it is only because I have had different experiences and opportunities.

What was of particular interest was the fact that Humanists would accept that structural factors (i.e., poverty or relative deprivation) played a part in a person's offending but yet they still adhered to a personalised ideation of rehabilitation. They, and none of the psychologists interviewed, seemed to recognise the inherent problems involved in this reasoning. It was for the individual to rehabilitate themselves, even from influences that lay beyond their control.

Returning to the point at hand, what we see here is echoes of what Muir (1977), in his classical text *Police: Streetcorner Politicians*, defines as a tragic perspective. He argues that in order for a police officer to become an effective professional, who can grow in their profession, they must necessarily reconcile two seemingly paradoxical positions: developing an intellectual ability to recognise those factors which can lead to human suffering/wrongdoing whilst simultaneously reconciling themselves morally to their coercive practice and the implications of that for those with whom they interact. He goes on to argue that not being able, or even disinclined, to reconcile these two states leads to the development of a cynical perspective which can lead to wholly negative practices and habits of denial and avoidance. What we see here with this Humanist is that intellectual understanding of the prisoners with whom they work. Others expressed similar points of view:

> Many of those I see it's ... a bad set of circumstances, some poor decisions and their life has gone wrong. Working here makes you realise this can happen to anyone, anyone can end up here [in prison].

> It sounds so simple but I had never really thought about it, and I know there are always exceptions to the rule, but generally the vast majority of prisoners I have worked with in my experience have had very, very difficult ... they have come from deprived areas; they have had difficult upbringings; they have had disruptive childhoods; they have had negative experiences at school ...

Humanists were still positivistic in their approach but were, in these terms, at the lighter end of the positivistic spectrum – positivist-lite. This affected the manner in which they perceived their rehabilitative role, which all saw in terms of co-production. They saw their role as aiding and abetting rehabilitation as opposed to imposing it. They were not there to force change upon people but instead to help those who wished to change:

> I will work with people and I think working in a prison it doesn't matter to me what that person has done in the past, it does not matter where they have come from, I will work with that individual and I will want to – I suppose – help them if I can in order to make the changes in their life which perhaps they want.

> A really important part of my role is helping to rehabilitate people who want to make that change whatever that may be.

> It is very positive to be able to help people to live better lives. That sounds really ... ... but it is true and you see so much misery and so many unhappy people.

Humanists were far more likely to talk about working *with*, as opposed to working *on*, prisoners. In terms of the tragic/cynical perspectives mentioned above, this becomes an interesting use of language. As noted, prisoners have little or no choice in their interactions with psychologists, so for Humanists to utilise such language, it suggests an element of denial or even avoidance. Other categories very much saw their role in terms of the 'treatment' or 'medical' model, as described by Towl (2004), and as such employed phrases such as *'interventions'* and *'programmes for'* prisoners. Language inherently communicating a sense of just power. However, this was largely absent in the responses given by Humanists who were far more hominine, yet avoidant, in approach.

This approach also informed their opinions of the public protection role that the institution and the criminal justice system imposes upon them. Many reframed this dual-relationship issue in terms of a means of helping the people with whom they work as opposed to using them as a means to satisfy this purpose. In practical terms, this meant that they saw public protection as a consequent of improving the lives of prisoners:

> It's simple really, if you have someone with anger control problems and you help them overcome those issues then you're helping the public ...

> I think we are there to improve people's lives and that is everybody, that's prisoners, staff, public. Because it is very easy to say we are there to reduce reoffending... but it is not just about that. Some of it is about keeping people alive, and some of it is about keeping staff safe and alive and all the rest of it. And if you can do those things and you can do them well and you can make prisoners lives better, you will make the public's lives better.

In a publication regarding the development of psychological services within NOMS, it set out a hierarchy of stakeholders, priority was given to the public, victims of crime, prison and probation staff, with the 'offender' coming last (Home Office, 2003). This prioritising may have been inadvertent but was nevertheless reflected in the responses given by psychologists in other categories. This was not true for Humanists who saw the hierarchy from the opposite perspective – as the quote above indicates. The second issue to arise from this quote is about the welfare of the individual, and the wider staff population, with whom they worked. In other criminological contexts, the notion of Repressive Welfarism has been used to describe an almost epochal shift in the dominant penal ethos of the late twentieth/early twenty-first century, whereby welfarist ideals were supplanted by a punitively focussed public protection agenda (Garland, 2001, 1985). However, as Robinson (2008), Sparks (2007), and Downes and Hansen (2006) note, it is evident that Garland overstates the division between welfare, punishment, and public protection policy in late modern penal practice. Instead what occurred was a synthesis between these two, seemingly disparate, forms of policy and practice. As Hudson (2003, 1987) points out that much of Youth Justice policy/practice in the 1970s/1980s was not strictly based around welfarist ideals but rather a combination of welfarism and punitiveness. Here the point is not that these ideations of juridical practice were separate and contiguous but rather that they had become so fused together that they were indistinguishable (see also Kemshall, 2008; Smith, 2003, 2005a).

One consequence of this is a variation of the dual-relationship issue discussed previously where practitioners become concerned with mitigating the control aspect of their role by use of their care role. In terms of youth justice, Kemshall (2008) describes a situation whereby the modern youth worker acts as a 'firewall' between the children clients and the full impact of the risk paradigm they are employed to implement. This she argues is due to many of the practitioners not sharing the objectives and values that underlie the policy which governs their practice. Phoenix (2009) takes this a step further and points out that it is now partially the role of the modern youth worker to actively alleviate both the form and reach of the punitive aspects of 'repressive welfarism'. This alleviation can only occur through the interfacial aspect of their role and thus for many is an integral part of their everyday work. However, she notes that one consequence of this is a certain amount of conflict due to the practitioner being consistently confronted by the punitive reality which is conjoined to the welfarist ethos of their discourse. Humanists in this study communicated a similar situation. Their concern for the welfare of the individuals with whom they worked was often hampered by occupational expectation:

> I think one of the most important things we need to do is to keep people safe. When they are in our care we should be making sure that they stay in one piece and alive. That is kind of the bottom line and I don't think we do enough of that.

Nearly all Humanists regretted that they were not always able to work in this way, as they were often called to other duties. Often this was as a result of their role being perceived, by the establishment in which they worked, as being risk-focussed. Nevertheless, many Humanists felt they should be doing more to help the prisoners in the prison to cope with their incarceration:

> If I were to describe my job then I would have said, when I first started, a lot of it was about how to help people cope with imprisonment. And that does not happen all that much now. Most psychologists would never see that as their job to help people cope with their imprisonment … I do, though.

> We probably do a more accurate job at predicting risk but the system is much less human than it used to be.

This intersection between the custodial needs of the institution and the role that psychologists play in these largely coercive practices and the motivation for care (dual relationship) can increase the level of emotional labour that the Humanists may have to engage in (Walsh, 2009), and speak to the difficulties that psychologists may face in reconciling their moral and disciplinary perspectives (Muir, jr, 1977). However, Humanists expressed a great deal of job satisfaction when, due to an establishment's understanding of their wider utility, they were able to work in what they considered humane ways:

You have got this environment which is difficult and hard and horrible for most people, that helping get people through that and helping things change in a positive way is what is rewarding.

This *emotive labour* (deflection) then enabled them to ameliorate some of the *emotional labour* that may be caused by the other relational or ontological factors that will be discussed in the following chapters. A related source of satisfaction stemmed from giving prisoners who may be in a very dark or chaotic place a healthy way of moving forward. In this sense, Humanists often perceived themselves as a beacon luring the offender towards the shores of rehabilitation and away from the destructive emotions that besieged them. As one particular psychologist noted:

> ...[often] they are in a bad situation ... they do not see the way out and just giving them a way forward, sensible steps not huge jumps, trying to tune in with them and giving them the right ways forward I think is a good thing.

This raised the notion of the third form of emotive labour, that of inversion – the processes of changing prisoners' negative emotions into more positive forms. As another participant noted:

> When you help someone who is in distress ... you see that a lot here, when you see that and can help them to change their thinking and the way they feel about their situation and the way they see their future ... That's when I feel I am doing good work.

It was clear that the main focus of inversion for Humanists involved improving prisoners' internal lives, without doing so for purely instrumental reasons. As this psychologist explained when relaying a story of a particularly problematic young prisoner they had worked with many years previously:

> He was seen as being ... a pain. Lots of trouble, lots of adjudications, lots of fights, always in and out of seg. It was clear from his file that he'd had an horrendous life, abuse, care, neglect ... everything that can destroy a person's chances, you know? He had been on a programme in his previous establishment but was so disruptive he was thrown off. It was decided at his lifer board that maybe 1-to-1 work might be more suitable. When I had to interview him first he ... I was ... not nervous really but ... apprehensive? I wanted it to go well but ... He was fine, the minute he opened up it all came pouring out. Really, he needed someone to listen to him, he'd never had that. He had such a negative view of himself ... it was heart-breaking. We worked together for three months and I listened and I helped him to see that what had happened to him was not his fault and that it didn't need to

define his life. We got to the point where he was much more positive about himself ...

Yet another spoke about the need to help people to see their lives and themselves through a more positive lens. They explained that much of their work was helping the men to have the confidence to be able to see themselves differently and begin to perceive their future lives in a more prosocial way. This particular individual went on to state that

> The role of the forensic psychologist is not just about helping prisoners to address their offending behaviour but ... but changing the way they see their possibilities.

The Humanist, though not necessarily reconciling their moral position and thus leaving themselves vulnerable to developing a cynical rather than tragic approach (as we will see later), is distinct from the other types due to their hominine, optimistic, and flexible approaches to psychological services, rehabilitation, emotive labour, and the manner in which they derive their job satisfaction. As this psychologist summed up:

> I know that probably most people in my groups or that I work with on a one to one basis that I am not changing their lives but I would like to think that for some of them, and I am not the only reason somebody changes, but I think if I am....if I am part of the process which means somebody's life improves then I am happy to spend the next 40 years doing that because I think what better thing to do with your life than help other people in theirs.

Functionalists

In both the sociological and anthropological fields, functionalism refers to the theory that societies can be understood by examining the functions that their constituent parts play in the construction and promulgation of the society (Fulcher & Scott, 2011). What is common to both these perspectives is the fact that, whether it be mental states or the constituent parts of a society, the defining factor is the function they play in some larger scheme. It is in this sense that the label Functionalist has been employed in this chapter.

For a participant to be defined as a Functionalist, it was necessary that they saw their role in functional terms, either protecting the public or rehabilitating prisoners. For Functionalists these were their prime directives; they were employed and thus tasked to achieve or enable some outcome:

> Society – public protection is the prime, the public if you like. So that is kind of where the focus is, it is always about protection, risk

and managing that. But obviously in balance there is duty of care to the individuals that we work with. But the end point is the public.

I do lots of different things … assessments, programme delivery, safer custody … lots of different things but they're always centred around public protection.

… facilitating or contributing towards public protection is obviously the fundamental element of our role.

Humanists placed the individual as the primary locus for their expertise and profession. However, Functionalists regarded the primary recipient of their service as the public and saw prisoners as considerably less important in a hierarchy of stakeholders. In this way they were, returning to Muir jr's (1977) analysis, much more able to morally reconcile the coercive nature of their practice with their intellectual understanding of the prisoners with whom they worked. In this sense they were closer to achieving that tragic perspective that could allow for the development of effective practice. However, this had a number of consequences for their professional approach both in terms of the rehabilitation of prisoners and in protecting the public. The first of these, a defining characteristic of the Functionalist, is the manner in which they conflate public protection with risk and risk management – a perspective that they share, to a certain degree, with the Retributivists. For the Functionalist, public protection *is* the reduction, or management, of risk. Under this viewpoint, prisoners are reinterpreted completely as risk subjects (Hannah-Moffat, 2005), with attendant risk identities, who pose a potential future threat to the wider public and thus must be assessed, managed, and controlled. This attitude was prevalent in Functionalist thinking:

…thinking about prison, organisational need, public[protection] risk assessment and I have heard people say risk assessment is the bread and butter of forensic psychologists and obviously there are those four roles and I do think it is very much equally – that is what it should be. But I think in terms of …maybe prisons and my experience I think good quality risk assessments timely assessment is probably key. I think that is important and understandably so, and rightly so.

…work with people to overcome risk and in some cases, for some people it might be just about managing and controlling risk.

For some, this was one of the motivators for having joined the Prison Service as a psychologist:

[My] motivation really was public protection and to work doing risk assessments, wanted to go to Parole Board hearings, so contribute to Parole Board hearings about risk.

The overarching ethos here is one of consequentialism – the notion that some greater good is achieved through acts which, regardless of individual cost, lead to an intrinsic good (Williams, 1993). The 'good' here is the protection of the public. It is the striving towards this good from which Functionalists can derive satisfaction in their work:

> The best thing that I have done this week for example ... is writing a risk assessment knowing that you are making the right decision for that person's progress and that that supports protection of the public.

The ultimate goal is public protection, which is achieved through the lowering or management of risk. The means by which that is seen to be achieved is the rehabilitation of the prisoner. Rehabilitation stands as the mechanism by which a prisoner can be changed and thus their risk reduced:

> I would say what I do helps people who have had a negative impact on society in some way or another – I am helping them to change their behaviour so that hopefully in the future they have a more positive impact on society.

> ... it is about that balance really between public protection and then enabling prisoners to change.

A consequence of this positionality is that Functionalists, unlike Humanists, make a separation between the wider public and the prisoner. This separation is due to both the crimes that the 'offender' has committed and the subsequent 'riskiness' that dictates how they are perceived. The Functionalists of this study all 'othered' the prisoner in this regard:

> [You] must remember that some of the individuals we work are very dangerous ... here for having committed some very serious offences and ... as I mentioned earlier what we do is centred around public protection so we must work to reduce the risk they pose to the public, their victims, and I suppose to themselves before they are released.

This positioning also impacted on the manner in which Functionalists perceived rehabilitative work. Humanists were much more likely to talk about rehabilitation in terms of co-production or collaboration. Rehabilitation was seen as something done *with* prisoners. Functionalists, however, were much more aligned to the treatment (medical) model and as such spoke in terms of *interventions, treatment programmes* and the like. As one pointed out, when talking about the role of psychology in sentence planning:

> You make an assessment of them and you know, it is not enough,
> ... it is bad practice, to just assess. You have got to give some

direction. You can't just say this person is high risk and that is the end of it. You have got to identify their treatment needs and then … You have got to give some recommendations about what treatment is suitable for that person to progress at the end of it and that is the key.

Whilst another, speaking on a similar theme, noted that

I think there is also an element of it that is not just about risk assessment but it is about actually doing the intervention yourself which like I said is why I wanted to get involved in [forensic psychology].

These responses also indicated their deeper positivistic outlook. The Functionalists were explicit in describing prisoners as people with '*cognitive, emotional or behavioural malignancies*' that needed to be '*treated*' before they would be safe to release back into society with the wider public:

I think the main purpose is to understand the offender's risk, to understand why somebody has committed the offence, what cognitive deficits they have, in terms of moving that person forward but in terms at the right time recommending that somebody has further work to do so you are protecting the public.

When doing risk assessments for the Parole Board you have to ensure that what was wrong with the offender has been treated. And treated thoroughly. Only then do you recommend release.

This 'othering' of people in prison was seen as a perfectly normal and unproblematic standpoint. Functionalists in this sample saw their role as being about reducing the risk that a 'prisoner' poses as opposed to improving that person's life *per se*. If that happens as a consequence of their interventions, then that is a happy correlate. Whilst not as a-hominine as the Retributivists, they are, as a consequence of their approach, much more procedurally focussed than Humanists. This meant that sometimes they were overreliant on the mechanics and bureaucracy of the job:

… if you're writing the risk assessment efficiently and as it's supposed to be written and you're using all the scoring guides and you know … then you shouldn't really have to worry because … it's standardised, so that's … it's … you're following, you know, protocol more than it being about your clinical opinion if you see what I mean?

This individual, like many of the other Functionalists, drew some comfort from the fact that there were guidelines and good practice instructions that governed their work. It meant not only could they shed some of the responsibility attached to their role but also it provided a means by which they could avoid some of the emotional labour inherent to their work. As one acknowledged: *The [protocols] enable you to objectify what could otherwise be a very emotive and difficult situation.*

However, one positive consequence of this reliance on procedure is that Functionalists often expressed a desire to do more than is required when it comes to risk assessments and interventions. Nearly all stated that they wished to see the prisoner as often as possible to do a thorough job of assessing the risk of that individual. This contrasted with Humanists who expressed similar wishes but in order to understand the *person*. This Functionalist explained:

> We are supposed to interview for the minimum of three hours, on each guy that you do, but I often see them for longer than that if they are there and they're available ... when you can just pop back and forth to ask them various things they often bring different information ... that allows you to be thorough and to do a good job in assessing their risk.

The language used by many Functionalists was also of note as it tended towards formality and neutralisation. For instance, when Humanists spoke about the prisoners, they may refer to '*background*' or '*history*', whereas Functionalists would speak of an '*offender's collateral data*' or '*contextual*' information. Another example is that when Humanists referred to the people they worked with they may say things like '*... one of the men I worked with last week ...*' or '*I was working with the guys ...*', whereas the Functionalists would use terms such as '*clients*' or '*offenders*' which imposed a linguistic distance between them and those they worked with. This Functionalist was typical:

> If I am allocated a risk assessment to do I would start by finding out the collateral data for that offender. So, I would look at previous psychology reports, I would have a look at the psychology file, I would have a look at his offender management file, so that would be like depositions; previous wing file if he had been to another jail etc. All of the reports, psychiatric assessments; presentence reports; I would have a look at all of that information before I was to see the offender.

A further aspect of the Functionalists' approach to their assessment and reha-bilitative work was the pragmatic approach they can often took towards the work, the prisoners they worked with, and the role of forensic psychology in general:

> My biggest bugbear is that we do not assess people early enough and then kind of determine where sentence should take them and to what establishment. We kind of... particularly working at [name of prison] was that you would get ... [someone] near to the end of their

sentence and then it would be this man needs a PCL-R – he has been in 25 years. It kind of feels a little bit wrong doing the PCLR now and that actually he needs to go back to closed conditions, surely somebody should have done that at the beginning of the sentence and said what would be suitable for that person.

There were two further aspects to this pragmatism. Many psychologists found the experience of being immersed in the sadness and chaos of the lives of prisoners both a 'pain' and a cause of stress. However, Functionalists were far less likely to talk in these terms, and though many found the work hard and stressful, they were less prone to prioritise this and took a much more pragmatic approach:

Well, yes, it is stressful and you have to put up with a lot of ... stuff but it's not like being a nurse in A&E is it? You just get on with it and switch off when you get home.

This sense of 'getting on with it' was quite common to Functionalists, who regarded resilience as both a desirable facet of their professional personas and also a fundamental requirement of the job. However, areas of frustration could arise when the ultimate goal of public protection and their pragmatic efforts were constrained by external influences:

What can be frustrating ... what can get to you is ... If you and me were having an interview now and I motivate you in some degree it is not going to be that influential if you have to walk out the door and then worry about your house. That impacts on what we can do ... and sometimes that is not recognised.

It is frustrating when you put the work in, do the intervention and then ... then it's all undone by [the prison]. You can only do what you can.

The pragmatism described here even extended to areas of the role which other groups, including both the Humanists and (some of) the Utilitarians, found to be difficult. Perhaps the most explicit example of this relates to the feeding back of negative reports. Humanists, in particular, found this to be a difficult aspect of their role, involving a complex interplay of the deflection and inversion forms of *emotive labour*. It was important for them to communicate thoroughly their findings and have those findings understood by the prisoner in a positive way. However, for Functionalists this understanding of their findings and recommendations was preferred but not necessary and was indicative of the forms of emotive labour that they themselves saw as necessary to operate with efficacy:

I am generally not that bothered if somebody does not get it because I think sometimes we have to make recommendations they are not going to like.

> It is not necessary that the client understands the report ... the
> recommendations ... all that matters is that they accept it.

It was clear that for the Functionalists the function of emotive labour was to
serve the greater concern of rehabilitation/public protection. Feeding back
negative reports only involves processes of deflection/inversion (or even
evocation) if that served the desired outcome – in order to achieve an 'acceptance' of the recommendations. This distancing was directly related to both
their procedural perspective and bureaucratic dependency. If the procedure was
a correct one and was followed to the letter, then they were, by definition, acting
properly. Their individual agency and power was not a consideration. There
was little moral contemplation beyond the immediate consequentialism of
gaining a prisoner's acquiescence. However, it is clear that such a procedural
approach indicates an ingrained and reflexive coping strategy which allows for a
separation between their work and the evocation of the attendant emotions.
Here then is a procedural objectivity which limit's the degree of *emotional
labour* that they must engage in to operate successfully as a forensic
psychologist.

Functionalists also saw it as their remit to educate others around them,
including both operational and governing staff, on the vicissitudes of risk and risk
management, crime and its causes, rehabilitation, and security:

> I think a forensic psychologist should have a good understanding
> of the origins of crime, why people commit crime, their
> psychopathology, and what can be done about it. And I think it
> is one of our functions to try and communicate that to everybody.

> That is what I see as the whole function of forensic psychology and
> how it fits into the prison or the probation service. Making sense of
> the why people have offended and communicating that to others in
> the prison.

Three-quarters of the participants mentioned indeterminately sentenced prisoners as both a burden in terms of the amount of work that those sentences have
produced and also as an understandable and proportionate sentence in the face of
large numbers of dangerous, or high risk, prisoners. However, this general support for the sentence is somewhat outstripped by the strength of the support
offered by both the Functionalists and the Retributivists. Functionalists located
their support in terms of the work that could be done (in theory) with individuals
serving these type of sentences as well as the public protection element of the
sentence:

> The concept behind it I think is a good one and I agree that you
> need some risk assessment to support progress rather than just
> being the least time you get out.

> I kind of do agree with the premise behind the IPP sentence and the need to get multidisciplinary say so about whether somebody has made progress or not. I do think that is right.

> The IPP ... I think in theory a brilliant idea. In practice a bit of a disaster.

> In principle I think the sentence is right ... it's right that someone is not released until it is safe to do so but in practice ... well I think they got some things wrong ... like the amount of time it takes to get someone on the necessary course may be longer than what their tariff is and that's not right ....

In these quotes it is the principle which is adamantly agreed with not necessarily the actual practice and administration of the sentence. This support lies in the fact that the prisoner is seen as a risk subject who needs to be managed and controlled and this being the fundamental function of the psychologist working in prison. Functionalists were far more concerned with the rehabilitation of the offender in order to reduce risk, as such they were more likely to focus on what work could be done. This was often the source of their frustrations with the sentence. For example, many of them noted that there was often insufficient time before the initial parole hearing to complete work that needed to be done to address the prisoners risk, which could result in delays in a prisoner's release – which would then have subsequent effects to their work. However, regardless of these frustrations, there was general support for the sentence due to both its promulgation of psychological services and for the fact it enabled them to do thorough risk assessments and treatment with those perceived as dangerous. As one noted:

> ... that to me is the ultimate risk assessment to actually have to assess, has this individual addressed their risk to the extent that they are now able to go out in the community and not be a risk of harm and not be a risk of re-offending. Or should they remain a prisoner. Because I think that – it is first and foremost a big responsibility to the public to make sure the people are not released who are still a risk of harm. But then you have also got a huge responsibility for the individual because as I have said earlier I would not like to think that anyone in the system was in prison for any longer than they needed to be. I think as soon as people can go back in the community and risk can be managed there, or they are no longer a risk then let's get them out of here.

Functionalists are categorised by their functional approach to psychological services, their consequentialist moral outlook, their reliance on protocols and bureaucratic procedures, and their pragmatic approach to the vicissitudes of prison work.

Utilitarians

In philosophical terms Utilitarianism is related to that branch of ethical thought which proposes that the *happiness* of the greater number is the one intrinsic good that actions and social arrangements are geared towards achieving (Williams, 1993). Therefore, in its simplest form, that which is moral and right is that which brings happiness to the greatest number; and that which brings happiness to the greater number must necessarily bring (in the long run) greater happiness to the individual, as they are inherently part of the greater number. In variant forms the Utilitarian argument regarding the happiness of the individual has come to be seen in quite paternalistic terms. The individual themselves may not know what is in fact going to bring about their happiness and therefore it is up to morally savvy 'others' to impose that which will bring about their happiness (Warburton, 1999). To a certain degree it is in this sense that the term is used – in general those psychologists defined as Utilitarians perceive imprisonment as a general good, which brings about some bettering of the lives of either the individual or the wider society, and as such this is the locus of their professional and personal approach.

Within the sample there were but three who could be classified as Utilitarians; however, in wider conversations with forensic psychologists, this positionality was expressed as being quite common. Nearly all those who have been subsequently spoken to have said that they have met a Utilitarian in one form or another. With regard to the three from the original sample, one was largely welfarist in approach, one was punitive in approach, and the other shared some aspects of both perspectives. The welfare-orientated individual saw imprisonment as good for prisoners because it enabled them to escape their chaotic lifestyles and thus improve their lives. The punitively focussed individual saw punishment as good for the individual as it maximises their opportunities to change and become part of wider society again. The other individual expressed opinions that fell, or swung, between these poles. However, regardless of attitudinal position, what categorised their responses, and thus places them within this field, was the manner in which they spoke in terms of what was 'good' or 'right'.

> It feels like it is a bit more meaningful than working in ... a load of other professions that I could think of. So, feel like you are sort of doing – your job has got some kind of purpose that you are trying to kind of achieve a great good if you know what I mean?

> Working with the prisoners here ... it feels like I'm doing some good, you know?

> Many [prisoners] here, they've not had good lives, they've been hurt and they've hurt others ... if we can help them to lead good lives and stop them from being hurt and from hurting others then it's only right that we do so.

For the Utilitarians in this sample, though they were focussed upon the prisoner, placing them high on the list of stakeholders, they were not so interested in 'palliating' the effects of the prison for they saw prison as a positive thing for prisoners. In this regard they were hominine in their approach but in a very different way than the Humanists. One particular individual who had worked with a lot of substance misusing prisoners (due to the nature of a previous posting) saw prison itself as an intervention in the very chaotic and hazardous lives of the prisoners they worked with:

> Coming to prison is often the first time that many of the [prisoners] have had any stability in their lives ... safety too, I suppose ... it's only here that they can even begin to think about changing and making their lives better. As I said earlier that's why I think prison can be good for some of them.

Whereas the more punitively focussed individual saw the prison from a less hominine perspective but still saw it as a place where positive individual change could be affected:

> I think we need to enable the individual to make positive changes but it is also about protecting the public and making sure that [their] time in prison is effective. ... If you have done your job well and if prison has worked for them you should not see them again, that's where we can do some good.

The third Utilitarian expressed much the same point of view as these others in their regard of the prison and its utility for both wider society and the individual. Each defined the prison as a moral site. They all saw the prison as a good. It was not that good works could be achieved there in spite of the conditions, which was a view expressed by some Humanists and Functionalists, but that the prison was a good in and of itself. This was a very different perspective than that expressed by any other psychologists. This was also something of an abstracted position. Each of their respective establishments had received negative reports from HMIP and had been highlighted as having poor conditions, high drug usage, and concerning levels of violence. Yet they still maintained that the prison, as an entity, was good for prisoners.

This moral positionality meant the Utilitarians were most comfortable with the power that lay inherent to their professional role. This related to their belief that they are involved in doing, or working on the side of, right. All three acknowledged that theirs was a role of power and accepted that as a necessary consequence of working within the prison. In this sense they were much more able than the Humanists to reconcile their own moral position in terms of their practice and the coercive reality in which they operated. These psychologists saw this coercive reality as being necessary because without it they would not be able to make the possibility of 'offender' change a reality. As one of them summed up: *It is a position of power, it has to be. What use would we be if we did not have that authority?* It is these psychologists, more so than even the Functionalists, who are able to achieve that tragic perspective that Muir jr (1977) argued was necessary for the development of an effective professional persona. Though there was a recognition and an acceptance of their power, this was not something to be taken lightly. The power was a tool and not something to be revelled in; it was the means by which they could achieve the 'good' with which they were concerned:

> ... but it's about doing the right thing. I suppose some may ... a very bad psychologist somewhere may enjoy that relationship, get off on it, but for me that's not what it's about. For me it's about being able to do what's right for them [prisoners] and helping them to realise where they have gone wrong and what they need to do to get back on track.

This last quote also reveals the approach that the Utilitarians took towards rehabilitation, which came about only when prisoners accepted what they had done and took responsibility for their actions. It was noted previously that one of the consequences of the introduction of New Public Management ideals to the penal estate was an attendant expectation for the responsibilisation of prisoners. Responsibilisation refers to the policy and practice of requiring prisoners, especially young prisoners (Muncie, 1999), to both be accountable and to take responsibility for their own actions (Cavadino, Dignan, Mair, & Bennett, 2019). This responsibilisation agenda, and the accompanying subjectivism, has been a dominant theme of both neoliberal and neoconservative criminal justice policy in the late modern era (Squires & Stephen, 2005). Though inherent to the approach by all categories of psychologists, this was a position held strongest by the Utilitarian who aligned the responsibilisation of the prisoner with their moral outlook:

> You can say what you like to people as long as you have hopefully persuaded them that you are saying it because you have got their best interests at heart not just because you want to be bloody awful to them. You make them confront some terrible that has happened – it was not something that happened to them it was something they did, they need to acknowledge that before we can move on.

> If someone comes into prison, they have ended up there for a reason. If you do nothing to address that reason, and if they don't, or can't, accept that reason, then nothing will change and they will continue to hurt those around them.

In this they have much more in common with the Functionalists than the Humanists in that they see their role in terms of '*interventions*' and the '*medical model*' of forensic psychology. They were also much more aligned with the Functionalists in the manner in which they approached the processes of emotion work and, specifically, *emotive labour*. As the quote above indicates, it does not matter if forcing a prisoner to confront what they have done evokes trauma as long as it serves the greater good. They were also less likely to be concerned with inverting any negative associations for the prisoners that may result from the responsibilisation agenda. When discussing the pain that can arise when forcing a prisoner to confront the harms that they have inflicted on others, one noted that the pain '*was necessary for the offender to take on board*' so they could '*then begin to change for the better*'. The emotive labour here then was one of harsh evocation rather than deflection or inversion. The emotive labour was concerned with breaking through the defences of the prisoner and making them confront the harms that they had inflicted. Unlike for other psychologists, this did not result in having to adopt processes of emotional labour to cope with their actions. This is perhaps due to the fact that they are far more positivistic in their outlook than the other welfare-orientated Humanists. For Utilitarians, the offender has, as evidenced by their offending, shown that they are in moral abeyance (Mathiesen, 1990), and that they must be bought back in line with the general good in order for them to return to society as productive and useful members. As this person explained:

> That to me is what psychology, a lot of it, is all about. It is about changing [prisoner's] behaviour so that it has a positive impact for others.

Unlike the Functionalists and Retributivists, they were much more hesitant about the promulgation of indeterminate sentences. They thought the sentence was okay '*in an ideal world*' where work could be done with prisoners but was impractical for implementation under the current system. They also felt that there was some question as to whether or not the nature of the sentence and its attendant bureaucratic problems undermined the good work that could be achieved with prisoners. In this regard it was felt that if the sentence itself became '*an impediment*', then it was not a '*good thing*' but that if these issues were resolved and that the good work could be bolstered and supplemented, then such sentenced would be '*appropriate and right*'.

A further consequence of the Utilitarian's moral outlook and comfort with their power is that they were much more able to cope with the types of stresses and everyday hassles that resulted in a great deal of *emotional labour* for other psychologists. For them, the moral lens with which they experience their day-to-day work shelters them and ameliorates the harmful effects of the penal world. They saw their work in contributing to the greater good, and as such if they suffer in its pursuit then that is justified. This 'martyr-like' attitude, whether a protective narrative or a genuine construct, acts as a shield by which the rigours of the professional world is kept at bay and their selves are protected. As one of them noted:

> ... yeah it's stressful, it can get on top of you at times ... but knowing that what you are doing is helping people, helping society, and that that's the right thing to do ... knowing that you're helping in some way, that you're doing some good, that's what sees you through the bad times and keeps you coming in [to work] every day.

As the sample for this group was so small, this is a more limited description than for the preceding two categories and it is recognised that there may be aspects of this group that a larger sample would reveal. However, what distinguishes the Utilitarian from the other categories of psychologists is their overt and overdeveloped moral sense of their work contributing to some greater good. This occupational morality dictates the manner in which they perceive, approach, and cope with the practicalities of forensic psychology work in the modern prison.

Retributivists

There were but two individuals who fell within this category. What categorised this group was the primacy of attention and focus given to the punitive and public protection aspects of their roles. However, although there was some similarity in general theme, the individuals in question were so widely disparate in their outlooks and approaches that they had to be separated into two distinct types. The separation was fairly straightforward as one of the individuals in question had a very different perspective on their role to any other respondent in the study – it is this person who has been described in terms of being a Retributive Idealist. The other individual was, in many ways, a Humanist in approach but seemed to be so disillusioned and cynical that their responses were often tinged with both punitive and public protection mantras. Therefore, it was decided to place this individual within the punitive/PP quadrant but separate them from the Idealist by defining their moral approach as one of Cynical Retributivism.

The Idealist

Within philosophical and economic discourses, 'idealism' is where all realities are mentally constructed, comprised of a set of ideated states, or that economic factors are inherent to nations and societies (Smith, 2005). In this thesis the Idealist is defined more generally as someone who 'prioritises ideals, principles, values, and goals over concrete realities' and therefore responds to the world 'as it might or should be', this being opposed to pragmatists who 'focus on the world as it presently is (Smith, 2005, p. 341). The Idealist interprets their reality in terms of what they think it should be and thus acts accordingly. The Idealist of this study perceived their professional world in terms of both the punitivity of the criminal justice system and of public protection ideals.

It must be noted that the Idealist was a distinct anomaly. This person's responses were consistently different from that of every other participant in the study, except in relation to notions of public protection and the dangerousness of prisoners. However, even here the similarity to the position of the Functionalists was only superficial. For the Idealist, not only was the notion of public protection the overarching impetus for their involvement in forensic psychology, and a driving motivator in their day-to-day practice, but also the very ideal against which they weighed and judged the very existence of psychology within the prison. When asked what the core role of the prison-based forensic psychologist was this individual responded '*I see my job in terms of protection of the public and risk to others. End of story*'. Every other psychologist, even when they had, like the Functionalists, public protection as a motivator, derived some of their job satisfaction from working with people – regardless of whether this was from a desire to help the individual prisoner (Humanist), a desire to understand the prisoner in order to be more proficient in carrying out their duties (Functionalist), or to enable them to realign the 'offender' with some notion of the greater good (Utilitarian). However, at no point did the Idealist express any such sentiment and I pushed them on this much more so than others. They freely admitted to deriving their job satisfaction solely from the rather abstract notion of protecting the public. As they stated:

> The best thing about being a psychologist, umm … a forensic psychologist, especially working here is helping to protect the public …

It was noted earlier that the Functionalist forced a degree of separation between the prisoner and the public in the manner in which they discussed both. However, for the Idealist, there seemed to be no connection in the first place. The 'offender' and the public inhabited separate realms due to one having committed an offence and being sent to prison '*to be punished*'. This removal from society meant that the individual prisoner was, for the Idealist, defined solely by their 'offender' status. The prisoner was perceived as a risk subject and a punishable other (Joffe, 1999). As they stated explicitly:

> If they end up here then … the courts have judged them and decided that they are dangerous … deserve to be punished. That's what we do … make sure that the offender is assessed properly so that the sentence can be carried out properly.

At a later stage of the interview this person also noted that the role of psychology in the prison was to '*facilitate the punishment ordered by the courts*'. This again was in stark contrast to every other participant. The Idealist seemed to view the prison as a place *of* punishment rather than as a place where people were sent *as* a punishment. Even the Utilitarians who held close the punitivity of the prison did not go this far in their assessment of the role of the prison nor the role of forensic psychology.

Coupled to this punitive attitude was also a high degree of abstraction of the prisoner. Their positionality here was reductive. The prisoner was seen only in terms of their risk, their dangerousness, and their sentence. This went beyond the neutralising and bureaucratising labels used by the Functionalists. When the Idealist used the terms '*offender*' and '*subject*', they were heavily value-laden and designed to convey a particular perspective of the prisoner.[2] There seemed to be

---

[2]At the time I thought this was directed at me personally as the individual in question was quite antagonistic and bought up my status as a former prisoner a number of times. However, upon reflection and closer examination of the transcript, this was dismissed as it flavoured their every response.

little sympathy or empathy for prisoners and they expressed no acceptance of the wider, or structural, circumstances within which offending may take place. Though not explicitly stated they seemed to be of the opinion that prisoners rationally chose their particular lifestyles and thus chose to offend and thus deserved their punishment without remittance. They noted:

> It always amazes me when an offender complains about having to do the [offending behaviour] course … I mean they have decided to commit their index offence … and that is clear evidence of poor decision making.

Their attitude contained a contradictory mix of the positivism displayed by the other psychologists and the Classicist attitudes that had informed the 'just deserts' era of the criminal justice system throughout the 1980's (von Hirsch, 1986). Consequentially, they saw the 'offender' as both rational and inherently dangerous and thus interpreted themselves, and the wider profession of psychology, as some sort of guardians safeguarding the public from the dangerous prisoners who were under their charge. As they noted when discussing the IPP sentence, which they saw as justified and proportionate, and the role of psychologists in assessing these prisoners:

> Some of the subjects we have to work with have done some very disturbing and horrific things … we have to ensure they are not released until it is safe to do so … that's our job.

> I have one subject, a rapist, IPP, my job as a psychologist is to ensure that he is not released until it is safe to do so. If it is ever safe to do so. It is my job to protect the public.

This also highlighted the degree to which they adhered to the responsibilisation agenda and the manner in which they viewed the offending behaviour courses that were necessarily part of their role. For the Idealist, the purpose of offending behaviour courses was '*to make the offender take responsibility for what they had done*' and to '*fulfil our public protection duties*'. Here the only emotive labour that the Idealist portrayed was in evoking a sense of responsibility and of punishment for the 'offender'. Given this individuals' attitude, it was no surprise that in terms of the hierarchy of stakeholders the offender was not even mentioned. In fact, neither were prison staff nor prisoner's families mentioned either. The question put to the respondent in this particular situation was who are the main beneficiaries of prison psychology work do you think? The response that came back was terse and to the point '*Future victims and the public*'.

In terms of both the power associated with the role of forensic psychology and the *emotional labour* that can be engendered by the realities of the work, the Idealist again occupies a different position to the other psychologists interviewed. With regard to power, this person accepted that they were in a position of authority but saw the power as belonging to the actual prison itself and therefore themselves as a member of staff. Power was not something that was inherent to either their profession or the expertise that they possessed. The Idealist very much saw themselves as just part of the machinery of the prison, or the wider criminal justice system, a cog in the wheel:

> Yes, I suppose we are in a position of power ... but that's only because we are staff members isn't it? We are employed by the prison and that place [pointing back towards the prison] is built on authority, we are part of that ... just like the officers, the Governors and everyone else ....

To some extent this was an attitude shared by other participants. However, where the Idealist differed was in two regards: firstly, there was their grouping of themselves with all the other staff members; and secondly, was their dismissal of the concerns voiced by some of the others – especially with regard to how prisoners may perceive their assessments and the manner in which the Parole Board may utilise those reports. These two issues were of some concern to a number, though not all, of those interviewed. However, the Idealist saw these issues as just part and parcel of prison work, and therefore of psychological work, and dismissed them out of hand. For instance, when asked if they ever worry about feeding back reports to the people they work with, this individual stated:

> No ... I know that some of them won't like what I have to say or recommend but that's part of the job, you accept that ... you just have to expect that and ... you have to just get on with it. In the end, it doesn't matter if they don't like what you're saying, you've got your job to do and they have to accept it.

Likewise, with regard to the Parole Board and their interpretation of the reports that the psychologists prepare for them they just noted, in an example of *post hoc ergo propter hoc* reasoning, that:

> If they [the Parole Board] decide that someone is not safe to be released, and base that on your report, then you know what you have done was right and your recommendation was justified ....

With regard to *emotional labour* and the manner in which they experience the frustrations of the job, they were, again, very different from the other categories. Whilst they did note workload as an issue, they placed this in relation to the greater workload that everyone in their prison was now being asked to do in the face of a growing prison population and a reduction of staff. What was more pertinent to the Idealist was that they felt increasingly alienated within the prison and that this caused them some occupational distress. Their team had been reduced in numbers in the recent past and they had been relocated within the prison to the administrative block away from the rest of the prison. This all served to highlight the alienation that they felt in the prison.

Idealist: Since we moved up into admin it's different. It used to feel like ... like we were included in the prison, part of the team maybe, a little bit, I don't know but now ...

Interviewer: How does that feel? Is it like ...

Idealist: It's hard ... it's like ... you know when you have friends who used to date and then they split up and it's awkward when you see the other one, no one knows what to say ... it's a bit like that. I mean not the same but ... not all the staff would talk to us, as I said before, but some would ... but now that we've moved, they tend not to ... it's not nice now.

This represented a particular emotional trigger for the Idealist as they saw themselves as part of the prison – this was a fundamental part of the *ideal* that they established for their role and their work. It was the clash here between their perceived professional reality and the corporeal reality of the prison that necessitated emotional labour. In many ways this is reminiscent of some of the problems that Carlen (2008) highlights with regard to imagined penalities and the ontological trauma that can arise due to the clash of realities. For the Idealist, this resulted in a sense of loss and therefore of both professional and personal isolation – they felt excluded from that which gave their occupation meaning.

The Retributive Idealist was an anomaly and only represents the moral perspective of one individual. This of course, as with the next category, impacts negatively on how much can be extrapolated from the existence of a single entity in a small sample. Nevertheless, the Idealist as described here offers an interesting counterpoint to the other categories thus far described. For this individual what categorised their professional outlook was their conservative, punitive approach to service delivery and an unsympathetic and unempathetic view of prisoners. Furthermore, their idealism leaves them vulnerable to both occupational uncertainty and ontological insecurity. These then become a vicious reinforcing loop that contributes to their conservative and punitive outlook.

The Cynic

This individual was defined by their descent into retributivism. They displayed overt aspects of occupational burnout, overimmersion in the prison, and professional disillusionment. Much of their account was anguished and laden in emotional labour. However, what defined them was their retreat into a cynical and bleak position from which they perceived and spoke of their role and profession. It is this aspect which distinguishes them from the other categories and, indeed, from the Idealist individual with whom they share the Retributive category.

At first, this individual presented as a Humanist but their responses involved an overt duality that meant they no longer fit into that category. The more they spoke, the more it became clear that they no longer felt the way they once had about either their career or their profession. Their responses became increasingly tinged with a lazy punitiveness. For instance, they noted that

> Cynic: ... yeah, when I first started, which seems like a lifetime ago now, I was interested in every aspect of the job ... the assessments, the courses, the advice and guidance, the training ... all of it. But now? Erm ... it's just, you know ... I come in, do what I have to do to make sure their sentence is being served, and then go ...

> Interviewer: It sounds like it's lost its sparkle ...

> Cynic: Yeah, exactly. I don't know ... I just ... maybe it's that I'm in a low period but I don't enjoy it anymore.

This disillusionment was pervasive in every response and evidenced their move away from a previous Humanist position. Though displaying some elements of the Humanist's hominine approach, they contradicted this with other, or later, statements. For instance, this person had stated that the best thing about being a psychologist working in prison was working with people and helping them to overcome their issues but then followed this by saying:

> My role, forensics, is not like a counselling role. It is not clinical, it is not counselling and that has been something when I have worked with people before and they might off load or they might tell me stuff and I think you have got to be careful to stick with .... I am here to assess risk, I am not here as a counsellor ....

They later explained that they were no longer interested in '*dealing with [prisoners] problems*' and that they now '*just do risk*'. Likewise, they had shared the optimism portrayed by the Humanists at one point in their career. When discussing what they felt their best experience had been, they related a story about a particularly infamous and recalcitrant prisoner they had worked with in the high security estate whom they had managed to make some progress with, where others had not. They went on to explain that this showed how everyone had the ability to change but then a few minutes later went on to say:

> Sometimes you think what is the point ... you can spend months working with people, thinking you've done a good job, got through to them ... then they get out, two weeks later they're back. You see them on the wing and they just shrug at you ... and it's just AGHHHH! That happens all the time here ....

Joined to the disillusionment and an increasing pessimism about those they worked with was an increasing unhappiness with their role, their establishment, and the profession in general. They stated repeatedly that they were not happy with where they were working, they found it stressful, tiring, and emotionally draining and they were only able to draw minimal satisfaction from their work. The *emotional labour* that this individual was having to undertake in order to maintain an effective presence as a forensic psychologist was immense:

> No, I have not been happy in it. I have enjoyed it in some ways but you know you get personally ground down, you get no reward for it, you don't get any positives apart from your own personal positives and then you have to cling to them.

> Every day you think to yourself ... you have to, you have to ... psych yourself up just to get through the gate. Then you have to psych yourself up to look at the ever growing to do list, then psych yourself up to open an offender's file ... every day. It's tiring.

This stress seemed to arise from the fact that they were not doing the work that they had originally enjoyed. This led to a great deal of frustration, not just with their work but also with their colleagues, the prison, and the wider criminal justice system. When trying to get this individual to talk about their experiences it was difficult to get them to separate their cynical responses from their positive ones. Often one was couched in terms of the other. For instance, when discussing the case of the difficult prisoner mentioned above they had stated that this was their best experience because they had made some progress with that individual but then immediately went on to say how rare a situation that was and therefore even seemed to see that good experience as a source of frustration. When asked specifically about the issue of frustration, they replied as follows:

> Interviewer: If possible can you tell me a time when you felt most frustrated professionally?

> Cynic: All of it really.

One key point about this psychologist was their overall level of defensiveness. They were clearly uncomfortable with their cynical perspective and therefore felt compelled to defend those responses and their self. Just as the conflict between occupational reality and ideal caused a certain ontological insecurity for the Idealist, the separation between the once held moral position of the Humanist and the extant held emotionally fatigued state of the Cynic led to a similar ontological precarity. This led to a vicious circle – the cynicism led to the conflicted moral position, which reinforced the negative experiences, which led to the ever-increasing dissatisfaction with their role and their profession, and so on. It was clear that this individual had utterly failed to reconcile themselves morally to the coercive reality in which they operated and thus they had moved from a once tragic perspective to a wholly cynical one (Muir, jr, 1977). This is the danger for Humanists, as they are unable to reconcile their dual moral positions, this descent into cynicism becomes a very distinct possibility.

This cynicism had a number of distinct consequences for their professional practice as they now took the path of least resistance with regard to work and had developed a range of avoidant habits (Muir, jr 1977). The quote above about being there to assess risk and not be a counsellor is one example. Not only was this indicative of the degree of *emotional labour* that they were undertaking but also was indicative of the forms of *emotive labour* that they were willing and able to engage in. They had become somewhat withdrawn from those they were working with and, whilst doing a lot more than going through the motions – professional pride prevented that, were limited in what they were prepared to invest in anymore. For them it was easier to just concentrate on the assessments, the risk, the public protection aspect of the role, and the management of the sentence. We have seen above that all psychologists were, in differing iterations, concerned with processes of evocation, deflection, or inversion. This was not true for this individual. When asked how they approached working with difficult prisoners and feeding back negative reports, they shrugged and stated that

> Some will get it. Some won't. That's their problem not mine. As long as I've done my job … I've fulfilled my [public protection] duties.

This is why they occupy a position between the poles of public protection and punitivity. Though they were clearly focussed upon the public protection mantra, their dismissive cynicism had unintended overtones of punitivity. In effect, it made their role easier and less emotionally harrowing or intensive to just concentrate on basic concerns and complete them with bureaucratic precision.

One Humanist accidently captured the appeal of relying on bureaucratic precision as a means of avoiding complex emotion work when discussing forensic psychology and the prison in general. This person had stated that they felt that psychology should be concerned with protecting the individual and aiding them to cope with imprisonment and therefore to aid in their rehabilitation. However, they went on to note that for some of their colleagues this might not always be the case and that sometimes

> … some psychologists … so quickly jump to the public protection stuff because it is a clear role. They can just focus on – I am here to risk assess, to report, to protect the public. And it is quite simplistic in that way. And that is an easier place to be in your head isn't it than having to constantly juggle should I, shouldn't I, how should I, how do I …?

This occupational position, which the Cynic had settled into, allowed them to resolve their moral conflict. They no longer asked the difficult questions that they once would have when they were a Humanist. Working within the prison had *'ground'* them down to the point where they were emotionally, morally, and professionally fatigued. Where once they may have attempted to ameliorate the effects of imprisonment for prisoners by engaging in varying emotive labours now, they no longer bothered. Everything they did professionally had become an extra burden and as such they took the path of least resistance in terms of caseload and emotional/emotive investment.

Conclusion

The differences in personal, moral, professional, and occupational outlook that emerged from the data meant that a typology of prison-based psychologists became inevitable. These differentiated yet native attitudes meant that though there was some commonality between in-group individuals, they were distinct from others in the sample. This is important because the differing positionalities of Humanists, Functionalists, Utilitarians, and Retributivists highlight varying occupational approaches and practices. For instance, each of these 'types' have, due to operative motives, distinctive forms of working with prisoners in terms of engagement and intended outcome. Each type prioritises different elements of psychological practice and this means that prisoners are necessarily in receipt of differential practice. This is especially true of the *emotive labour* that differing types of psychologist are engaging in. Where some psychologists are concerned with ameliorating prisoner's experiences of the prison and the psychological 'interventions' they are subject to via processes of evocation, deflection, or inversion, some are not. Such differential practice represents an interesting conundrum for those who manage psychological services in the prison estate because it is testament to just how subjective their service can be.

A further consequence of this typology, to be explored in more depth in the next chapter, is concerned with how psychologists in this sample perceive their ontological positioning within the penal landscape. As each type has a differing view on their role, it means that occupational relationships can be dependent on how they are utilised within the establishments in which they work. If they are utilised in such ways that it competes or clashes with their sense of psychological self then this can negatively impact on their working lives. Not only is their engagement with prisoners dependent upon whether or not their role adheres to their professional positionality but so too is their relationships with other staff, their in-team colleagues, and even their wider profession.

Chapter 5

Occupational Experiences of Forensic Psychologists

Its quite weird what we do, and prison is a weird place to work. In the excitement, the rush to get in and get going, you never really stop to think about that and what it might do to you. Now, a few years in, I think about that a lot.

–Trainee Psychologist

One absence in a lot of the prison literature is an acknowledgement of just how peculiar the prison is a place of employment. These disciplinary megaliths are coercive entities in which a great deal of misery is visited upon our fellow citizens. They are often brutal and brutalising environments where horrors upon horrors can be heaped upon our fellow citizens ('prisoner' and 'screw' alike). As Oscar Wilde (1898) once noted in his famous Ballad 'The vilest deeds like poison weeds, Bloom well in prison-air'. Yet ... yet, they are also mundane places of employment. A place where people get up and go to in order to earn a salary. In them people have their tea floats, they gossip, they idle, they bicker, they laugh, they cry, they push paper, they fill out forms, they have to do mandatory manual handling training(!), they have line managers and performance reviews, in essence, they go about their ordinary working lives.

This chapter is concerned with exploring this reality. It is concerned with how psychologists experience their work and occupational environment. The typology a psychologist belongs to, and the attendant ontological positioning that this represents, can have consequences for how a psychologist interacts with their place of work. However, this was not the only relevant factor. It is the interaction between these factors, some of which were universal to the sample, and the typological attitudes that shall be explored here. The first section details what psychologists found positive about working in a prison, what conferred occupational satisfaction, and what ensured professional well-being. The second section looks at the factors that affected occupational practice and professional well-being in more negative ways and which caused dissatisfaction for those psychologists who experienced them.

Forensic Psychologists, 91–122
Copyright © 2021 Jason Warr
Published under exclusive licence by Emerald Publishing Limited
doi:10.1108/978-1-83909-960-120200006

Occupational Satisfaction

The US Corrections study conducted by Mackain, Myers, Ostapiej, and Newman (2010) noted that economic factors, organisational support, and interpersonal relationships were all heavily correlated with job satisfaction or lack thereof. Although an important factor in the US study, very few of the psychologists interviewed in this research raised economic or fiscal factors as an issue. Therefore, this aspect of the discussion shall be limited to a single point. Of the three who did speak to remuneration, one indicated that being a prison psychologist was sufficiently well paid to allow for a comfortable and secure life. The other two who raised the issue of economic factors both perceived other aspects of their professional lives as unsatisfactory and therefore saw their level of remuneration as insufficient:

> The pay. We are not properly compensated for the work we are expected to do ... and working here demands a lot from you. Physically, emotionally, professionally.

> I don't think that our pay reflects our skill and I think that that very often ... affects motivation.

Nonfiscal concerns were ranked higher in terms of what would impact on occupational satisfaction. Variances in moral positionality shaped the manner in which psychologists approached issues of emotional and emotive labour as they relate to the minutiae of occupational experience. However, with regard to the sources of job satisfaction, there was a certain amount of uniformity amongst the sample. These sources fell into three main categories: first, seeing the fruits of their labours; second, the satisfaction derived from the wide variance of people with whom they worked and the intellectual challenge this engendered; and, third the positive relationships and support that came from working within a progressive and prosocial team.

The Product of Labour

It is a sad reality of our particular political economy that often a person's notion of value and self-worth is enmeshed with their labour. As such, a close relationship to the product of one's labour is heavily correlated with how an employee will view both their occupation and their toil (Ashman & Gibson, 2010). However, it was often the case that, due to the episodic contact that prison psychologists had with prisoners, they only saw them for a brief and limited period of time, and were thus often deprived any evidence of that product. As these psychologists noted:

> ... because people go and we don't really get to know what happens ... unless they come back again and then you know it hasn't gone well.

I don't get to see an awful lot of positives if you like, when people have done OK because in the prison they go off to another prison.

They were usually unaware of what happened with the prisoner after their contact with them had ceased. A number of participants spoke in terms of only seeing '*snapshots*' or '*glimpses*' of the lives of those they worked with. This often resulted in a situation where they would work with an individual and then receive no feedback as to the impact or efficacy of their input. Having no sense of achievement or accomplishment at work can be closely correlated with job dissatisfaction (Weiss & Cropanzano, 1996). As this person noted in response to being asked about the frustrations they experience:

Not seeing cases through. It's frustrating when you only get a snapshot ... when it's that fragment of their life.

For all but the Retributive Idealist it was seeing the fruits of their labour that was the greatest source of satisfaction. This was primarily because it validated their role both professionally and personally. What this 'seeing results' meant depended largely on the individual and their typological perspective. However, these did fall into three broad categories: seeing a change in the perspective/behaviour of the prisoner they were working with; seeing some change that would result in a reduction in risk/harm that the 'offender' may pose; and seeing evidence that they had done good work, whether that be an assessment, a report, or programme.

With regard to the first source of satisfaction, many participants located the best aspects of their job in their ability to help affect changes in the outlook/ worldview of prisoners. This was seen as an important aspect of the role of psychology, especially by the Humanists and Functionalists. For instance, one Humanist explained that:

The best thing about doing what I do is helping the prisoners to change their lives around and see the world differently.

For the Humanists in this sample this was a source of satisfaction because this changed perspective enabled the prisoner to lead a better life. In contrast, a Functionalist noted that for them the best thing about being a forensic psychologist working in prisons was:

... about helping them to change, to see themselves, their victims, their families, their lives in a different way.

This was because such an altered outlook was seen as necessary for the prisoner to be 'rehabilitated', i.e., reduce their attendant risk. In both cases, the change of perception adhered to their typological motivations and attached to the perceived purposes of their profession. Given the rarity of seeing such products of their labour, it is no surprise that when they see evidence of it this is cited as a primary source of job satisfaction. As one Humanist pointed out:

> What I really enjoy... what keeps me coming into work every day, is that moment when one of the lads gets it. They get that their life does not have to be the same as it was ... that it can be different for them.

This particular psychologist, who had plainly stated that they were in a 'down' period of their working life, was at pains to note that this 'light-bulb' moment offered them a real sense of achievement and a connection to their work. What this quote shows is that these satisfactions exist on a sliding scale from the fairly minor triumph described to some of those indicated in the quotes below:

> There was a gentleman who was the first ever guy I worked with I think in terms of doing a risk assessment and it was difficult, it was a difficult piece of work because of the way that he responded to me because he was my first guy I was working with in that respect, and we got to his parole hearing and it was just very difficult, probably one of the most intimidating aspects of my entire training period was definitely ... it was a nightmare. And anyway, he stayed in. The outcome was that this guy should stay in prison for a while and do some more work. And then he came up for review two years later and then I worked with him again and actually he had progressed and some things had gone really well. And then I went to his hearing, again and then he eventually got transferred to open conditions. And that is good, but that very rarely happens, to be able to see something and yes, it worked. It does work!

> It's seeing the work you have done, perhaps with a difficult prisoner, bear fruit. It's rare but now I have seen it a couple of times where I assessed someone early on in their sentence and then saw them much later and was able to recommend parole. I've had that twice now, but it makes everything worth it.

> I think one of the best examples for me was when I recommended release for somebody but I think that was because I was kind of recommending release and you do not often get to do that.

These quotes highlight the last two issues described – seeing a progression that will reduce the harm someone may pose and knowing that a good piece of work has been done. Returning to the point made above by Weiss and Cropanzano (1996), it is important for people to have a connection to the 'output' that their work creates, for this enables them to invest 'into' the work that they do and to receive back both meaning and a sense of professional self-worth. These are, they argue, core aspects to job satisfaction and can be essential in both the productivity of the worker and the well-being of the work force. For many of the uniformed staff you see this when they say that there has been a quiet day and everyone has gotten to go home safe and sound. They often have material evidence of their product – they have maintained order. In terms of this study, it was evident that only when the psychologists could see some outcome could they shift from seeing their role in abstract terms, from which it was difficult to draw any tangible satisfaction, to seeing it in concrete terms which allowed them to invest and derive a sense of worth. The following psychologists all noted, when describing the best aspect of their work, that in some way or another seeing these 'wins' was what made the job worthwhile and what they most remembered about their 'good' days

> Often there is a … what's the best way of describing this? Umm, a … separation, no a … disconnection between the work you do with a prisoner and then what happens to them, due to the limited involvement we may have with any one person. We are not like the OM's who get to see … we … we don't … this means that often you are left in the dark as to what, if any, benefit you have been. That can make it … difficult to … there is no product if you know what I mean. So, when you get that product, when you see someone progress or make a real change, then, then you have to grasp on to that … it doesn't happen much but when it does it's like YES!

> … I thinks it was probably when a group member that I had who did really well on the course, the sex offenders treatment programme, got released and then he umm … a few months later wrote in from outside to the governor you know saying how … umm S.O.T.P and specifically us as facilitators of that programme had really changed his life and that he'd told us what he was doing now and that he was really successful and that he had pulled it all together and I think that … probably … stands out for me,

> For me the, to repeat what I have already said, it is helping make change. So, I still remember … the people that I made a difference to.

> Interviewer: What is the best experience you have had?

> Psychologist: Probably working on the sex offender group with a man who then rang up after he had been released from [name of prison] to tell me how well he was doing. I think that is what you do the job for.

> Psychologist: … you see people actually grow up and you see them put learning into practice. That is positive. That is a really positive experience.

> Interviewer: How rare is it that you get to see that?

Psychologist: You don't see it a lot. You don't see it a lot at all. But when you do you can have ten thousand complaints and it kind of makes up for every single one of them.

One Utilitarian specifically linked this notion to providing evidence of their having done a good piece of work which also added to their sense of job satisfaction

I think it is when you see people progress you feel people are progressing, I think that is good, I think that is the best. And you are like – yes that works really well – that was a good assessment ... that was a good piece of work.

In contrast, a staunch Humanist put this in the following terms:

I love people ... I just find people really interesting, there's nothing that interest me more than you know ... humans as they are so I think that now I get to interact with so many different types of people every day and that makes every day different ... which I love. And I really, really enjoy seeing a change in people and ... you don't see much ... humph [smile] but you see a small amount of change ... or just, even if just a small increase in confidence or self-esteem and that I find really rewarding.

Intellectual and Professional Challenge

In the quote above, you see reward accruing from the very nature of the job being undertaken. Judge and Church (2000) argue that though core self-evaluation is highly correlated to job satisfaction, this evaluation process is influenced by how the worker perceives the actual job itself. For instance, Judge and Church (also see Saari & Judge, 2004) argue that if the job offers sufficient variance, maintains interest, offers up sufficient challenges to the workers professional skill set, then the job will be perceived positively. This will then allow for positive self-evaluation, and thus job satisfaction. This was indicated by the psychologist above noting that they '*loved*' seeing so many different people that it made every day different. Others also cited, as a source of both personal and occupational satisfaction, the intellectual challenge of the role and having to relate their training and expertise to practical cases. As such there were two sources of job satisfaction derived in this sense – the variation of working with differing people with different problems, and then relating the skill that they had learned to their every day job. This form of intellectual and professional challenge is important for the personal development of all those who work in therapeutic and counselling fields (Skovholt & Ronnestad, 1995) and is acknowledged as being especially important for psychologists working in criminal justice settings (Garland,

McCarty, & Zhao, 2009). Here, it is actually getting to practice being a 'psychologist' and the intellectual and professional challenge of being able to disentangle the psychological puzzles that individuals and their offending represented made the job worthwhile. Often this was expressed in terms of discovering or exploring what made people *'tick'* and *'why people had done what they had done'* as these psychologists explained:

> I think I enjoy the assessment side and I enjoy trying to understand the function maybe of an offence, why that happened, what the developmental factors are. I really enjoy that. It is really satisfying, being able to unpick that.

> I was always intrigued by what made people tick and why people committed crimes that they did ... now I really would like to know why people do what they do and I kind of fixated with what makes somebody so very different, even if they have the same kind of upbringing.

> I enjoy the interviews, I enjoy trying to understand, thinking about it, presenting that person with some ideas so we talked about that... I am thinking this, what do you think about that? I enjoy that. Sort of formulating, understanding, thinking about theory and how that can apply. Hypothesizing some of the reasons why that person might be where they are now. What had led them that way? What influences have driven that behaviour or shaped that behaviour?

> From a much more selfish point of view I find it utterly fascinating. I think working with other people – I get to spend my day listening to how other people think, how other people tick, what motivates them and that to me is absolutely fascinating ...

Worth noting the epistemic power represented in some of these quotes in terms of the 'expert' interpreting and imposing understanding through the lens of psychology. Anyway, a further point that contributes to job satisfaction and positive self-evaluation is perceiving the work as being worthwhile or morally productive (Judge & Church, 2000). Many participants referred to the job as *'important'* or it being a position of *'responsibility'* or of it having *'value'*. All these descriptions indicate a sense that the job is a worthy one and therefore this can ameliorate the negative effects of the job and refocus the bad into work positives. As we have seen in the last chapter, this was particularly true for the Functionalists and the Idealist who had a more deontological positionality and thus drew their satisfaction from performing their duty. However, others also drew some satisfaction from this moral aspect, as this Humanist noted:

Interviewer: Would you say you have been happy in your work?

Psychologist: No, not at all. I have been absolutely traumatised by it but it is fulfilling and it is something that I feel is worthwhile.

As was argued in the studies of Mackain et al. (2010) and Walsh (2009), working relationships and team dynamics were heavily correlated with job satisfaction and the amount of emotional labour that an individual may have to perform. Negative work relationships were a major factor described by many of the psychologists of this study. However, with regard to good working relationships, two aspects were significant in producing occupational satisfaction. These were the working relationships that they had with prisoners and the relationships that they had with their team members, especially their supervisors.

Although many of the psychologists interviewed were aware of the negative attitudes held by some prisoners towards their profession, were aware of the negative press in the national prison newspapers, there seemed to be an impression that this was a position held by a minority. In fact, nearly all those interviewed claimed that, on the whole, the working relationships they had with prisoners were good and that this offered a significant source of job satisfaction. Many in fact went on to explain that poor relations were the exception rather than the rule:

> … it might not be because of me necessarily but what I represent they might take a disliking. I have had that. But then a lot of the time as I say if it is assessment they want it done. If it is something that is going to hopefully progress them often just they will engage in that process. I have never had anyone sort of … outwardly show real dislike.

> … we are all human. There are going to be people that find me irritating and other people that find me easier to work with but that might be just more of a personality thing. But I have never had anyone [say] I hate you and what you stand for and your profession.

> Umm, I think I have a good relationship with most prisoners that I come into contact with. Umm, and I try very hard to maintain a good relationship with those that I … find particularly difficult.

> I have never had any seriously strong reactions to the fact that I am a psychologist or I am a member of the psychology department. I have never had anyone be abusive to me or refuse to see me or anything like that.

This last individual also noted how their engagement could impact on the relationship between them and the prisoners they were working with. They stated that there was a difference between working with someone in a group or in a one-to-one setting, where there was more of a therapeutic focus, to when the interaction revolved around assessment, as they explained:

> In terms of doing things like risk assessments whether it be for a parole report or anything else I think I would say an understandable level of wariness because they know that I am there to ask them questions and to make judgments about their answers and to make decisions about recommendations about what should happen and I think there is that sort of stereotypical view that ... you are analysing everything you say and everything you do and every move they make and you are sort of making inferences about it. It is not necessarily like that. I have never had any strong reactions but I suppose it is understandable....

What is being characterised here is justifiable wariness before trust is established, and not the open hostility that is suggested by accounts in the literature or in the open forums that prisoners have access to. There is an evident discrepancy between the way that psychologists perceive and describe their relationships with prisoners and the way that prisoners perceive and describe their relationship with psychologists (see Crewe, 2009; Maruna, 2011; Warr, 2008). This discrepancy was prevalent in all but one of the accounts given by those interviewed of their relationships with prisoners. The one exception to this was one psychologist who worked in an establishment that held a significant number of indeterminately sentenced prisoners and who had claimed that a number of complaints had been made about them. However, even for this individual, these problematic relationships were considered to be the exceptions rather than the rule.

Prosociality and Support

Satisfaction was also drawn from working within a prosocial team and having a supportive supervisor. As will be discussed below when these relationships are malignant or 'toxic' then they can add to stress levels, compound emotional labours, as well as hamper motivation and work quality. However, when these relationships are good, they can have a significant effect on the manner in which the workplace and the job itself are perceived (Belilos, 1997). This was echoed by the participants of this study:

> Interviewer: Do you find the work stressful?
>
> Psychologist: Not really. I am pretty sure that is not typical. I find... I am aware ... I consider myself to have a responsible job but because I never feel like I am on my own ... and although it is stressful in terms of when you are in a session you are working with very difficult characters, very challenging characters and people with a lot of problems as well which can be difficult to listen to and deal with – but then I feel I have got a lot of support from my colleagues and so I guess it helps to deal with the stress.

And similarly, within the department I have a very good boss, very good line manager.

Another participant gave a similar account. This person had recently moved to a new prison and a new team who they described as being motivated, helpful, and supportive. Since moving to the new team their work life had improved enormously and so had their perception of their role and their profession:

> I consider myself to be fortunate to be part of the team I am part of now. It is not that the other teams were not good but I consider myself to be fortunate.

They also stated that their new 'boss' was a much better team leader than the one they had worked with previously and was much more understanding and caring. This was an important element of the working lives of forensic psychologists – their team leader could have a fundamental impact on the professional experience of those who worked under them. Team leaders who encouraged supportive and collaborative working were considered the ideal. One Humanist explained that if a team leader was a '*people person*' who was confident and '*managed all the characters of the team effectively*' and ensured that they all supported each other it '*made the team a team*'. The importance of a good supervisor was mentioned by nearly all the participants, regardless of type. Two psychologists who had worked with the same team leader in different establishments noted the significant positive effect that this person had to their respective team dynamics. This exchange with a different psychologist, whose team had been allocated a new supervisor after a particularly turbulent period, captures both this facet of the relationship and the impact that it could have:

> Interviewer: Okay going back ... you said before that the supervisor you have now is more supportive and more receptive to the needs of [their] team and made it more of a team, do you think that's helped in any way with some of the problems that you have been discussing ... and if so in what way?
>
> Psychologist: I think there's much more a culture now where it's okay to say if you don't feel okay ... umm, if that makes sense? Yeah? Whereas before it was almost frowned upon and it was like you're weak like ... you know ...
>
> Interviewer: So ... you've got to be more stoical ...
>
> Psychologist: yeah ... umm ... [they] saw, [they] saw ... I think [they] liked to think of [themselves] as really robust and that was you know brilliant ... umm, what a fantastic quality ... umm and if you didn't live up to [their] own level of robustness, if that's a word, then [they] would look down on you as being weak and punish you for it. Whereas ...

Interviewer: Punish you in what way?

Psychologist: Erm … [long pause] [they were] very manipulative so in some way it would come back to bite you on the arse or whatever … through work not like … or [they] would bitch about you behind your back or something. [They] just wasn't a very nice [person] … but now it's encouraged that you say what's going on for you, that you're open and that you stay healthy. Unfortunately, the level of work is still the same … umm, so that hasn't changed but we look after each other a lot more now.

Interviewer: Okay, so your working relationship within your team is much better now?

Psychologist: Yeah.

What was pertinent to the good supervisor was the degree to which they were far more emotionally supportive and gave recognition of the stress and difficulty of the job. It was often noted that a good manager helped to alleviate the other stresses that may be experienced and thus made the work, and its attendant stresses, bearable. This is one of the factors outlined by Saari and Judge (2004) when they noted that when a supervisor encourages a team and is supportive and understanding of them, then not only does morale rise but so too productivity. The psychologists in this sample echoed this. The good supervisor or team leader reduced the necessity of, and the form of, emotional labour that psychologists needed to perform in order to conduct their daily work. This in turn made psychologists more productive at work as this psychologist explained:

As I said before when [name of psychologist] took over [they] made sure everyone was supported … No one was left to struggle. Not like before. We're happier now. All of us, I think. Our workload has increased [laugh] … but it doesn't feel like it because everyone pulls together and gets it done, you know?

What was evident was that the wider range of supervisors that a psychologist had access to, the more beneficial it was for them, their practice, and their view of their profession. Not only did this protect them from being stuck with a bad supervisor but it also opened them up to differing perspectives on their role. This broadening of their occupational horizon was important as working in one establishment, performing a limited role, with the same team over time could negatively affect a psychologist's working life. Yet this could be offset by changes to supervision and management. This was captured by one psychologist who'd had the benefit of having had a number of supervisors in the past:

I have had the opportunity to work with different supervisors. I think that has been really helpful because they all may approach things in a different way and it is just great to have different perspectives on things and encourage you to think about things in maybe a different way than another supervisor might. So, I think that has been helpful and rewarding as well and maintained my interest and motivation.

We have seen here that there are a number of factors that either promote or cause job satisfaction for those psychologists interviewed. These are, primarily, concerned with having the worthiness of the job reinforced, seeing the fruits of their labour, the diversity of experience and practice, and the benefits of having good working relationships with prisoners, colleagues, and supervisors. However, there are also a number of factors that have the opposite effect.

Occupational Dissatisfaction

Of great concern to many of those interviewed were the working experiences that led to occupational dissatisfaction. It is to these contrasted but yet binary reflections that I now turn. There were, in essence, five forms of generalised negative experience relayed by the participants. These are categorised as role ambiguity and ontological insecurity; occupational factors which relate to volume of work and working conditions; negative peer relationships and team dynamics; training and career advancement; and finally, the relational/social frustrations of working with prisoners.

Occupational Role and Ontological Ambiguity

Psychology work, in general, is a difficult and complex practice which is only compounded by the prison setting (Towl, 2004). In this locale, psychologists are working with some of the most damaged and chaotic individuals that our society has to offer (Gannon & Ward, 2014). If you couple this to the fact that forensic psychologists in prison do not necessarily have a fixed role, as their duties can cover a very broad range of activities, then psychological work in custodial setting becomes dilemmic in nature:

> I think that is one of the things I really underestimated about the job and that is why it can be difficult sometimes. It is not all black and white you are trying to work out what is best for people and it is difficult.

A factor made clear by Weiss and Cropanzano (1996) and Judge and Church (2000) is that there needs to be a clear understanding of occupational role in order for an employee to have any attachment to, or derive any satisfaction from, their work. In this study, it was found that two early indicators of workplace stress for psychologists were related to when there was either ambiguity in the role or when that role changed. The first of these issues were often experienced when, as discussed by Crighton and Towl (2008), the individual had been recruited under misunderstood terms, i.e., when a governor had a position to fill but not the clear-cut work to offer the new psychologist. This in turn led to a situation whereby some psychologists were not doing psychological work as part of their occupational remit which resulted in frustration; as a number of participants explained:

> It was frustrating because the job I wanted to do, which is what I thought I was being employed to do … perhaps was not always the job other people wanted me to do.

> Lots of us get sucked off into doing all sorts of different things for the prison, for the governor and become the governor's right-hand person for lots of things and … we're taken away from the psychology work.

Changes in the role were felt more keenly by those who had been in service for a long time. For instance, one who fell into this category noted the frustration that came with the changing role of psychologists:

> One [frustration] of mine was, many years ago now, working with a guy who suffered from insomnia due to real childhood trauma …. I did not reduce his risk of reoffending by treating his insomnia but he was extremely distressed and unable to sleep … we managed to find a way to help him. But now? If you were a guy in prison who suffered like that the psychology department would not be there for you.

This participant went on to explain that by aiding them to overcome their problem, the individual was then able to progress in other ways but such longitudinal practice was no longer viable. Others too noted that the nature of the work being asked of them was not always compatible with the rehabilitative ethos that they had once adhered to. This was echoed by one of the more senior psychologists interviewed for this project for contextual material who relayed a very similar story to that above but this time involving the treatment of nightmares. For this individual, the fact that psychological services within the prison could no longer, in general, engage in such therapeutic work was something to be lamented. However, this was not just a factor that impacted on those who had been in service for a long time as it could also be a source of frustration for those whose department had shrunk, the prison had rerolled, or when outside political influence/events impacted on the role being conducted. For instance, one of the psychologists interviewed stated that in their prison the introduction of the IPP prisoners and the shift in focus that forced upon them led to a situation where:

> … everything changed, in just a couple of years, we had all these people who needed assessments and programmes and … some were very challenging in their behaviour and their mental health problems and I know I, and some of the others, were not really trained for that so that was difficult … frustrating.

Whilst another, a Humanist, noted that:

> It's when you see a young man who has such ... desperate
> problems but you can't do anything to help them because ...
> because that is not the type of work you are doing with them.
> You're doing an assessment or a ... whatever. That's what makes
> me frustrated with the service ... you know?

A shift to more narrowly risk-orientated work, predicated on measurement
and management rather than disciplinary change, meant that their role had
become ontologically ambiguous which resulted in frustration and dissatisfaction.
Unlike some of the more generalised issues discussed below, some of these concerns impacted on specific types of psychologists more than others. Those who
were most vocal in this regard were the Humanists who became frustrated by the
lack of person-centred therapeutic work they were able to do or engage in. This
was less true for both Functionalists and Utilitarians as the move to more risk-
based work did provide them with perspective appropriate anchoring. However,
even here unanticipated changes or ambiguity in role expectation could cause
frustration – especially if there was a reliance on *ad hoc* rather than professionally
guided practice. For instance, one psychologist related a story about their
Governor, in response to an HMIP report, asking them to implement an anti-
bullying strategy that he had devised but which ignored the psychologically
informed practice previously utilised. Such, *ad hoc* practice caused this psychologist, and others in similar situations, a great deal of frustration. The Retributive
Idealist again proved the exception because, as long as the prison was acting as a
place of punishment, then their role adhered to both the ideation of their profession and their ontological position. This enabled them to avoid the sense of
ambiguity and ontological insecurity that others experienced in a move to
narrowly defined practice.

Occupational Factors: Workload

A major cause of discontent among the sample was the sheer volume of work that
was expected of them. As one psychologist employed in an establishment with a
large and rapidly changing population noted:

> The absolute worst thing is the churn. I've worked here for a
> number of years now and it's just getting worse. There's less of
> us now too.

Another pointed out that:

> ... the pressure on people to churn these reports is immense,
> absolutely immense.

This issue was not specific to those who worked in such large establishments as in the cases above. Nearly all of those who participated in the study made some comment about the *'churn'*, or *'merry-go-round'*, of prisoners and how this was both difficult to cope with and, at times, led to impossible work schedules. Here, the primary issue was the pressure created by the volume of people they were expected to report upon, which they felt they were only able to do effectively once they had formed some sort of relationship or rapport. For instance, one individual spoke of how having a short amount of time with any one person could be frustrating:

> Yes, definitely in terms of the fact that I think it is too restrictive what we can do, and who we can do it with and for how long. And I think it is not necessarily realistic in terms of thinking if you look at somebody that is so damaged and troubled and had problems for ever you need to be putting in more services and work with that person longer, addressing more things, so like I was saying before have a more holistic approach to treatment. And I do find sometimes it is very much – right OK you have got ten sessions to work on something. It is not realistic. You are just scratching the surface and that is frustrating.

Another pointed out that this pressure could create further frustrations, as well as consequences for the individuals who needed to be worked with:

> At some point I have to say well I am going to do this report or whatever for this guy and actually that guy is going further down on the list. And that is just a difficult every day decision that you have to make.

This individual was one of many who pointed out that the pressure within their office to produce reports was increasingly intense. Another psychologist explained that the waiting list for assessments/reports in their prison grew exponentially and that often there were times when individuals were just bumped from the list. They explained that one prisoner might need an assessment for decategorisation but some other person needed an assessment for parole and *'obviously that person got priority'*. This in itself led to frustration or even a sense of guilt as they recognised that they were contributing, through no fault of their own, to a situation that would have future repercussions for prisoners. Psychologists were feeling both pressured due to the amount of work requiring their attention and feeling guilty because of the consequences of not getting that work done. This caused a very particular form of emotional labour – whereby psychologists were having to not only reconcile these emotions in order to operate effectively but also to hide their own frustrations from the affected prisoners.

A further factor which compounded this issue was the recognition that the bureaucratic nature of modern prison work exacerbated this problem *'The worse thing for us is the caseload and the paperwork. It's non-stop. That can get you down'*. It was evident that for every one of the sample, the demands of administrating paperwork was *'an acute burden'*. This is consistent with the findings of Mackain et al. (2010) who noted that the toil of administrative work can have definite negative effects for psychologists in the workplace:

> The only time I probably don't enjoy it is when I am feeling overworked because if I am busy I am feeling a little bit stressed with the amount of paper work I have got to do.

> I feel a bit overwhelmed and therefore something that would not normally rile me on one day might really upset me or frustrate me or anger me on another day because I feel like I have too much on and not enough time to do it.

> For instance, this month … I am so busy that … the amount of paper work I have to catch up on I just don't have the time, I still have assessments and the course to run as well … all the paper work for the reports and assessments and courses it's just piling up and when I look at it I'm just … GRRR!

> If I have got a lot of work on and I am worried about when I am going to fit it all in, I don't sleep very well, but that is more about not necessarily the content of it, it is more about the volume of it.

What is somewhat ironic here is that the discipline of forensic psychology was integral to the development of a scriptural economy within the prison, predicated on the disciplinary capital of their expertise. It was within these bureaucratic mechanisms that their power became manifest. As such, not only were they net contributors to this bureaucratic workload but they were also dependent upon it for their discourse to have any efficacy. This also highlights one of the problems with bureaucratic legitimacy as defined by Crewe, Liebling, and Hulley (2015) and Liebling, Price, and Shefer (2011). This professional dimension of their Moral Quality of Prison Life study examines the prisons transparency and responsiveness in terms of its systems, and the degree to which these hamper or not the institution's moral regard for the prisoner. A low score on this measure is particularly telling for how the prison is perceived and experienced. However, as practitioners, and contributors to the bureaucratic systems within the prison, it seems that forensic psychologists experience a different but related form of bureaucratic legitimacy. The degree to which this aspect of their role dominated their occupational lives was heavily correlated with their experience and perception of the prison in which they worked and their quality of working life. This seemed particularly pertinent for those employed in establishments where the majority of prisoners were on parole sentences, especially IPPs, or where there were a large number of courses being run by the psychology department. For many, this had a huge impact both on the prisons in which they worked and on the workloads that they themselves faced:

> When I first started here the IPP sentence was not in [here] and there were 50 lifers, something like that, so what we have now in percentages it is just massive, we are looking at kind of 300% more work, but we have not had that many more staff. So, what I mean ... so yes that has been a burden.

> I think it has been a challenge in terms of the organisation because certain sentences you might have to prioritise ... The treatment places, risk assessments. So, yes that kind of change has probably increased ... also I think the challenge in terms of meeting their [ISPP] needs was not leaving behind other people who we also want to work on.

> ... the need for psychology assessment has increased massively. So, for example here we have probably a third of our population IPP so a big proportion. I don't know if it is roughly half of that, but a big chunk of that will need a psychological assessment. So, the impact on forensic psychology is massively increased workload.

Related to this was the level of bureaucratic interference in the delivery of their day-to-day work. For instance, a number of participants identified Key Performance Targets as a particular source of frustration:

> You have got pressures of key performance targets, so you have to deliver a certain amount of programmes so then that pressure in order to meet KPTs, to meet milestones, to meet targets balancing that with delivering good quality intervention, not just having bums on seats for the sake of it, you want to make sure the right people are on the right programmes... I think that is an organisational pressure I can imagine most people probably have felt at some stage.

> I think the main problem is the rate at which we have to deliver these programmes ... so we have KPT's that we have to meet and that's why we have to run a certain number of sessions a week ... and do the paperwork ... and we have to just keep on going because if we don't meet our key performance target then we fail and then we lose money ... So, the focus is absolutely 100% on meeting those targets ... it's not on the staff or their welfare.

A significant further factor was the budgetary issues faced by departments and the manner in which they were able to deliver their work. One of the most significant realities to emerge in England and Wales in the last decade has been the politics of austerity. The criminal justice system stood at the forefront, and took the brunt, of the budgetary cuts that came in the wake of the neoliberal, ideological policies of austerity introduced by the Conservative governments in Britain from 2010 onwards (for a wider discussion of how this impacted on the wider criminal justice system see Secret Barrister 2018). Prisons and probation were particularly eviscerated by these policies, seeing cuts after cuts after cuts to budgets that were predicated not on necessity but on the ideological imperative to reduce the costs of the State (Allen, 2013; Ismail, 2020). The psychology teams and departments reflected here did not escape this fiscal scythe. Nearly all participants spoke of how the need to save money was a major factor in the dynamics of their working life and contributed to the habitus of stress:

> I think that is the constraint, the strictness of budgets etc. is a massive thing.

> ... when we found out that we were losing two of the team due to ... all the money is in programmes and that's only part of what we do ... but because we no longer offer the [name of course] we lost a big part of our budget and had to lose staff. That has affected the team massively.

> We have to reduce costs; all the time reduce costs and that impacts on what we can do.

> We had a budget cut. Less staff. More work though, and that adds to the general level of stress we all feel.

A number of psychologists noted the growing competition from private firms, who would do risk assessments with a very quick turnaround. Many of these firms are staffed by forensic psychologists who have, at one time or another, worked within the same prisons as those who participated in this study. They had often had the same training, had done the same work, and even qualified in the same way. Yet they were held in something approaching contempt by the psychologists interviewed. Most, when asked about this reality, just grimaced or tutted disapprovingly. It was felt that because the private firms did not have the same ethical standards and practices, and thus could do a two-day return on a report, they were being put under further unfair pressure. The budgetary constraints, coupled with workload expectations, meant that people felt they were not able to fully perform the tasks that they needed to. This then resulted in further frustrations, stresses, and, in some cases, a further loss of motivation. One aspect to this increased pressure was the reduction in scope of the work that was available to the psychologists, as they were needed to churn out reports or meet treatment needs:

> It can get boring doing the same thing day in day out. I thought, ... when I went from assistant to trainee I would be doing research, training, working with lots of people. Instead ... because of the IPPs and the workload, I'm just doing the same thing as I was then – facilitating the courses that they want us to run and doing all the admin.

Repetitive work can negatively affect motivation and perceptions of work, the organisation, and their professional selves (Saari & Judge, 2004). As one psychologist who had spent the majority of their career doing the same programme noted: '*doing the same thing over and over ... it gets you down*'. However, for some participants, some of these stresses were ameliorated through the new working model of regional service delivery:

> Now I am region I get to do much more psychological work than when I was in [name of prison]. There it was all paper work and programmes, now I do more ... it helps, I don't get down as much.

> Interviewer: Is being a psychologist in prison stressful?

> Psychologist: I think so – I think if I compare when I worked in the prison to where I work now in the region, then yes [it's] more stressful I would say. Now, I get to see lots of different aspects of the job ... I work just as hard but it's not as stressful.

> We have just undergone a change where we are now a regional model so we have been removed from the management kind of capacity so basically, we are doing what psychologists do, and only what forensic psychologists can do rather than doing generic [work] ...

The change in working practice this move allowed facilitated a complete concentration on the job of forensic psychology. This freed them up from a number of the 'generic' aspects of prison work, allowed them to concentrate on areas suited to their expertise, and meant that much of the workload that they had previously shouldered alone was now manageable.

Negative Peer Relationships and Team Dynamics

It's not surprising that a significant source of occupational dissatisfaction arose due to certain working relationships and team dynamics. This was especially true when it came to being supervised poorly or having bad relationships with senior members of staff, as a number of the participants in this study explained:

> Interviewer: Have you ever had a bad supervisor then?

> Psychologist: I would rather not comment.

> Interviewer: Fair enough.

> Psychologist: But yes.

> I was probably deeply traumatised by all the work I did because I did not get any proper supervision. I didn't get any reflection time for me and some of the offences that people had committed were absolutely nightmarish.

> I had a manager who was not very nice ... [they] was quite a difficult person and just made everything really difficult. You couldn't talk to [them] and any criticism [they] took personally ... it was very awkward and unpleasant for everyone.

Other psychologists gave examples of poor management practices. These included managers/supervisors who would isolate team members, single out team members for public criticism, be dismissive of personal problems, and act in hostile or discouraging ways. Such practices contribute to an unhealthy or 'toxic' workplace that allows for the generation of negative work practices (see McMahon, 1999). Dismissive behaviour from managers was a particular source of occupational stress and dissatisfaction. As we saw in the section above, one of the psychologists noted that a manager would just intimate to their team that '*they should just get on with it*' and that they should be stoical about the work they did. This made the workers in the team feel inadequate if they did not cope and were left unable to address such concerns with their line manager. This in turn led them to not only perceive their boss in negative terms but also feel as if their concerns were not being taken seriously, all of which increased stress levels and the amount of emotional labour needed in order to remain operative. As this participant explained:

> ... over time that 'getting on with it' actually really starts to change you. ... changes ... who you are I think, definitely. And has had an impact on my personal life ... yeah ... and ... because ... oh ... I guess ... there's no, there's no vent for any of this stuff you're just taking loads of, loads of stuff on board and umm ... there's not really anyway to get rid of it.

However, frustrations did not just arise from the internal dynamics of the psychology department. Some arose directly from working with other staff members, especially uniformed or operational members of staff. These ranged from dealing with the obstructiveness of some uniform staff to coping with divergent attitudes:

> I find it very frustrating working with staff or dealing with staff who are not as positive and enthusiastic about rehabilitation as I am. Well not even enthusiastic I suppose just – I get frustrated by staff who have negative views on things like that because I think ... why are you in this job if that is your view, what are you doing here?

> Probably other than that [not being listened too] the most frustrated I have ever been at work is through staff issues and interpersonal difficulties with staff members, not in terms of being frustrated at anything psychological or being frustrated with any prisoners or anything like that. It is generally staff.

> Often, they [uniformed staff] can be quite ignorant with very
> entrenched, ill-informed views ... that can make it a difficult
> place to work as what we do is misunderstood, undervalued, and
> viewed with suspicion. You try address this but ...

Some of these issues will be discussed in greater depth in the following chapters. However, what was evident was that for nearly all the participants in this study, uniformed staff, and their attitudes and behaviours towards psychology and psychologists, were a distinct source of workplace stress. Partly because during the working day psychologists were located in the same environment and could not escape staff attention. As one joked *'we're locked in here with them'*. Often these negative associations and interactions with the uniform body could further exacerbate the problems within a team adding to the negative work environment. This was especially so if the manager of the team was dismissive or ineffective in ameliorating these tensions:

> As I said I had problems with a member of staff and it didn't help
> that my manager took their side. The others saw that ... it made ...
> no one wanted to speak up after that.
>
> Interviewer: Did your line manager help, or do anything to stop ...
>
> Psychologist: No... They ... They made that clear. We wouldn't
> get help, not in that way ...
>
> Interviewer: How did you feel about that?
>
> Psychologist: Well, two left. I just ... got my head down.

Not only did these negative interactions add to the stresses that psychologists endured at work but they could also impact on the manner in which they perceived themselves, their role, and the importance of their work. One psychologist, who had experienced a number of problems with uniform staff, noted that when their line manager had sided with the prison officers it had made them *'question everything about what I do'* and that this *'made [them] feel like shit, everyday'*. If a person's professional persona and practice is challenged in such a way as to undermine their sense of moral worth, then this can affect their ontological security. If this situation does arise and is not mitigated by managers and team leaders who are in a position to do so, then this can result in a sense of abandonment and a much greater need to engage in varying forms of emotion work designed to enable them to maintain operational efficacy and a sense of well-being (Marroquin et al., 2017).

Training and Career Advancement

Another strand of frustration derived from the Chartership process itself and the opportunities for becoming 'qualified'. Trainees are those who are working towards their Chartership, or the British Psychological Society's Diploma in Forensic Psychology. For those who participated in this study, the process of Chartership that they were engaged in involved them having to complete both Stage 1 and 2 of the Diploma (BPS 2008). Stage 1 of the Diploma is split into two parts: the first part comes under heading of Knowledge and involves written assessment/examination in four areas – the context of practice in forensic psychology, the applications of psychology to processes within the justice system, working with specific client groups, and using and communicating information in practice. The second part comes under the heading of Research and involves the assessment of a research project of publishable standard and, on occasion, an oral exam.

Stage 2 of the Diploma involves the production for assessment of four portfolios of written evidence demonstrating proficiency in the four core elements or roles of forensic psychological work, which are:

(1) The delivery of applications and interventions – this can, and does, include conducting various forms of prescribed risk assessment and the facilitation of the accredited offender behaviour treatment programmes.
(2) Research – this role is concerned with designing, conducting, analysing, and evaluating a self-generated piece of applied psychological research in the forensic setting of the prison/probation field in which the candidate is employed; for example, developing a psychological assessment tool or method for that setting.
(3) The communication of forensic psychological knowledge to other professionals – this can include such activities as advising on aspects of investigation strategy, design of service delivery, the planning of treatment protocols or giving expert testimony to tribunals, courts, or other decision-making bodies.
(4) The training of other professionals – this can include imparting psychological knowledge which may improve the service delivery of other professional or training in interviewing, stress management, hostage awareness, and psychological interventions.

In order to satisfy the assessment of these core elements, trainees are required to produce two exemplars for each of the four portfolios that they are to submit. Also, along with these portfolios, they must submit a practice diary, a supervision log and supporting evidence (which should include an overview of how competency in each core role has been achieved).

Once these course requirements have been met and submitted, the candidates are assessed by those assessors allocated by the Qualifications Officer. These assessors are chosen, or allocated, based upon their availability and, in cases of resubmission, their previous assessment history. Once the materials have been sent to the relevant assessors, the candidates should have their results within 3 months of that date. After this process, the matter is handed over to the Chief Assessor for final scrutiny and ratification and then handed to the Board of

Assessors who, upon receipt of a letter from the candidate's supervisor confirming their fitness for practice and any other clarification they deem necessary, will award the Diploma in Forensic Psychology.

According to the Handbook utilised by the majority of these psychologists (BPS 2008), this process should take a minimum of three years and a maximum of six years (unless exemption from Stage 1 has been granted in which case it is 2 and 4 years, respectively). However, many of the psychologists who participated in this research found that it took much longer than this if they were employed within the Prison Service, unlike some others, when they began their training. In some circumstances, psychologists were employed to do a single role and this led to difficulties in gaining sufficient evidence of variety of work to satisfy the British Psychological Society's assigned markers. For instance, one of the participants noted that the usual, or standard, way 'in' was to:

> ... do a degree in psychology, then get a job as a psychological assistant in the Prison Service and then when they get a job as a trainee, sort of do the masters and Chartership then.

However, many of the studies participants had not taken this route. Nearly a third of the sample had not specifically studied psychology at undergraduate level. These participants had to take a more circuitous path involving various jobs and some form of post graduate diploma in psychology. Others had specifically sought careers in psychological fields but not always forensic ones. Commonly, the interest was in doing clinical work with vulnerable persons, rather than in the criminal justice system *per se*. Half of the sample indicated that they had been unable to secure work in their chosen field so had made the pragmatic choice to apply for trainee positions in their local prison. These varying routes, coupled with individual's differing roles, often caused delays in the process of obtaining Chartership. As one said:

> That training, 8 years of like ... it was the most stressful thing I have ever done. It was absolutely horrendous. It was just the hardest thing I have done, not the Masters but the actual working towards Chartership.

Whilst another pointed out that for them the major stress of their work was:

> Not being able to complete the Chartership. It's been ... years. I'm still no closer.

This was a common complaint for those unfortunate to be employed in a prison where the psychology department was utilised in only one or two ways. Usually this restricted role was concerned with high levels of risk assessment and course delivery, which could lead to both frustration in achieving qualification and a loss of impetus. It also meant having little opportunity to push on with the Chartership as they were stuck in necessarily repetitive work. The sheer pressures of work and the churn of clients with their varying needs also affected this issue, with one person saying that:

> There is no time for reflection. There is no time for 'did I make a difference today' it is just getting through it. That is not training psychologists.

This was echoed by another participant who pointed out that such working practice could cause delays which could then impact on their motivation:

> Umm ... I had so much enthusiasm and motivation but then the years have sort of rolled on and I don't feel like I'm really getting anywhere ... personally.

A number of other participants mentioned that satisfying the criteria could be difficult due to 'moving goalposts' on the part of the British Psychological Society. This specifically related to what work could be included in portfolios and thus taken as evidence. A number had work rejected and had resubmitted with little guidance or feedback with regard to their work. It was difficult to ascertain whether or not this was a matter of poor supervision (of those who mentioned this problem the majority had also mentioned having a poor relationship with their supervisor) or a problem with the evidence criteria and Chartership assessment.

Frustrations also arose from trying to impart psychological knowledge, a key component of the Chartership process, to the management of an establishment where there was little interest in that form of knowledge. This could occur even when psychologists felt the management of their prison was generally prop-sychology. They noted this most when institutional interests were prioritised over and above that of identified 'treatment needs'. A repeated example concerned the prison's response to prisoners who were seen to threaten the *'good order and discipline'* (GOAD) of the prison. As one participant explained:

> I tried to impart knowledge from an assessment to an individual who is a manager in the establishment about what was suitable for that prisoner and I didn't think anybody was taking any notice of that assessment and I felt really frustrated. Actually, there was a wealth of information that was held that could structure how that person was worked with and it kind of met with resistance. That was frustrating ...

This issue related to the increasing 'service' nature of psychological work within a prison. Some participants noted that the prison and its management could sometimes treat their forensic psychologists as commissioned professionals whose opinion is only sought in certain circumstances. They noted that, especially in the cases of younger or less experienced psychologists, there was the risk that their service delivery was becoming more like that of private companies who take an atomised approach to the work, spending very little time with the prisoner during the assessment period, and with little interest beyond the risk assessment itself. This lack of an holistic approach to a person's case, they felt, was eroding a wider recognition of what was effective about their work:

> That is how we are being shaped – you are this external person who comes in, risk assesses – it is all about protection of the public – and then goes out and has nothing else to do with that case. There is very little follow up. Very little interest in what the impact of the report might have been or how that prisoner felt about it. The caseload is too great that, there is no thought to how we are impacting on people and how it impacts on us it's just … next case, next case, next case.

This could lead to a situation whereby the psychologist was neither treated nor utilised as an integral aspect of the prison and as such their input could be dismissed when the excuse of security or the GOAD of the prison came into play. This represented a particular challenge to not only the Retributive Idealist who saw themselves as an integral part of the penal enterprise but also the Functionalists who perceived this approach to their expertise as a barrier to the very function of psychological practice. Further to these concerns was the implication this had to achieving 'qualification' when one of the core requirements, imparting psychological expertise, was difficult to evidence.

The move to a changed model of service alleviated some of these concerns and stresses for some of those undergoing the Chartership process. One of the forecasted benefits of the move to a regional model was that it would allow those psychologists working in the various regions to have greater access to a more varied psychological skill set from which they could learn. Though not exhaustive this did seem to be borne out by those in this study who had been through this change. They noted enthusiastically that they were, or were soon to be, engaged in a far wider range of forensic psychological work, including the opportunities to undertake research[1] and imparting psychological expertise (requirements of the Chartership process), as this person indicated:

> I think personally now, working for the region, I have had more opportunity I think and the supervisor I have in terms of carving out those opportunities – I think in terms of meeting organisational need as well so the pieces of work I have done have met that so if there is an assessment need at that particular prison, the region will say we need this picked up, you have trained in that you know how to do it. So, having more opportunity, personally, that is a good thing because it means you get more experience and that helps with becoming qualified.

---

[1]Research for forensic psychologists is problematic even beyond the prison. See Wilson and Noon (1998).

What is relevant here is not that the regional model was a panacea to the problems that some faced in obtaining Chartership, rather that it allowed the forensic psychologists to more easily satisfy the requirements handed down by the BPS. In a professional body where becoming 'qualified' was seen as both an occupational and a professional necessity – not achieving it, or being prevented from achieving that, had negative consequences. As one psychologist noted, '*being frustrated*' in the Chartership process got them '*down*' because it impacted on not only their achievement and advancement but also:

> It makes you feel like you're not good enough. Even though you do good work and … and … there's a nagging little voice at the back of your mind saying … well, you know. That's all down to not getting there yet, after so many years.

A further issue with training was for those few psychologists who experienced the power related to their profession as another emotional burden. One of the psychologists, who had over seven years of experience, stated that they thought it was '*very bad practice*' that psychologists do not receive any training on an issue that was central to their practice. They went on to say that '*at no time during all my training has anyone really spoken about [power]*' and that they felt unprepared for what they encountered and unsupported in this area of their professional life. These sentiments were echoed by the few others who addressed this issue. For instance, the one Functionalist psychologist who spoke to this stated that they had been completely unprepared for the power dynamic to be so overt, especially when dealing with particularly vulnerable prisoners, but that when they had raised this with their supervisor they had received an unsatisfactory response:

> … [they] said to me that I would just have to get used to it … I didn't think that was very helpful. They should prepare you more for that aspect of it. Some of the men I see are so vulnerable and damaged that you run the risk of making things so much worse for them if you're not careful. There should be training around this area … but there isn't.

Another participant claimed that there was '*absolutely no preparation for dealing with that dynamic*'. Yet another pointed out that they felt they needed some form of training because they were concerned about doing more harm to clients who were '*vulnerable and psychologically fragile*'. This individual went on to say that they were constantly worried that using '*sometimes quite blunt*' psychological programmes and assessments on the '*very vulnerable*' was doing '*much more harm than good*'. This not only increased the degree of emotion work that they had to engage in, so that the worry would not impede their work, but also resulted in anger with their supervisor and mentor who had told them that they just needed to '*get on with it*'. What was clear is that for these few psychologists being confronted with the reality of their power and its impact was a cause of deep emotion work. Emotion work that they were not prepared for and received little support with.

Relational and Social Frustrations

Finally, frustration and stress could arise from the relational difficulties inherent to interactions with prisoners. Some participants, primarily the Humanists, stated that this relational aspect of their work could cause a great deal of strain, yet was often overlooked, especially where meeting targets had become seen with increasing import. This was not true for all, those with good support networks at work and an understanding supervisor were well catered for, as one notes:

> I never feel like I go home struggling with something that I have never been able to talk to anybody about. And if I did that would be my choice to do that rather than there not being the capacity to deal with it at work.

However, for others this 'strain' could be invoked in a number of ways; for instance, a number of psychologists mentioned the anxiety that could arise from having to deliver bad news or having to report back negative findings to prisoners:

> ...and it was one of the most negative reports I had ever written. And we had to go and disclose them and we had to either read them out loud or give them to the people and then discuss them. And I spent the night before literally crying because I thought – he is going to kill me – he is going to be so angry it is going to be awful.

Others spoke of the sadness that was often inherent to working with lifers who had little hope of progressing or reducing their risk:

> ... but knowing they are still in prison, and knowing some of the stuff I do know and thinking this is really quite sad. That can get to you.

> When you see a lifer who is so damaged, so ... you know they are unlikely to be released. Working with them becomes very hard.

However, perhaps the most common 'strain' related to hearing about the traumatic experiences of prisoners themselves. Many participants had not expected, nor had been trained to deal with, this aspect of the work:

> That is what gets to me more – I find myself driving home from work thinking about that rather than thinking about the poor victim ... but I think that is just because I am working with that individual. And that came as a bit of a surprise. I thought I would find it harder to listen to their accounts of what they had done to others... which obviously is not always easy but it is always having to listen to people talk about what has happened to them that I find difficult.

Others found that listening to prisoner's experiences could cause them distress. This was especially true when people spoke of childhood abuse and childhood sexual exploitation. Two participants, both of whom worked primarily with prisoners convicted of sexual offences, made this point explicitly when speaking of having to maintain their professional facade in the light of these revelations:

> ... because of the questions you might ask that individual – and that can evoke quite strong emotion. In my experience I have had that. It is something I need to manage. It is not helpful to the client if I am getting upset. Not professional or helpful. So, I think at times it can be quite challenging hearing some of those things.

> I remember interviewing one young man and he was telling me how he had been repeatedly raped by his father. And how his father had made him abuse his little sister. He was in a terrible state ... I just wanted to cry, to give him a hug ... but you can't. You have to bite it back. You have to go on with the interview, do what you're there to do.

In such situations, it is clear that psychologists were forced into engaging varying forms of *emotional labour*. Different psychologists spoke of the need to '*hide*' emotions or to '*mask the things you feel*' when hearing the trauma of prisoners. Without this masking of emotion, it was felt that maintaining professional standards was compromised. A further example of this emotional labour came with working with those convicted of the most severe sexual offences, where they explained that it was often necessary to fake '*empathies in order to disguise the revulsion*' that they felt. Not doing this would compromise their efficacy as a psychological practitioner and would hinder the 'treatment' or rehabilitation of those being worked with. Often psychologists would focus on their emotive labour in such situations in order to mitigate the emotional labour. For instance, one Functionalist noted that they would:

> ... concentrate on getting [the prisoner] to think through their actions and why they had happened. Concentrating on that allowed me to ... yeah, not think about the awful things they're actually telling me.

This was true for nearly all those interviewed yet seemed to be only formally recognised for those working with prisoners convicted of sexual offences where programme breaks and peer-led debriefing support were a given.[2] This is distinct from more clinical fields where such support is standard operating procedure (see Ducharme, Knusden, and Roman (2007) for a discussion of these issues in drug

---

[2]Though three of the participants in this study who worked mainly with prisoners convicted of sex offences had noted that they had not been given these breaks and given little peer support either.

treatment work and Farber (1990) in psychotherapy). Participants who had previous clinical experience had noted this difference and had lamented its loss in the forensic field. Where psychologists were not getting this support from colleagues and in the workplace, then the emotional aspects of their work were taken home, impacting their domestic lives.

Emotional Labour and the Problem of Spillage

Emotion work is inherent to prison work (see Mann & Cowburn, 2005; Nylander, Lindberg, & Bruhn, 2011; Walsh, 2009). However, as Crawley (2004) argues when this work spills over from the professional realm into the personal one, and begins to impact on more personal interactions, then this has gone beyond the norm. Many participants spoke about the effect that working within the prison could have on their social or private lives. This was particularly true for those who worked in programmes or were involved in intensive work with prisoners, especially on SOTP type courses:

> Yeah ... It makes you over analyse as well ... I think It makes you over analyse yourself which you then carry, I find it difficult to separate this from my personal life. So, then you know I was going and like found myself speaking to my ... to my boyfriend in the same way that I was speaking to a prisoner on a S.O.T.P group saying that you know like ... even giving him treatment needs ... you know? It's not intentional it's just like sub conscious at this point ... so I was trying to facilitate change in my boyfriend because it all becomes clouded.

This psychologist went on to say that:

> You have to be very skilled in leaving it all here [pointing to the prison] ... but it becomes who you are after a while, you become a facilitator and that's how you think. Umm ... so if it is just innately you it becomes even more difficult to recognise that ... you know, not everyone needs ... to change. Not everyone does have treatment needs. Not everyone is a sex offender ... [nervous laugh] yeah.

Another psychologist echoed these sentiments when they noted that

> You're looking out for things more. So ... so it ... it just takes away all innocence from your life, you know? So, you could be in the park, for example, and there's a guy with a kid and you just look at him slightly differently than you would have before you started this. Or ... you know ... I was on the bus the other day and there was a woman with her two children and there was an older

> man sitting in the seat next to them and you know he seemed to be very interested in the children ... and he was probably just genuinely very happy to see some children but ... you know, I assumed 'what are you looking at them like that for?' and I think that if I see something what am I gonna do because I feel responsible.

This conflation between the professional and personal habitus, and the implications this had for the performance of self, was just one aspect of this 'spillage'. This loss of innocence echoes the findings of Crawley (2004), who found that prison officers found some prison work so 'profane' that it could contaminate or stain their personal lives. Other participants of this study also experienced the prison itself as contaminating their personal and social lives. In the same way that some of the officers in Crawley's study noted that the prison could 'pollute' the home by introducing the 'filth' of the prison into the 'clean' home, some psychologists felt the need to shed the *'dirt and smell of the prison'* before being able to continue with their personal lives. One psychologist noted that:

> ... the minute I get home I have to shower, get changed. I need to get the prison ... you know the, the ... prison off me. I need to get changed into clean clothing and get rid of the day.

This symbolic contamination was expressed by one participant when they discussed having to put distance between the prison and their loved ones. They noted that if they were meeting friends/family after work or were going out they would have to '... *take a change of clothing ... items that I have not been wearing in the prison'*. When asked why this was the case this psychologist noted that it was because:

> ... it wouldn't be right, meeting my partner, my family, my friends whilst still having the smell of the prison all over me ... No, I wouldn't feel right about that.

Whilst not all of those interviewed expressed this notion, a significant proportion did note the need to keep those whom they cared for separate from the realities of the intramural world. Often this was achieved by not talking about their work or the prison with those whom they lived or associated. This 'shedding' of the prison seemed to suggest a recognition of the manner in which the prison work could 'spill over' and one means of coping with the emotional weight of the work. Others took different measures in order to ameliorate this problem:

> In terms of taking it home emotionally, sometimes, I do tend to almost go that is work and that is home. I think I do that quite well, or I go to the gym or just do stuff to try and get it out.

> Of course, you take it home. You see so much misery ... so much
> pain ... How do you deal with that? Vodka! Ha ... no, I go out,
> socialise, see people ... put myself in normal situations.

Nearly all participants spoke of the need to do 'normal' things and to 'socialise' with people not related, or attached, to the prison in any way. However, as the following quote suggests, this was not always possible or desirable:

> There was a guy in [name of prison] who I had worked with a
> couple of times and who had killed a baby ... it was a Friday
> afternoon, I was trying to finalise this report and I had gone
> through what we had talked about and he had been very drunk,
> ... it turned out that he had actually been so drunk that he picked
> the baby up several times and kept dropping it. He didn't just drop
> it once on the fireplace, he dropped it three times. And he was so
> upset when he was telling me this, we were talking and I got to this
> place where I actually heard the baby falling from his arms into the
> fireplace and I was really upset and it made me feel really ill ... I
> went home and I was physically sick all weekend. I was just
> vomiting the whole weekend ... on the Sunday I was just sitting
> there in the garden thinking what am I going to do – what am I
> going to do. And on Monday I just went back to work.

Emotional labour is associated with processes of coping at work. The individual undergoes processes of hiding, faking or mitigating the emotions evinced in the workplace in order to maintain occupational efficacy (Mann & Cowburn, 2005). However, what is evident here is that some of the psychologists in this sample were also having to utilise the same processes of emotional labour in order to maintain a balance in their domestic situation and in their personal relationships. The prison, and their work, weighed heavily upon them and required substantial emotion work in order to maintain their health and well-being beyond the walls.

The Retributive Idealist, once more, offered a very different perspective in this regard. At no time did this psychologist refer to the need to shake off the prison as others had. The evocative accounts relayed by prisoners which provoked emotional responses in others were not a source of personal trauma. Instead, this individual perceived these as a necessary aspect of their role of making the person confront their offending. When asked if they ever thought about those people and what they had been through in their lives they responded:

> Of course, it is good to see them be confronted with what they
> themselves have suffered as you can use this to make them
> understand how they have made others suffer. That is why they
> are here and ...it's part of my role.

When then asked if they ever felt sorry for the people they worked with and whether or not it upset them they responded with a curt '*No*'. Here, then the accounts which others found difficult and resulted in the need for emotional labour was reversed. Instead of evoking emotional labour for the Retributive Idealist, the accounts of trauma provided were ammunition for the psychologist's *emotive labour*. In effect, the Idealist was operationalising the emotion associated with a prisoner's communications in order to evoke, deflect, or even inverse emotion in that person in order to force them to confront the harms they had caused. This operationalisation meant that the Idealist was not internalising the emotion which may necessitate emotional labour but rather reflecting it back to the people with whom they were working.

This chapter has explored those influences that can impact on the occupational satisfaction or dissatisfaction of forensic psychologists working within a prison. Whilst some of these factors can be procedural or organisational in nature, such as workload and the increased service nature of the role, many were relational in nature. From the pleasure and satisfaction taken in seeing those who they work with progress and develop personally to the negative aspects of poor supervision and management. The relational dynamics in the workplace are strongly associated with how psychologists experience their occupational reality and this corroborates findings from Mackain et al. (2010). However, this study extends those findings by showing how the various forms of prosociality that can and do exist within psychology teams can mitigate the procedural factors that can lead to occupational dissatisfaction. It is the absence of these prosocial elements that exacerbate the problems that psychologists experience and effect how they perceive their work and their professional selves.

What is evident is that psychological work in prison is emotion work. Where we saw in the last chapter some of the processes of emotive labour, here I have explored those elements of psychological work that evince varying forms of emotional labour in order for the psychologist to maintain professional efficacy. Whereas emotive labour was closely tied to the moral positioning of the psychologist, it is clear that with emotional labour the causes were less specifically tied to typological position. Those elements that evince the need for psychologists to regulate their own emotion were more generalised. They also related to elements of occupational experience that often lay outside of their sphere of direct control. Here then we see that if triggering occupational phenomena occur, which lie beyond the direct control of the psychologist and are not mitigated by the others, then it creates the need for emotional labour. A consequence of this is that emotional labour is not only necessary to cope with some elements of psychological practice but that it is inevitable within the prison where many facets of experience are imposed. It is to this aspect of the experiences of psychologists that I now turn. There are further aspects of the professional and occupational lives of forensic psychologists that relate more directly to the dynamics of power that exist within the prison.

Chapter 6

Adjuncts of Penal Power

> I mean, you know, it is a position of authority but ...but ... I don't
> like to think of it that way.
>
> —Trainee Psychologist

Power is central to the prison and fundamentally shapes the practices, cultures, and relationships that occur therein. It is multifaceted, complex, involving an entanglement of forms, and infuses and is manifest in every element of the prison. No discussion of prison is complete without an exploration of these dynamics. Power in prison, as noted by Hepburn (1985), often takes six particular forms (coercive, reward, legitimate [signification], exchange, expertise, and respect) and can derive from structural, interpersonal, or discursive sources (see Carlen & Worrall, 2004; Carrabine, 2005; Foucault, 1979; Sim, 2009). By exploring differing manifestations of power, these authors highlight how systems of influence converge within the prison to construct complex matrices of interconnected forms of control and constraint designed to achieve a disciplinary end. The prison is, in effect, designed to impose societally desired change on the disciplined individual (Mathiesen, 1990). However, as Crewe, Bennett, and Wahidin (2008) note, the power that permeates prisons impacts on all those who work or abide within them. These next two chapters will focus on these issues. However, as prison staff are often seen as embodiments of penal power (Liebling, Price, & Shefer, 2011), I shall begin by exploring how psychologists experience acting as adjuncts of disciplinary power.

Forensic psychologists in prison are central to a diffuse yet pervasive and profound form of penal power. This power is a blend of both coercive authority (Hepburn, 1985), prisoners have little or no choice but to interact with them (Crewe, 2009), and a form expertise imbued with a great deal of disciplinary capital. Theirs is a power that enmeshes differing forms of extant types of power in order to create a new, and profound, form of penal power that is both potent yet diffused. This is also a power that is inescapable and has the potential for long-term consequences. It is also a unique form of penal power as the source of its potency lies beyond the prison itself, yet has become a foundational facet of the everyday carceral habitus.

This chapter is concerned with exploring and explicating how they themselves perceive, respond to, and enact the power that is associated with their expert discourse and practice. As discussed previously, there are varying aspects to the

Forensic Psychologists, 123–141
Copyright © 2021 Jason Warr
Published under exclusive licence by Emerald Publishing Limited
doi:10.1108/978-1-83909-960-120200007

power of psychology within the prison that are particularly pertinent to the experiences and occupational lives of those interviewed in this study. These can be categorised as the medicalisation of the field and the reality of the psychologist as an 'Expert', their involvement in soft and bureaucratic forms of control, the coerced involvement of prisoners in psychological practice, and the manner in which individuals may engage in processes of neutralisation regarding their own power. It is these issues which will form the focus of the following discussion.

Medicalisation and Psychology

The development of contemporary forensic psychology in prisons has adhered to the processes of medicalisation of deviance as described by Conrad and Schneider (1992). The authority of psychology in prisons is one of expertise and is thus predicated upon its disciplinary capital. The consumable and risk assuaging nature of psychological discourse both supports and furthers the interests of the prison. Consequently, practice centralises around the assessment/treatment nexus (Otto & Heilbrun, 2002; Towl, 2004) because doing so serves the disciplinary needs of the prison and cements the position of psychology. In effect, the medicalisation framing becomes both the lens through which the profession is perceived and the overarching ethos of practice. This occurs because psychological issues are perceived in distinctly positivistic terms – they have an objective element (offending behaviour) that can be addressed and redressed. This also establishes the extramurality of their expertise. Unlike the prison officer described by Hepburn (1985) and Liebling et al. (2011), whose expertise is personal and derives from their experience of navigating and managing the prison and its inhabitants (jail craft), the expertise of forensic psychologists is derived from without the prison wall. It is not primarily expertise derived from personal experience but rather expertise that is prepackaged by an established discourse that is independent of, yet is infused throughout, the prison.

The different types of forensic psychologist in this study perceived medicalisation in very different ways. The Humanists were uncomfortable with the medical/intervention model of practice and preferred to see their position as one of working with people rather than imposing some sort of '*medical intervention*'. Many distanced themselves altogether from this medicalised model of practice. This was also true for the term 'offender' – Humanists were far more likely to say '*prisoner*', '*client*', '*men*', etc., than use the symbolically laden term that others would routinely use. One stated:

> A lot of people jump in with – right we must risk assess you within an inch of your life, quite early days, and we will then treat you. And I hate the term 'treat'; I hate it. It is a medical model ... but [what we do] it is not a pill. It is not an injection. It is not a treatment. It really winds me up.

They went on to note that they did not like the term *intervention* either because:

> Intervention is something that we do to someone ... but there should
> be a more appropriate co-working kind of word ... And to me treat
> and intervene are really inappropriate words. I work with people,
> I help people. I don't intervene ... treat, it's ... it's ... inappropriate.

This sentiment dominated the Humanist approach – the discomfort with this 'framing' of their professional practice was often palpable. One individual voiced this discomfort, as well as disdain for those who adopted this professional script, by noting that these psychologists had '*Dr envy*' and that this was a '*... cover for some rather poor people skills and practice*'.

However, other participants held very different positions and saw their role very much in this light – they were in the prison to 'treat' prisoners. The Functionalists, the first of those who saw their professional practice through this particular lens, did not refer to this as the 'medical model'. Rather, this was just forensic psychological practice. One psychologist when asked what they thought of the medical model responded:

> What it that? Is that not just what we do? We assess the offender
> and we design a course of treatment or management. That is what
> forensic psychology is for. In order to protect the public, we must
> intervene in these prisoners' lives. It would be rather odd for us to
> do any different.

This particular psychologist captured the occupational positionality of most Functionalists. The position was a forthright one, assessment/intervention was what the profession was and should be. There were subtle differences, which adhered to their relative position in the Functionalist typological quadrant, in the manner in which they utilised the particular signifiers of this position. For instance, those who occupied the middle ground might refer to '*interventions*' and '*treatment*', whereas others closer to the public protection/punitivity axes tended towards a more surgical vocabulary. It was not uncommon for those to use phrases such as '*diagnosing*' offending behaviour and then 'excising' those issues/ factors. One even noted that it was similar to an '*invasive exploratory surgery*' to uncover the '*root causes*' of an '*offender's behaviour*'.

This 'rooting' out of criminogenic causes was echoed by the Retributivists. However, the Utilitarians took a slightly different approach, regarding themselves as facilitators, and it is in this regard in which they perceived the forensic psychologist role. So, they often spoke of how it is their role to '*help the offender get their life back on track*' or to assist the prisoner in '*getting better again*'. Here they are framing their work in terms of helping with the treatment not just in terms of diagnostics or intervention. If the others could be thought of as following the Doctor or Surgeon ideation of their role, then the Utilitarians were definitely the Ward Nurse.

Once more the Idealist was distinct from others in their perception of authority and power. As these individuals saw themselves as an integral part of the institution, they perceived their power not only coming from their professional discourse but also from the coercive reality of the prison. As they described here:

> As with any staff position it has ... it has authority to it. That's only right. We wouldn't be able to do our job, not properly anyway, if we didn't have the authority of other staff. Remember, some of the prisoners we deal with have done horrendous things, we need to be in a position to manage them ...

This psychologist shared some commonality with Utilitarians who felt that their authority enabled them in making the prison experience one of benefit for the prisoner. However, where the Idealist differed was in the sense that they saw their power as facilitating the retributive role that they had within the larger narrative of the prison. The Idealist was more comfortable with their own power and embraced it in ways that none of the others did.

These variated perceptions of practice necessarily resulted in very different ideas on not only where authority came from but also how it was to be utilised. The more medicalised the ideation, the more profound the belief in the 'rightness' of manifesting their power by working 'on' prisoners. However, the more hominine approaches were uncomfortable with this usage of their power and sought to mitigate this overt imposition of their disciplinary power.

The Psychologist as 'Expert'

Arising from the medicalisation of deviance and the contemporary construction of forensic psychological discourse is the premise that psychologists are experts in terms of modern disciplinary practice (Scull, 2006). It is they who are able to both risk assess and risk assuage. It is they who are able to diagnose the needs and risks of prisoners, formulate plans by which those needs and risks can be addressed, and ultimately judge whether those needs and risks have been addressed. Psychologists are wielders and purveyors of the symbolically weighty signifiers which both underpin and extend the disciplinary infused prison. Herein lies the central facet of psychological power within the prison. Not only are they staff members who wield the coercive authority of the prison but, they also wield an extramural 'expert' authority that can influence how other members of staff implement and utilise their forms of power.

What was evident however was that not all forensic psychologists held concordant awareness or attitudes to either their power or the expertise upon which it was predicated. Humanists, for instance, were especially concerned with the impact that their power could have on prisoners:

> I agree I am in a position of authority, there is a clear power imbalance between staff member and prisoner. It is not something that I am particularly – how can I put this – I did not come into the job because I was... this job never appealed to me because I will

have the opportunity to have power over other people. I never sort of sit and think isn't it great that I get to decide other people's futures. That does not really – I don't really like to think about that. I am not really conscious of it.

I don't think generally [we] psychologists understand that power perception. I mean the majority of psychologists are in because they want to do good. They want to help ... So, I think lots of people would be really surprised to hear how it feels to be on the receiving end of even a positive report.

It was clear that the majority of Humanists, who had often given some thought to these issues, had a deeper comprehension than other participants of the power dynamic that existed between them, those they work with, and other members of staff. This made them uncomfortable with their own power and the position of authority that they and their role were assigned within the disciplinary apparatus of the prison. As these participants noted:

Interviewer: what sense do you get from the prisoners about their regard of psychology in general?

Psychologist: I think that... I think that they are understandably wary, we can have a very profound impact on their lives and that ... that makes them wary. That makes me wary ...

There are some assessments and they carry so much kit with them that actually you start putting out all these blocks and tools, you might as well be like pulling out the scalpel and tweezers and it must feel a little bit like that sometimes I think for prisoners. I am always aware of that and ... and ... it's uncomfortable for me.

I wanna be sure I got that [a recommendation to deny parole] right you know? Umm ... it's quite scary having that much responsibility and that much influence over someone's life.

Often for the Humanists, this discomfort was centred around the impact that their power could have on the carceral lives of prisoners. A negative report could have major impacts on parole chances, IEP status, and even well-being. These psychologists were more in tune with that facet of their work and the manner in which their power could have the kinds of delayed consequences for prisoners that Crewe (2009) discussed. However, as was noted previously, Humanists were less likely than other types of psychologists to have reconciled their occupational reality, and the power inherent to it, and their moral position. This then, as noted by Muir jr (1977), meant that they were much more vulnerable to the cynicising effects of their profession than others as well as suffering from a wide range of ontological anxieties. There were other senses in which unease was invoked for Humanists, and this related to how their profession was perceived by some of their peers. As one noted:

> It does worry you. I have a colleague, who doesn't worry about it, [they] seem to ... not enjoy ... how to put this? They seem to ... I don't know, thrive on it? Maybe that's wrong but they are certainly comfortable with it. Which I don't understand ...

Another Humanist also noted that one of their senior colleagues seemed to thrive or enjoy the authority of the job:

> I have always been uncomfortable with it, you try and ... but some people are very different. For instance, I worked with someone, not here but when I was at [prison X] ... who I spoke about before, they ... they seemed to relish that part of it. They would speak about how they could do this or do that when writing reports ... and would make jokes about it. I don't really understand how you could be that comfortable [to make jokes].

Here the unease is not just because of their own positionality but also that held by their peers. The attitudes of others both affirmed and compounded their own sense in regard to their role and authority. This discomfort was not just related to their power but also focused on the roots of that power – their psychological expertise. It was not uncommon for Humanists to express hesitancy or even discomfort with regard to the notion of 'expertise'. As this psychologist, a more senior Humanist, explained:

> A young IPP lad I am working with recently showed me his parole decision where the Judge had referred to me as an 'expert witness' ... that made me really, I mean ... I am not quite sure ... I ... we are not the same as a pathologist or a toxicology person. Referring to us in those terms ... it doesn't feel right, you know?

In terms of considering their own authority and the related expertise, Functionalists and Utilitarians, who were both more reconciled to the dual realities of their profession, held very different views to those expressed by the Humanists. These psychologists were more concerned about the manner in which the power dynamic could hamper or inhibit their 'rehabilitative' efforts and thus the efficacy of their practice. As one Functionalist noted, it was important for them not to be too closely associated with the authority of the prison as this could *'alienate the offender'* and result in them not being able to *'do the rehabilitative work that the offender needed'*. Here then, as with other aspects of their occupational perspective, concerns relating to the prisoner came low down in their thinking. Even when discussing their power and the potential impact on a prisoner, this was cast in either functional or utilitarian terms, as exemplified in the following quotation:

> You have to be careful you know? Some of the prisoners we work with are very vulnerable ... we have to be careful, mindful, that our

work does not compound that vulnerability ... if it does it can really impact on what we can do in terms of rehabilitation.

Their unease with regard to their own power was a motivation or an impetus for good and careful practice. This was true of both groups who saw the need for a careful management of how they were perceived so that it did not get in the way of their function or role. For some this meant '*carefully managing relationships*' in order to maintain the '*rehabilitative relationship*' and for others the careful management of their status by '*maintaining a good standing in the eyes of prisoners*'. This identity work is similar to the emotive labour that was discussed previously – here the intent was not so much the controlling of prisoners' emotions but their regard, oddly mirroring the narrative labour that prisoners themselves are engaged in when dealing with authoritative others, especially psychologists (Warr, 2019). For these forensic psychologists how they were perceived as practitioners was important in determining the efficacy of their role. In this regard, both groups were much more comfortable with the notion of 'expertise'. For many of the Functionalists, the expertise of psychology was an integral part of not only who they were and how they saw themselves but also a necessary condition of their effectiveness. One Functionalist captured this sentiment where they discussed this issue in terms of the Chartership:

> It was when I finally completed the [Chartership] that I felt that I was fully acknowledged as the 'expert' that we are required to be. It was then that I felt I could run programmes or give evidence at a parole hearing and have the authority to do so without being second guessed. Obviously, I was doing those things anyway but ... but getting the qualification made ... it rubberstamped my expertise.

Another, when discussing the proliferation of psychologists throughout the criminal justice system, noted:

> It is much better now that you have proper psychological experts conducting risk assessments and managing prisoners. Before it was just ... well, you know?

This last sentiment was one echoed by both the Retributivists who were both much more comfortable with their power and embraced the expert ideation. For both of these individuals, though coming from quite distinct perspectives, the expertise of forensic psychologists was both a necessary and sufficient condition for the protection of the public and the ensuring of just punishments. Both welcomed the advent of psychological practice in prisons. The Cynical Retributivist noted:

> Before we came along it was all done ad hoc – there was no coherent risk assessment, everyone was doing different things. It

was, to be frank, rather rubbish – the public certainly were not being protected. Disgraceful really.

Here then 'expertise' was a good that was to be embraced and promulgated. For the Retributivists, this did not however necessitate any identity work or emotive labour as it did with the Functionalists and the Utilitarians. These two psychologists felt that they embodied their expertise and their power. They did not need to perform this overtly as it was evident in the position and role they had. As the Idealist noted *'we would not be here if we were not best suited to be assessing and managing the risk prisoners pose'*.

As has been shown, the notion of expertise and the manner in which this relates to power was a source of some contention for those who could be categorised as Humanists but not for others. These differing perspectives impacted on the manner in which psychologists perceived themselves, themselves as professional entities within the prison, and on how they approached their practice and their role.

Psychology and Bureaucratic Forms of Power

Bureaucratic power in the prison is concomitant with discursive trends in wider society. de Certeau (1988) highlights the phenomenon, especially in the post-Enlightenment era, of what he calls scriptural dominance. He notes that in the move away from orality traditions, written information is given ever greater probity and symbolic weight which confers a scriptural economy in the trade and exchange of these inscribed forms. He goes on to note that, in this era of scriptural dominance, the repetition of inscribed signifiers (packets of symbolic information) cements both the probity of the information being communicated and the reliability of the source (see also Dean (1999) in his discussion of the processes of Governmentality). The conjunction of these two issues means that data that are written, and seen as specialist and/or authoritative, carry a great deal of power within systems of symbolic interactivity. Crozier (2010) argues that it is here, in the ability of the inscribed to constrain, shape, and influence practice, that bureaucratic formulations become both the embodiment of a system of power and the mechanism (via symbolic communication) by which that power becomes manifest. This facet of bureaucratic power was evidenced by the psychologists in this study when it came to discussing prisoners' files. One stated that *'yes, file data always, always comes first'*; they went on to note that when interviewing a prisoner *'you assess what an offender is saying in the context of the accurate data held on file'*.

This comment establishes that, for at least this individual, there is a distinction between the truth of the scriptural form and the suspect form of that data gathered from the untrusted source – the prisoner. Levine and McCornak (1991) argue, in their examination of Situationally Aroused Communicative Suspicion and Generalised Communicative Suspicion, that there is a distinction between suspicion that is evoked in a particular context and where suspicion is generally aroused due to the source of the information. For these psychologists, communications from prisoners are perceived as generally suspicious, whereas information provided by other 'expert' psychologists is trustworthy. This is perhaps a consequence of the stigmatised nature of prisoners who are, in general, perceived as untrustworthy entities (see Armstrong, 2014). Due to both the penal context and the prisoner as a tainted source, information gleaned from them must be handled and checked carefully. As this psychologist noted:

> It's not that you can't trust prisoners, but ... It's being professional. You have to be careful with the information they give you. You have to think why is this prisoner telling me this? Always check it against file data, check it against whatever you can.

What such generalised suspicion does is to further cement the authority of the bureaucratic data held on that prisoner. It is this file data that all other information is checked against; each instance of where this happens solidifies the perceived probity of that data.

There was a degree of correlation between typological position, depth of positivistic ontology, and the privileging of bureaucratic data over and above interactional data. This was perhaps most evident with the Humanists who would often qualify their statements in this regard and note that they '... *would probably weight the file information more heavily than self-report, if there was no other evidence to support the self-report'*. However, other Humanists were more accepting of the problems of bureaucratic constructions of the prisoner. These were much less likely to privilege formal bureaucratic ideations of the prisoner over their own interaction and perspective, as this individual captured:

> I would like to consider myself not to be a judgemental person, I would like to think that when I do a risk assessment I put in a great deal of time and effort to make sure that I read all of the reports, but I look at those reports from a balanced point of view so I don't read someone's report and think well that is what must be the case – I read all the reports, and of course take them into account, but it is when I meet the person the assessment begins. I remain open to the person and what they have to tell me.

Another Humanist noted that, early in their career, they had encountered a situation whereby the file data were filled with '*wild inaccuracies*', including the age of the victim, which were '*very disturbing'* given that '*some of these errors had shaped sentence plans wrongly for years*'. This meant that they were somewhat suspicious of what went into files and determined to check and investigate if the person they worked with provided disparate or contradictory information. However, for other types, this process may not occur as they were much more likely to adhere to the bureaucratic ideations of the prisoner they worked with. For instance, Functionalists and Utilitarians, who were more deeply positivistic, were more likely to treat prisoners according to how they were bureaucratically constructed. As such, they would be much more likely to privilege the file data, as this Functionalist explained:

> If I am allocated a risk assessment to do I would start by finding out the collateral information for that offender. So, I would look at previous psychology reports, I would have a look at the psychology file, I would have a look at his offender management file, so that would be like depositions; previous wing file if he had been to another jail etc. all of the reports, psychiatric assessments; presentence reports; I would have a look at all of that information before I was to see the offender so I would know who they were.

Another phrased this in a similar way when they noted that they focused on the file data in order to gain *'an accurate sense of the real person, rather than who they wanted me to see'*. Again, we see here the nature of the bureaucratic power of psychology in play – the constructed idea of the prisoner that exists on paper is that which is responded to as the real.

Both Retributivists held extreme positivist positions and as such held very 'imagined' ideations of the prisoners they worked with – for the very different reasons discussed in previous chapters. This resulted in them not only privileging the information held on file about a prisoner but they did so over any impression they garnered from interactions with the prisoner which they tended to interpret as *'representations'* or *'performances'*. The idealist described this perspective when they said:

> Before [doing] ... risk assessments you must look to the file data, you must read all the reports to learn who the offender is. Only then can you get an idea of how to approach the offender, how to see beyond their representations and get to the truth.

The Cynical Retributive held a similar perspective to that of the Idealist. They noted that they could not *'necessarily trust what prisoners say or how they present themselves'* and thus would pay much more attention to *'file data'* when forming their professional opinions. Here their cynicism held sway over their professional practice and resulted in them rejecting, in a similar way to the Idealist, what they saw as representational 'scripts' from prisoners. Instead, they preferred to see the bureaucratic construction as the prisoner's master status. This individual went on to explain that they were *'very careful'* in constructing and drafting their reports so as to *'ensure that what was there* [in the reports] *conformed to the existing data* [on file]' so that they could ensure that *'any prisoner manipulation'* of information was *'excised from the files'*.

The Cynical Retributive had given this issue a great deal of thought and was explicitly clear that they saw their role as maintaining the conformity of the scriptural representation. They explained that *'every offender will try and manipulate you'* when it comes to parole reports/sentence plans. They acknowledged that the representations proffered by prisoners often contained '*kernels of truth*' that were '*wrapped in what they think we, or the Parole Board, want to hear*' and that this needed to be carefully unpicked. They continued by noting that they mitigated this by using the file data in order to maintain the accuracy of the knowledge held (and presented) on that prisoner. They said that this '*was the real skill, the expertise, of psychology*'. They linked their expertise to the bureaucratic power of the discipline by noting that the expertise of psychology lies in cohering the information presented to them via the lens of the extant data (often produced by other psychologists) held on file. Here then we see a further manifestation of the disciplinary capital of psychological discourse in that it acts as both tool and lens for other psychologists too, and not just other disciplinary authorities within the prison.

Other psychologists echoed these sentiments by speaking about '*maintaining accuracy*' or ensuring '*precision and coherence*' in the file data. For instance, one psychologist had noted that it was important to maintain a sense of '*coherence in the reports*'. When asked for an explanation of what this meant, they had said '*to ensure that [their] reports address the same issues as others*'. A different psychologist had made a similar statement about 'coherence' and when asked to explain had noted that '*Obviously, coherence is important for any parole dossier*'. Whilst these statements are not as explicit in their descriptions as the Cynical Retributivist, the accounts of other psychologists do support this notion of maintaining coherence within the scriptural economy of risk, risk assessment, and the implementation of their expertise. These cohering processes are what Darley and Gross (1983), and later Kassin, Dror, and Kukucka (2013), highlight as the circularity of logics in the assessment process which result in forms of confirmation bias. Fundamentally, the more these cohering logics are implemented by successive psychologists, the more they shape the data produced but also the manner in which that data are then perceived, which then in turn shapes the manner in which the next psychologist produces their data and so on. Circularity.

However, one aspect of maintaining this bureaucracy which, though acknowledged in discussions of the pressures of caseload (see previous chapter), was omitted from any discussion of power or authority was how 'managing' caseloads and prioritising cases could have a profound impact on prisoners and impact on the general bureaucratic legitimacy of the prison. It was highlighted that the need for varying types of risk assessment meant that some prisoners were inevitably bumped from lists as others who had more immediate needs were prioritised. Yet this was never acknowledged as the exercising of their everyday power, even where it was acknowledged that such practices could have both short- and long-term consequences for the prisoners who were 'bumped'. These consequences could mean delays in progressing through the system and even in delays in completing mandated offending behaviour courses – both of which could further deprive these prisoners of their liberty by adding years to the amount of time that they may spend in prison. Nor was there any acknowledgement of how such practices could contribute in the wider sense to the bureaucratic legitimacy of the prison (Liebling et al., 2012) and how the prison was perceived and experienced by prisoners. As Crewe, Liebling, and Hulley (2015) show, bureaucratic legitimacy is frequently the lowest scoring dimension in tests of prisons moral climates and can have implications for the good order of a prison. Here forensic psychologists are contributing to this dimension in potentially negative ways, through the everyday exercising of their power, with little or no acceptance or understanding of this. This highlights how psychological expertise, their disciplinary capital, the bureaucracy that underpins its practice, and their role in the wider scriptural economy of the prison are not distinct aspects of the penal power of psychology but are necessarily entwined and self-supporting formulations of that power.

Coerced Involvement and Ethical Blindness

Trotter and Ward (2013) define ethical blindness as when practitioners fail to perceive the full weight of the consequences of their actions due to the limiting professional lens through which they understand and conduct their professional practice (see also Ward & Syverson, 2009). When this is coupled with the coercive nature of forensic interactions in prisons, there is the potential for serious consequences for prisoners. The coercion here is different from that that exists with prison officers as it is not predicated on either practices of physical force or of sanction (Hepburn, 1985), but it is still necessarily coercive in nature. The coercion here derives from the 'expert' judgements of psychologists, their disciplinary capital within the scriptural economy of the contemporary prison, and what consequences they may have both for the prisoner in their immediate carceral lifeworld and over their carceral life course. These potential harms to the prisoner become an unconsidered factor in light of the delivery of institutional concerns (see Brown, Shell, & Cole, 2015). Though many were concerned with the harm that could be experienced by vulnerable prisoners, this particular issue was given little attention by my participants. Many accepted that *'prisoners have little choice'* in their dealings with psychology, yet they rarely looked beyond that to what the consequences of that may be nor how that may be experienced. Every psychologist was asked about this issue and the most common responses fell into two broad categories which were *'I had not really thought about that'* or that such consequences were *'unknown and unknowable'*.

The exception here was with a few Functionalists who understood this issue as acting as a barrier to what they could do with *'unwilling participants'*, and thus it was seen as an impediment to treatment efficacy. As this psychologist noted when talking about those on parole sentences in their prison:

> There has always been the issue of lifers and IPPs that they are not really willing clients if you like. They are not really of their own free will engaging in any work with you. That impacts on what we can do with them ...

Whilst another noted that when prisoners were *'forced to deal with us'*, it would make the psychologist's job much harder as they had *'to deal with that'* issue first *'before anything useful could be achieved'*. What was not considered was the impact that this coercion could have on the person in terms of their perception of psychologists and the honesty with which they then engaged. As I have argued elsewhere (Warr, 2008), the coercive reality between the prisoner and the psychologist results in a situation whereby it is difficult to trust, and thus achieve any real candour with, psychologists in prisons. Crewe (2009) adds that, in actuality, the power of psychology in terms of the prison may be counterproductive and can prove a barrier to truthful and open disclosure (see also Towl & Walker, 2015).

No participants raised this as a concern when discussing these issues, and many appeared not to want to consider it in general. One psychologist, a Humanist, even stated explicitly that they '*couldn't bear to think about*' the coercive nature of their profession as it would mean that the work was '*more difficult, more traumatic than it was already*'. A Functionalist seemed resigned to the fact that some harm may come to the prisoner by the 'system' coercing their involvement, but this was seen as a necessary aspect of their sentence so the '*prison can maintain the protection of the public*'. The Idealist, however, was both more explicit and understanding of this dynamic and how this was an extension of the carcerality that was imposed upon prisoners:

> They have no choice but to work with us, it's part of their sentence. The criminal justice system works that way. To a degree what the offender wants is irrelevant … we have a job to do, and that job is to assess and reduce the risk they pose to the public. If they want to progress in their sentence then …[shrug]

Here, we see the central dichotomy of power as discussed by Muir jr (1977) and how forensic psychologists relate to that issue. Whilst some psychologists clearly did not want to consider the reality of the prisoner's situation, others saw the coercion as an inherent and justified aspect of their work. Nevertheless, the implications of this coercion were little considered by the participants of this study. A combination of their typological positioning, their professional perspectives, and the bureaucratic lens governed their understanding, or willingness to understand, this particular dynamic. This is what Gannon and Ward (2014) describe as being the fundamental bases of both the dual-relationship issue, which those operating under the risk/needs model of service delivery are subject to, and ethical blindness. These authors (see also: Haag, 2006) argue that ethical blindness occurs when there is not a reflexive and responsive professional dialogue (see again Brown et al., 2015) that focuses on the experiences of those under assessment. This is because the carceral priorities of risk, security, and disciplinary concerns are privileged and conflated as if they were therapeutic concerns. This conflation means that the interests of the prisoner becomes subsumed and hidden (see also Greenburg & Shuman, 1997). Consequently, the potential harms that can be imposed by coerced interaction with psychology remain unconsidered.

Psychology, Power and Neutralisation

Some participants recognised the issues outlined regarding their position of power and the authority that their role entailed. However, others seemed to deny either the inherent and unequal power relationship between their professional selves and the prisoners with whom they worked, or the impact of this imbalance on prisoners. When speaking to forensic psychologists at conferences and presentations, the same processes of denial have been evident and a source of discussion (as well as discomfort). A common response from my participants was that they were not powerful within the prison and did not feature highly in the overall hierarchy of authority of the prison. For example:

> I don't ever think of it as being a position of power. I like to think of it actually as an opportunity for somebody to be able to – that is why I always try to tell people or motivate them by saying it is actually an opportunity for them to get to the nitty gritty of what has happened and just see it as a tour really ...

> I don't see us as being in a position of power ... I mean that's not what we ... we are here to help the prisoners.

They saw others, mainly discipline staff and the Senior Management Team (SMT), as those who wielded power within the prison. One psychologist, who sat on the SMT of their prison, even expressed the same sentiment – excluding themselves from their own assessment. Many located power as belonging with the prison itself, as a carceral institution, rather than being located in and of their profession and its perceived expertise:

> ... it's not us; the power doesn't come from us does it? It's the prison ... they [uniformed staff] hold all the power here.

> I don't think I have ever stopped to think about it as being an authoritative position but just I kind of think we are a little cog in a big wheel or something like that.

> ... prisoners are very vulnerable. As a staff member I have some authority you know? In some circumstances at least ... but that's as a staff member not as a psychologist.

Such participants expressed a tautological position in regard to this: they did not see power as originating with them because they, in and of themselves, did not see themselves as powerful. Partly this was to do with the relatively low numbers, as a staff group, that existed in any department/prison, as one person noted '*there are too few of us to have any real authority here*'. This meant that they did not see themselves has having much collective efficacy in the prison when compared to other staff groups. A further aspect of this sense of powerlessness was concerned with the quotidian reality of being a forensic psychologist in prison delivering rigid and regimented programmes and assessment tools, designed by others. This speaks to the peculiarity of the power of forensic psychologists operating in the prison. Unlike officers there is not a power that is derived from the physically coercive practices of the institution, rather it is one that emerges from a combination of the disciplinary interests of the prison conjoined with an external, and independent, source of expertise. One Functionalist captured this notion when they explained that the authority of psychology, in this circumstance, belonged to the assessments themselves and whoever had created and sanctioned the tools which psychologists were asked to employ, rather than the person doing the delivery:

> These tools are standardised, you know? So, if you're following the correct format for the report and using the scoring guides properly, as they are designed to be used then ... you know, then you can't really go wrong. It's not your 'clinical' opinion it's a standardised ... you don't have to worry because ... it's not really based on you, or it being about your clinical opinion or ... authority, if you see what I mean?

Another psychologist bluntly stated that often they felt more *'monkey than organ grinder'* in their day to day work. They had been delivering the same programme for a number of years and said that, because it was *'formulaic in content'* without *'much room for input or innovation'*, they were just a *'tool in the OBP cog'*. Here we see a recognition of the incomplete and extramural nature of this nascent penal power. The psychologist is not only an embodiment of psychological power but acts as a channel for a form of power that exists beyond them, and outside of the prison. This recognition results in a perceived lack of autonomy which then played a significant part in the manner in which they understood their own power.

As noted previously, one of the reasons that psychologists were perceived as powerful by prisoners was their influence in the parole process and the impact that this could have in the carceral lives of prisoners (Crewe, 2009). For prisoners, especially indeterminately sentenced prisoners, the power of forensic psychologists is both acute, in that can impact on their daily lives, and chronic in that it can shape their future lives within and without the prison. The influence of psychological assessment on the decision-makers within the prison and with the parole board is profound and can go largely unchecked. However, many of those interviewed sought to relocate responsibility for these parole decisions from themselves to the Parole Board:

> I've read the articles in Inside Time too, the whole 'psychobabes thing', and whilst I sympathise ... erm, I don't really understand where they're coming from. We don't make those decisions; the Parole Board do.

> You've seen Inside Time? We get blamed for their [Parole Board] decisions. They make decisions that affect our clients, really affect our clients, and then we get the blame ... when they have to do more offending behaviour work.

> You see the Parole Board decision and ... if it's negative ... you
> know, you know that we will be blamed for that.

The reporting of forensic psychologists in the national prison papers has
increased in the last decade. Often these articles concentrate on two interrelated
factors: the flawed nature of psychological expertise and then the perceived
unwarranted influence of psychology over the Parole Board. However, there is a
personal element to this reporting in Inside Times and other publications which
must be noted.[1] Each article and each complaint necessarily have a referent who is
being attacked in a media format. Whilst not explicitly named, if the complainant
names the establishment that they are in, then the psychologist in question and
others will know who that individual is talking about. That can be personally
distressing. As two of the participants mentioned:

> You see the articles in Inside Time and ... you're being attacked. It
> is really horrible. Properly, properly horrible.

> Personally, I think it's irresponsible of the paper because it's very
> hurtful for those involved. You're only doing your job, it's the
> Parole Board makes the decisions ... you don't want to be attacked
> for it. It's really not nice.

Returning to the issue of parole reports, others blamed the Prison Service for
this phenomenon by stating that they felt that often the fault lay with the
paperwork and files that were submitted alongside psychological reports. One
noted that the quality of these reports and submissions could *'be shockingly bad'*
whilst utilising *'quasi-psychological mumbo-jumbo'* that they feared might *'unduly
influence the board'*. This type of displacement was often rooted in the limited
contact that forensic psychologists had with their clients. Being divorced from the
products of their labour made practitioners blind not only to the end results of
their consultations but also the probative weight which their input and recommendations are afforded. Nevertheless, there is a degree to which this attempt at
avoiding responsibility for those decisions, which are often predicated on the
recommendations of forensic psychologists, has distinct overtones of neutralisation. Montada (2001), expanding the conceptual framework of Sykes and Matza

---

[1]Converse for instance or some of the other forums that have begun in the last few years.
Also, increasingly, on social media. Many further examples of these sentiments can be
found in the accounts, letters, and complaints of prisoners detailed within the national
prisoner newspaper Inside Time. In the period since this research began, the topic of
forensic psychology has almost been a constant in the pages of the paper and, though
many of the larger articles are authored by a small minority, subject to a wide range of
queries from a wide range of individuals (Inside Time, 2013). Many of these articles and
complaints are pejorative in tone if not in content. There are also a range of gendered
influences at play in this issue, whereby those forensic psychologists employed by the Prison
Service are referred to in many of these articles as 'psychobabes' (see Chapter 8 for a further
discussion of this issue).

(1957), explains that the denial of responsibility is aimed at protecting oneself from blame, reprisal, and feelings of guilt. For psychologists, this denial of power and responsibility can be understood as a form of emotion work. They seek to protect themselves from blame, reprisal, and, perhaps more profoundly, feelings of guilt that may arise from being unable to reconcile the central dichotomy of their practice.

Participants attempted to displace responsibility in another respect. One particular distancing practice was with regard to the allocation of risk levels to prisoners. Such levels can determine what work the prisoner can do, where they are housed within units and what activities they can engage in. Psychologists can play a role in these assessments, especially for those serving indeterminate or parole-based sentences, but many put a distance between themselves, their recommendations, and the risk characterisations that prisoners experienced:

> It's so managers can, um ... make the best decisions on how to manage the offender ... in the prison. Our reports are part of that but we're not responsible ... [for how] reports are used.

> All I can do is do the risk assessment and then advise, give my professional opinion ... what the prison does with that, well ... I don't have any say over that ... not really.

> When writing a general risk assessment for an offender you ensure that you get all your boxes ticked and that you have done a good job. You can then go home thinking 'Yes, I have done a good job'. It is frustrating though that you don't have much say on what happens after ...

> I may write a report and comment on an offender's risk level ... but I have no power over how that report is used by the prison.

> We don't make the decisions about risk ... we just make assessments of risk, you know?

Only a few of the more experienced Humanists recognised that their role in transmitting, amplifying, and consolidating notions of risk attached to prisoners had a powerful impact on those prisoners. These forensic psychologists had some understanding of the disciplinary capital of their expertise and the manner in which this could affect the prisoners who were in their care. However, for many their adjunct status went unrecognised and denied. This form of professional denial relates to a type of attention withdrawal, such as that noted by Anshel (2000) regarding the Police and stress events. Some officers withdraw their attention from the consequences of their power so as not to confront the impacts to which they have contributed (see also Muir jr (1977)). This emotion work becomes a means of pre-mitigating or even preventing the negative emotions that can arise from coercive practice. Similarly, for psychologists, not confronting the experiential reality of prisoners and denying the consequences of their interaction and interventions, it enables them to avoid any evocation of guilt. Here we see a form of self-imposed 'moral blindness' that is distinct from the ethical blindness discussed previously. Ethical blindness, as defined by Ward and Syversen (2009), occurs when the professional lens blinds a practitioner to the consequences of their professional practice. Whilst these forensic psychologists certainly experience this, it is a distinct phenomenon from the moral blindness that arises from processes of denial. Bauman and Donskis (2013) argue that in the liquid modern society moral blindness arises in circumstances where technologies of knowing, employed by the powerful, result in an insensitivity to the very human that is subject to those technologies. This goes beyond just not seeing the consequences of one's profession to not seeing the person with which that profession is concerned. Here, with the denial of their role in decisions made by the parole board and the devastating consequence of their power on prisoners, we see forensic psychologists being morally blind to the humans (prisoners) whom they have dominion over.

Furthermore, this distancing is not only a manifestation of attention withdrawal but also of implicatory denial as described by Cohen (2001). Here we see, for the majority of the sample, both normalisation and discursive defence mechanisms being employed, which both deny the implications of their profession whilst at the same time building in ideations of normality to the risk diagnosing power of their role. It also allows psychologists to cast their authority in a benign, and thus defendable, light related to principles of rehabilitation and treatment whilst at the same time covering up the insensitivity of those processes which are geared towards achieving the disciplinary ends of the prison. Both forms of denial are, in effect, defensive in nature and allow these psychologists to perform their role without having to confront their own power, their adjunct status, and the emotional labour this may evoke.

This chapter has explored how psychologists experience being adjuncts of power in the modern prison. What is evident is that the power of psychology, due to its confluence of intra- and extramural sources of authority, is both profound and somewhat remote. Whilst they influence both the present and future life course of prisoners and the manner in which other staff operate disciplinarily, many had little awareness of this. This may not be surprising given that the power inherent to practice or action is often concealed from those who are acting (Arendt, 1959). Nevertheless, they operate both a noncorporeal coercive and expert form of authority, underpinned by a distinct and pervasive scriptural economy, predicated on a conjunction of the disciplinary interests of the prison and a 'medicalised' discourse. Whilst it is true that some psychologists were uncomfortable with the framing of their discipline in terms of medicalised practice, this was, nevertheless, the manner in which psychology defined its practice. The analysis/management of risk and the treatment of 'offending behaviour' both established the grounds for the disciplinary capital of psychology within the prison but was also central to the 'expertise' which practitioners held. This is especially evident in their reliance upon, and contribution to, the scriptural dominance of bureaucratised data. Their laminating of psychological signifiers in that data added to the probity of that data for both other psychologists and others within and without the prison. The circular logics of assessment therefore increased psychology's symbolic capital within the prison. In consequence, regardless of the typological perspective, psychologists were in service to the prison and concerned with furthering its interests.

Herein lies the core of the dual-relationship issue for forensic psychologists working in prison. This goes beyond the simplistic notion of the care/control problem that nurses in the prison may experience and highlights a deeper symbiotic relationship to the disciplinary power of the prison. Psychology, as a discourse, has become a predicate of disciplinary power in the modern prison. However, many psychologists, of all types, perceive their practice in terms of its impact on the prisoner's behaviour rather than as power acting on the prisoner directly. It is this reality that caused a great deal of the emotion work that individual psychologists undertook and led them to deny, or neutralise, the power and influence they had in the prison. Yet this denial had consequences in terms of ethical practice as it meant that many psychologists were blind, both ethically and morally, to the coercive nature of their practice and the implications that this could have for the prisoners with whom they worked.

Chapter 7

Subalterns of Penal Power

> I don't think many people in here, or out there, realise just how intimidating the prison can be for those of us not in uniform …
> –Psychology Assistant

The previous chapter discussed forensic psychologists as adjuncts and wielders of power within the contemporary prison and how they perceive and respond to this aspect of their role. Muir jr (1977) notes in his discussion on the police that they experience a fundamental paradox when it comes to power. They are both powerful yet not absolutely powerful, and the disjunction between these two states can result in a complex relationship to the profession from which their own power derives. As noted in the previous chapter, though forensic psychologists are indeed wielders of a pervasive penal power and have a great deal of disciplinary capital within the scriptural economy of the contemporary prison, they do not often recognise this. Those interviewed for this study were much more likely to locate power within the prison with other staff groups. This chapter looks more closely at how they themselves felt subject to the wider influences of various forms of penal power. Here we begin to see how they can be both fundamentally powerful whilst simultaneously vulnerable. Specifically, this chapter will discuss two core ways in which those interviewed were subjected to issues of power. These include the territorial dynamics that exist between psychology and other disciplinary infused discourses within the prison and the relationship between psychology and the more coercive power wielded by uniformed staff.

Territoriality: Offender Management vs Psychology

Foucault (1979) and Sim (1990) highlight how the prison is constructed from varying carceral and disciplinary discourses, each of which is supported by systems of practice, expertise, and bureaucracy. In organisations, if these systems of power overlap in their interests and duties there is often a competition in terms of resources, influence, and practice (Liefooghe & Mackenzie, 2001). This often results in behaviours that Hall (1990) would define as territoriality. Brown, Lawrence, and Robinson (2005) note that though there are differing aspects of territoriality in the workplace, from the benign (i.e. personalising one's own desk/

Forensic Psychologists, 143–163
Copyright © 2021 Jason Warr
Published under exclusive licence by Emerald Publishing Limited
doi:10.1108/978-1-83909-960-120200008

office space) to the malign (i.e. processes of exclusion), there are fundamental elements which define these practices. These are the enactment of behaviours designed to indicate ownership of particular physical, social, or symbolic objects that exist within the organisation. Though some of these behaviours can lead to social cohesion and in-group organisational identities, they can, in some circumstances, also have negative effects on individuals and the organisation. This is especially true where territoriality results in a wholesale 'preoccupation with communicating and maintaining proprietary claims' (p. 577) within the organisation itself. Proprietary signalling, behaviours designed to specifically mark out realms of influence, can become a significant aspect of dysfunctional organisational culture and practice (Brown & Robinson, 2007).

Brown and Robinson (2007) go on to argue that two of the most pernicious aspects of territorialism in organisations are when these behaviours result in 'ineffective knowledge sharing' and 'territorial infringements' (p. 254). Ineffective knowledge sharing was a situation which most psychologists thought pervaded their prison, to its detriment, and underscored a great deal of their quotidian working life:

> It feels like there are lots of barriers within a prison to getting information from other departments. That actually if we could all work together we would get more done ... I still think we work in silos a lot, everyone has their little fiefdom and you can't go beyond that. It's not a good way for us to work ...

> Ah, the most frustrating ... is trying to get file data [from] other departments.

> I understand it but perhaps another frustration and a constraint is sharing knowledge from a security perspective and how that would and can inform risk assessments; and sometimes I think we are not fully aware of everything of what is going on and actually if you are making a recommendation I think that can make you quite vulnerable. If somebody has got some information somewhere that potentially could shape how you would pull together your assessment and you are not aware of it.

> I spend a lot of my time just chasing information from other departments. The worst culprits are always security, healthcare and OMU. It's not that they won't give you information you ask for but it's ... it's always late or partial, or not the bit that you need. It takes up so much of my time.

Many participants highlighted that such behaviours had impinged both on their efficacy and their working lives. One participant captured this sentiment when they noted that everyone in the prison should be *'working together, to achieve the same ends'* but rather, what often occurs is everyone *'working at cross-purposes'* because they are only interested in *'what they are doing and their little bit of the prison'*.

In terms of territorial infringement, the two parties most often accused of these behaviours were Security and Offender Management Units (OMUs). Many psychologists (comprising all types) noted that they had experienced problems with 'Security' attempting to stamp their authority in varying ways. For instance, one stated that in their prison the security Principal Officer would send missives to the psychology department, and only the psychology department, on a weekly basis concerning various issues such as trafficking, inappropriate relationships, grooming, etc. Another said that:

> Whenever we have a new member join the team the security officers will pick on them during the security briefings, every time. They did it when I started here and ... they still do it. It's like they are trying to ... I don't know, it's like being in the playground again 'my sand pit', you know?

Another expanded on this issue when they said that:

> I ... for example we had training ... the err ... security training officer ... I remember him saying to me 'I wouldn't ordinarily talk to your kind but, you know, I've been ordered to so I will.' He made it clear that he thought that we were a security risk and needed reminding that security comes first!

However, sometimes this territorialising by security went beyond this 'security first' positioning. Where it did it often presented ethical problems for psychologists in terms of their professional practice and the ethics dictated by their governing body. For instance, one of the participants described how they had discovered that security officers were regularly accessing prisoner's psychology files looking for 'intelligence'. When this psychologist had raised this with the officers in question, and the Senior Management Team in the prison, they had been told that '*security could do whatever they wanted*' with any information held in the prison and that they '*should concentrate on their job and let security do theirs*'. Another stated that security officers would often come to their department demanding personal and file information that they '*could use against so and so*' and was perturbed that their colleagues would just comply. This psychologist, who had worked in a clinical setting before coming to the prison, found this behaviour deeply troubling and unprofessional but noted that when they had spoken to their colleagues about this it had been dismissed as '*it's just what security do*'. Partly the discomfort here was because of the ethical problems that this posed for the psychologist and their team in terms of the British Psychological Society (BPS) guidelines and protocols around confidentiality. When they were asked what they themselves had done about it they said:

> What could I do? It's security ... everyone did what they said. In the end, I just carried on and tried to ignore it. I just became more careful what I would put in my notes. I still feel uncomfortable about it though.

A different psychologist noted that they had been told by their line manager to give 'Security' whatever they wanted otherwise they would '*throw a tantrum*'. They noted that their department had traditionally acquiesced to Security even when this had been '*not in the best interest of our role*'. This presented an ethical conundrum for some staff which was peculiar to the prison environment:

> We work in an entirely different setting [than health or education], some of the BPS/HBC stuff does not apply as simply to us. It clearly applies to us but you have to think … it is great chatting to forensic and clinical chums in health and they just kind of roll their eyes, but I say we get told to do that and you can't not, and people say well just say no. No, you don't understand because three men in uniform will just come in and just take the file.

A more senior psychologist had noted that they had found a similar tradition of acquiescence when moving to their current position and had '*put a stop to that*' and made sure that any communication with security went through themselves. When asked why they had done this, they had, after some hesitation and whilst refusing to give details, admitted that in the past there had been some '*influencing of reports and assessments by security staff*' that they felt was '*at best inappropriate*'.

Though mentioned by fewer psychologists, these attempts at influencing reports were a further territorial imposition by Security staff. This could be subtle; for instance, asking psychologists to focus on particular issues that may have little or nothing to do with someone's offending behaviour but was an institutional concern. One participant recalled a Security Governor demanding that the report that they were producing provide a post hoc '*justification for a decision that they had already made*'. This tended to be the focus of other psychologist's accounts when it came to their interactions with Security personnel. One had recounted that '*security will always come first, irrespective of what I think about somebody*'. Another explained how a security officer had wanted them to change a report that was to be submitted to the Parole Board after discovering that the psychologist was recommending a move to open conditions:

> …[the security officer] said that that prisoner was too high risk. I asked him what evidence he had to support that and he said 'I just know'. He was quite insistent that I change the … my recommendations.

Another noted that they had been asked to omit details from a report as security did not want the prisoner to know that this was an area of investigation/intelligence that security was interested in. There were only a few who mentioned this aspect of territoriality directly but what was consistent was the attempt by security staff to impose their interests and concerns on the work and practice of psychologists.

What was more often reported was a conflict between psychology departments/ practitioners and the OMUs. As Robinson (2005) highlights, the advent of the National Offender Management Service (NOMS) in the early 2000s also created a new paradigm for the management of prisoners both within and without prison. This created the OMUs, normally run by probation and specialised prison staff, who ideally would oversee the management of a prisoner's sentence from beginning to end. In this regard, they are charged with assessing, monitoring, and managing the prisoners risk via OASys. They also have input into sentence plans, deliver offending behaviour programmes, compile parole reports, and input into Multi Agency Public Protection Arrangements (MAPPA) for qualifying cases. This was work which also dominated the day-to-day practice of the psychology department. Here lies the crux of this territorial dispute – though coming from different discursive traditions, both departments are doing much the same work and therefore must compete for the same resources, opportunities, and influence. In effect, both departments are competing for disciplinary capital within a limited symbolic economy.

All participants spoke of a strained relationship with OMU in some way. Some stated how psychology and OMU hadn't '*always seen eye to eye*' whilst others noted that in the early days '*there was some stepping on each other's toes*'. However, nearly all noted that these issues had become increasingly compounded by the advancement and entrenchment of the Offender Management (OM) model:

> With the OM model as I am sure you know, you have key workers. That is where psychology should fit in … but they are not part of the OM model, they are somebody that you call in to do something and then go away, which is really unhelpful.

Another put this relationship between OM and psychology in a more conflicted light:

> I think there is that little bit maybe – battle is probably too strong a word but certainly challenge in terms of promoting psychology in an accurate way within the OM paradigm and say, 'no, this is what we can do!' Don't just think of us as programmes……there is nothing wrong with delivery of programmes but maybe the skill is in the treatment management and making sure the right clinical decisions are made … that's what we should be doing but … OM [does that].

Most associated OMU with the prominence of probation services within and without the prison, as one participant noted: '*OM? That's all probation really…*'. However, what was central to this frustration with the OM model was that, increasingly, it was they who dictated the input and practice of psychologists and their interactions with prisoners. Some considered this reality unwelcome in terms of their wider position within the structure of the prison:

> We're now in a position where probation and … [OMU] they, really, they call us in when they need us to do a report or an

> assessment but ... it's not great. We should be involved in managing those offenders ...

> It means that psychologists become synonymous with particular pieces of work rather than being something that is part of the system.

> I do feel ... I don't know ... separate? With OM we don't really input we just do a risk assessment here and then do a programme there. We're not really a part of it and ... and that's ... it's not ideal.

One of the occupational realities that faced the psychologists interviewed was an increasing shift towards 'episodic' psychological services. This led to psychologists not being seen as an intrinsic part of the prison system but increasingly as a service brought in to assess and fix the offender by delivering certain forms of 'intervention' or treatment. Psychologists felt that as OMUs gained in influence and dominance (secured greater territory) within the prison, they, and their departments, were being pushed to the periphery of the 'treatment' work. This frustration was compounded by psychologists feeling that they were more qualified than Offender Managers to take this lead. One even noted that they and their team were the *'experts in offender and risk management'* and thus should be *'central to OM'* rather than on the periphery.

Though this seemed to be an issue for most of the participants the Retributive Idealist expressed the greatest frustration. Their ontological security was inherently tied to their being a member of the prison's staff and playing an integral role in the functions of the prison. However, with psychology becoming a distinct body of experts who were called upon for discrete pieces of work by OMU, that would aid and further the interests of OM, they felt *'pushed out'* and *'sometimes side-lined'*. They felt that the work of their department was not utilised in the *'way it necessarily should be'*. This was exacerbated by the fact that their unit had been relocated away from the core prison to the administrative block, whereas OM had been given a larger more *'privileged'* locale within the *'heart'* of the prison. As Hall (1990) argues, territoriality, and in deed notions of proximity and distance (Simmel, 1971), are inherently tied to the manner in which humans denote and perceive status. Here distance from the centre of the prison was perceived as a loss of status within the structure of the prison. This further impacted on this individual because they then felt that the prison was, to a certain degree, preventing them from doing their role:

> ... how can we properly protect the public and ensure an offender's sentence is being ... when we are not involved directly?

This was a distinct pain for the Retributive Idealist but it also echoed the concerns of others. One Functionalist noted that, like the Idealist mentioned above, their department had been relocated to one of the more distant regions of the prison (a former workshop), whereas OMU had been relocated to one of the core residential wings. Another highlighted how they had been moved to the administrative area away from the residential wings where they were once based and that the OMU now occupied the space they once had – in the heart of the prison. Here then we see OMU not only subsuming the work and influence of psychology but also the physical territories that they had once occupied.

This aspect of practice was also a source of worry for one Humanist whose management had not yet moved to a regional model of service delivery. They had noted this episodic, or 'on-call', practice had increasingly become the norm in their prison where they too had been moved away from the core prison to a more remote area. This caused them some worry but they blamed their own profession for this situation rather than OM or the prison:

> We don't potentially integrate ourselves enough. Separate entity almost. And I think that has only got capacity to be worse when we are a regional team and we kind of only just drop in rather than being very integrated into the establishment.

One Functionalist, who had been in service for nearly a decade and had seen a number of changes to their role in that time, noted that this imposed practice could have wider implications, especially with regard to privatised forensic psychological services. Crewe (2009) noted that for some prisoners going through parole proceedings there had been a growing tendency to retain private and external psychologists to produce reports that challenged the orthodoxy provided by HMPPS psychologists (see also Forde, 2018). This was a source of anxiety, as one psychologist stated:

> It's much more common now. Once upon a time you would never worry about a different psychological perspective being proffered to the board but ... and it's umm ... unpleasant, I suppose, when you're challenged by the board based on a report produced by an external [psychologist] that is not as rigorous ...

However, of greater concern was that the increased move to an episodic service in which the prison viewed them as a resource to be called in as and when necessary, made them vulnerable in terms of private practice replacing them as a preferred model of service. This potential for outsourcing, they felt, was much more likely in light of increasing budgetary constraints:

> Of course, we run the risk, as we move to a regional model, ... and as there are ever greater pressures to save money, of becoming seen more as a service to be called upon rather than part of [NOMS]... Not a big leap from that, is it, to replacing us with the privateers, many of whom used to work with us, who can do it cheaper. Not as effectively ... but cheaper.

This concern was recognised by senior psychologists. The profession was increasingly being shaped by external budgetary constraints. This forced them into being an '*external person*' who would be called upon to deliver a risk assessment or a programme and then have no more input into a case because there was '*... not enough time. There is just not enough time, there is not enough money, there is not enough resource*'. This person stated that historically a psychologist could spend weeks getting to know a prisoner, and establishing consent, before doing a report but that:

> Now the demand on resources is such that if a psychologist is doing a lifer report, if they see them three times it will be for consent, interview and disclosure and that is what private companies do, actually the private companies do not want to do the disclosure either. And they do not really do the consent. Private companies will tend to see somebody all day for one day and that will be it. I think we are still doing better than that but it is reduced. And the pressure on people to churn these reports is immense, absolutely immense.

Psychological services are shaped by the power not only of others within the prison, such as OM and the fiscal diktats of budget holders, but also of the private sector. This is particularly true where prison and probation are a joined entity and operate through an OM ethos dominated by contemporary austerity politics. All of this creates a situation whereby psychology and individual psychologists are subject to the territorial constraints (power) of these other disciplinary entities. This speaks directly to the manner in which psychologists can, professionally, be subaltern to other bodies within the prison who have an interest in limiting the disciplinary capital of psychology. However, there are other areas of their experiential reality where they are more directly subject to the carceral power of others.

The Uniformed Body: Intimidation and Bullying

It was evident that there was a strained relationship between the psychologists interviewed and the uniformed body with whom they work. It was these inter-relational aspects of working in the prison that caused a great deal of the stress that forensic psychologists experienced. Many participants saw the uniform body as being both very powerful, wielding direct power over them, but also as the principle power holders within the prison. As these individuals noted:

> Power? Well, it ... it comes from the prison ... they [uniformed staff] hold all the power here don't they?

> Staff, officers ... whatever you want to call them, their job is there to keep control and order and a lot of that is I guess is telling

people what they can and can't do, where they can and can't go ... and they have the authority for that.

Prison officers ... as a group they have a lot of power and I think they do remain quite unaccountable for their behaviour ... that's the bottom line.

I think it's quite scary, when you really think about it, how much power prison officers have ... even with other staff. We are all dependent on them, they know that and ... and sometimes they like to remind you.

This last quote speaks to assertions of dominance (Haugaard, 1997). Arendt (1970; 1959), and later Barnes (1988), emphasise that within systems of authority it is not sufficient for those with power to possess it, it must also be displayed (see also Tyler, 1998). Each performance of the officer role acts as an instance by which others in the prison are reminded of the authority that officers have. Theirs is a 'power over' other inhabitants of the prison. Here, then, what these psychologists are experiencing are daily displays of 'power' within the wider structures of authority. However, there were other behaviours described by the participants of the study that spoke of more naked or direct displays of power by uniform staff:

But it seemed to be accepted as a, as a ritual abuse of people who weren't prison officers. And, and I thought that was really a bit ... er ... bizarre really. I mean it's a very protected world. Prison officers are highly protected and have a lot of power over others.

It is evident that some of these more direct displays of power that the women in this study were subject to represented forms of intimidation and bullying based upon gender (see next Chapter). However, psychologists reported other behaviours that were not gender specific but could be classified as bullying and emotional abuse (Einarsen, Hoel, Zapf, & Cooper, 2002). Farrington (1993, p. 382) defines bullying as when behaviours involve 'repetitive and unprovoked physical, verbal and/or psychological attacks based on an imbalance of power and intended to cause fear or harm to the victim'. Other theorists (see Salin, 2003; Smith & Brain, 2000) extend this definition to include more nuanced behaviours. Ireland (2002) specifically notes that bullying behaviours can either be direct or indirect. As such, not only are direct physical attacks included but so too are behaviours such as shunning, gossiping, rumour spreading, and derision which are designed to exclude, alienate, and immiserate.

Elaine and Peter Crawley (2008) noted that cynicism and suspicion can play a major part in prisoner officer culture and dominate officer 'in-groups' (a group of mutually identifying and reinforcing staff members). In such circumstances, officers may perceive themselves as being threatened and besieged by defined 'out-groups'. Often these out-groups are prisoners but this is not always necessarily the case. What arises in such situations is defensive and reactionary behaviours towards the out-group. This 'diffidence' with regard to out-groups can lead to exclusionary behaviours and a delineation of an 'us and them' boundary (Warr, 2014). Many of the psychologists in this study experienced this form of behaviour as a daily reality:

> I think that in the Prison Service generally there's, there's a divide between uniformed staff and civilian staff and that's particularly evident.

> They intimidate you sometimes, on the wing, you know? We are there to do a job as well but because you're not in uniform ... well, you know?'

> Oh, there's definitely a them and us mentality, they make that very very clear.

> There is a lot of myths that grow up within an establishment about psychologists and the department and it is a them and us thing.

This separation between uniformed and non-uniformed staff was reported consistently. Many felt this situation was more prevalent with them and probation than other non-uniformed personnel in the prison. In some regards this makes sense as these are the staff populations who, by the very nature of their practice, are more socially divorced from both prison officers and prisoners. They operate in a different disciplinary space. Uniformed officers are concerned with, and focus their power upon, the day-to-day obedience of prisoners (Liebling, 2011), whereas probation and psychological staff are more concerned with punishing and addressing the 'risk' that those prisoners represent more generally. Herein lies the fundamental disjunction between these staff bodies: one is concerned with utilising their power in terms of the everyday life of the prison and the other is concerned with utilising their power for the aims and objectives of the criminal justice system. One is immediate, one is more abstract. This distinction in terms of power both creates and cements the difference between these staff populations and, given the natural in-grouping of prison officers (Crawley, 2004; Liebling, Price, & Shefer, 2011), results in an us/them disjunction.

Some specifically thought this 'us and them' mentality arose from their role, stating that their training, expertise, and their professional role seemed to evoke negative feelings with some of the uniform body with whom they worked.[1] They explained that officers seemed to mistrust the psychologists that worked within

---

[1]Certainly, a number of uniformed staff with whom I spoke to, across multiple prisons, about my research felt that forensic psychologists were immensely powerful in terms of the prison. These officers related, in rather disparaging terms, that this power was not just relegated to prisoners but was evident in the manner that their prisons (and the wider Prison Service) were run and managed.

their prisons, even when accepting that their work was necessary and desirable in terms of the stated goals of rehabilitation:

> Interviewer: You mentioned a lack of trust?
>
> Psychologist: Yeah ... it's because ... I think they're scared of us, you know? Like we can see inside their heads, all their dirty little secrets; that makes them not trust us.
>
> I think they think that we think that we are really clever and they think we're snobs and ... umm, that we haven't seen life you know? That creates a them/us relationship
>
> Psychologist: ... I think it's partly because there is a lot of ignorance surrounding what we do. Not with all, some work with us on delivering programmes and they have a greater understanding ... but others? They don't see it, they have no experience of it and ... and they don't trust it.
>
> Interviewer: Do you think that means they don't trust you?
>
> Psychologist: Yes. Definitely.

Being confronted with this lack of trust and open hostility often came as a surprise to participants, who had expected a sense of camaraderie amongst prison staff. Such experiences represented a significant cause of occupational shock:

> My first day, during induction, I nearly had a fight with one of them. He was so rude and disrespectful ... well I'm not a shrinking violet and can look after myself and I was not putting up with that. He was like that with all of us. I just avoided him after that.
>
> I was struck by the sheer rudeness and unpleasantness of some prison staff. I was quite taken aback by that.
>
> It was always the staff that surprised me – how they felt about psychologists ... but my approach to that was just wear them down. There was one officer on the gate once – it took me two years to make him make eye contact and say hello to me. I made him. There is only so many times you can ignore someone if they are in your face going, 'hello'.
>
> They were very closed ranks and suspicious. The psychology department did not look right to the prison officers and that made them hostile.
>
> ... the just plain bloody-minded staff that were not very nice were actually much harder to cope with than any problems you have

with the prisoners, because the staff are meant to be on your side, but you know they aren't always.

Psychologists entering the job had generally been warned by supervisors, older colleagues, and university educators that their role might be emotionally demanding. One relayed that before starting as a trainee psychologist their supervisor at university had asked them if that was what they really wanted to do as it *'would be very tough on you'*. However, even those that had expected the prison to offer a more challenging working environment expressed surprise at the reception that they received at the hands of uniformed staff:

> Prisons are a hostile environment, aren't they? So, I think you have to go into prisons knowing that you are working within a hostile environment where you have to be quite emotionally, personally robust. I just wasn't expecting as much of it from the staff as I probably got.
>
> Psychologist: I knew it would be tough, it is prison after all but ... but the reaction I have had from staff ... just wow!
>
> Interviewer: What do you mean?
>
> Psychologist: The hostility, the sheer levels of hostility ... I ... you know?

This was a common theme and one which transcended typological position. All of the psychologists interviewed relayed stories which highlighted the hostility of prison officers. None had really been prepared for the overt in-group behaviour and hostility from those who were supposed to be colleagues.

Banter

A number of psychologists had mentioned that they felt like prison officers thought they would be *'able to see into their heads'* and see their *'darkest secrets'*. One participant, a trainee, pointed out that a particular group of officers would go silent whenever they passed by and had heard themselves referred to as 'Starling' after the character from *Silence of the Lambs* (1991). This moniker was used in both a friendly and non-friendly manner, fitting the wider experiences of other psychologists who were subject to such 'banter'. Banter was noted by nearly all of the interviewees as being an important aspect of prison work and life. Tait (2011) argues that banter plays an integral part in prison officer work and can be used both to draw distinctions between the officer group and the prisoners who are in their care and to reduce tensions and hostility. Paull, Oman, and Standen (2012) also note this duality to the role of banter. It has the potential to be a positive aspect in the workplace, especially when it lubricates working relationships, reduces stress, and builds camaraderie. However, banter can also have a darker edge when used by in-groups to hurt, alienate, or immiserate a member of an out-group. Many participants spoke to this duality:

> You need banter in a place like this. Keeps morale up, I know that … but some of it's … not nice.

> You're not included in the banter. It's an officer thing. They make fun of us. I think it's 'cause they're scared of us really, afraid we will see inside their heads or something.

> You get the odd … you do get people who do it in a jokey way like … some of them call us trick cyclists…. psychologists….and it is kind of derogatory…. done with a laugh and a smile but you kind of think….it is not really that respectful either is it?

> I guess in any kind of organisation there is lots of banter and I don't think it is like the only banter that happens, or the only discrimination is against psychologists, it just … it just feels like that.

The consequence of such banter, however, was to make the prison an unpleasant place to work. Some participants felt alienated and disrespected beyond the safe space provided by their office. This is a further facet of Brown et al.'s (2005) analysis of territorialism, and the spatiality of bullying within the organisation identified by Liefooghe and Mackenzie (2001). The uniform in-group are rendering the spaces beyond the psychology department as hostile territories. Entering into these environments the psychologist is reminded of the power of the uniform body even if they are not directly exposed to any 'banter' on that occasion. One psychologist explained that they (and their colleagues) needed to '*brace*' themselves when they left the office as it was '*inevitable*' that they would have to '*confront the banter of wing staff*'. This 'bracing' was then another aspect of the emotional labour that psychologists must engage in. In essence, they must gird themselves to enter the wider prison and to prepare to encounter the staff that inhabit those territories. For some participants, being exposed to such hostility could lead to a pervasive sense of disrespect and insecurity:

> Psychologist: I don't think we're that well respected …

> Interviewer: By prisoners or by …?

> Psychologist: Just in general …

> Interviewer: How does that make you feel?

> Psychologist: Pretty worthless to be honest … it makes you question … it makes you think what's the point? You get over that but at times …

For some, the emotional labour that this required presented a further laminating of the emotion work that going onto wings required – as they had not only to prepare themselves for the challenging psychological work but also to face the officers whom they might encounter. Thus, negative 'banter' could be a significant cause of workplace stress and job dissatisfaction. This could pertain far beyond the end of a placement:

> I think the on-going stress is just something that you don't really realise, and maybe sometimes when I have revisited places, when I have actually been going back … certainly to [name of prison] which was one of the most horrendous experiences I have had for lots of personal reasons as well as the … [officer] behaviour that was going on there, going back about a year later and driving back there I began to feel really ill, and I thought this is just stress, this is just how I must have felt every day I was going in. That really shook me because you just get in such a state you don't realise that you are hanging on to sanity or what you think of as sanity.

Nearly all participants believed that they alone had to cope with the negative impact of such 'banter'. Even if there was support available then it would be difficult to ask for. Often this was because the behaviours were not seen as serious enough to be perceived as bullying. Many participants also feared that challenging such practices risked making matters worse or alienating further members of the uniformed body. Several stated that they did not want to be perceived as '*weak for getting upset*' or for being '*silly*' and '*over-sensitive*' or not being able to '*take a joke*'. Due to such internalised 'gaslighting', they were left to devise their own coping strategies:

> You have to build up a rapport, you had to if people were taking the micky you had to be rude back to them. In a pleasant and jovial bantering way … not to punch people is a good thing.

> You have to learn to give as good as you get, or learn to ignore it … there's not much else you can do.

> My trick was always to be very efficient and professional, eventually it helped … the comments got … I didn't get … there was some respect shown after a while.

All of those interviewed highlighted this aspect of their daily working lives as something which impacted negatively on, not only their experience of being a psychologist but also of how they viewed the prison. One individual noted that:

> The banter … when it's not nice, when it's directed at what you're trying to do … it makes you question everything.

Another noted that:

> It really makes you look at the prison in a different way. You see
> the staff and they are not very nice, the things they say. Every day
> ... it just not nice here. I know that sounds silly it's prison after all
> but ... but, I don't know, it's dark and horrible and ...It's a real
> struggle to come in some days.

Negative banter and the creation of hostile spaces beyond the psychology
department are distinct examples of dominance assertion by prison officers. In
this sense, there are two facets of dominance assertion: The first, of which negative
banter is a form, can be thought of impositional dominance – whereby staff
evidence their power by inflicting it upon others directly. The second can be
thought of as isolational dominance – whereby prison staff withdraw or withhold
their power in ways very much designed to emphasise that power. I will explore
this latter iteration below. However, to return to impositional dominance there
were other examples provided by psychologists that went beyond 'banter'.

Impositional Dominance by Uniformed Staff

Many participants had been subjected to practical jokes by the uniformed body:

> We used to have really silly things like locking the chairs in really
> low positions, or unplugging keyboards or gluing bits of paper to
> the desk. One time the office was full of balloons. Sometimes it was
> funny but ... mostly not.

However, for other psychologists, practical jokes were a source of great irri-
tation. This was especially true when the practical jokes, like the unplugging of
keyboards in the above example, impinged on their ability to perform their role:

> It doesn't happen anymore but ... our offices are down [below
> ground level] ... and we don't really have any windows and ... and
> we went through a stage of the staff removing the lights from our
> offices. Like Ha ha very funny. Not. We've got bloody work to do,
> you know!

> There's a toilet that only we use ... the officers from B wing used to
> block it up which meant we had to go through B wing to get to the
> other women's toilet which was back by the admin block. It was a
> long walk away and grrrrr ... You'd see them in the office
> sniggering like naughty school boys.

The first psychologist quoted here also expanded on this issue by noting that
not only were these 'jokes' by uniform staff an annoyance but that they took on a
more '*sinister tone*' because they were directed only at them. This then made the

psychologists feel singled out. Lewis and Gunn (2007) note that behaviours are more likely to be regarded as bullying when they only involve members of a selected group. This singling out rendered the behaviour as one that was ultimately immiserating, even if intended to be harmless. However, as these psychologists noted, some pranks were not so ambiguous in intent:

> They used to put things, like nasty little cartoons through my door.

> We came in one day and someone had hidden really horrible photoshopped pictures around our office. It happened again a few times after that.

> Porn. I used to find porn in my desk drawer. I didn't bother reporting ... I still don't know who it was, I just ... threw it away but ... urghhh!

This last psychologist repeatedly stated that some of the uniform body in their prison should be screened for the SOTP course as they '*clearly needed it*' if they were using such materials to attempt '*intimidation*'. The porn pranking, like the nasty cartoons, were not just focused at psychologists but at particular individuals, over extended periods of time, and had extremely negative impacts on the individuals who were subjected to this behaviour. Two who had experienced this expressed a great deal of weariness about coming into work and confessed that they were actively seeking employment outside of the Prison Service because of this. Others explained similar experiences which included, but were not limited to, name calling, or gossip about private lives, or hinted at inappropriate relationships with prisoners, etc. Three quarters of the sample noted that these behaviours from uniform staff had made them seriously consider leaving the service at some point in their career.

Other examples of impositional dominance included active disruptions to psychological practice. This included a wide range of behaviours by prison officers. For instance, one psychologist noted that whenever a particular officer was on gate duty they would end up getting a 'random' search which did not seem to occur to others. Another, who worked directly with OMU, pointed out that the officer in charge would treat them like '*a secretary rather than a forensic psychologist*' and impose administrative duties on them constantly, then demand that they prioritise the paperwork above other work. This psychologist noted that they:

> ... used to get very frustrated that I was being asked to focus on things like have these pieces of paper been sent off to the correct person at the correct time as opposed to doing my job. Obviously, I am expected to do both but it was almost like, I saw myself as a ... well treatment. Too often she seemed to think my priority should be paper work being in order, boxes being ticked, audit results being filed, scores being noted, rather than what I was being paid to be there for.

This psychologist explained that such interference in their duties resulted in the need for '*in-office meditation*' in order to get through a shift with that particular person. Such interference is a further aspect of officer territorialism, and concomitant with the descriptions given by other psychologists of how some officers would try to prevent them performing their psychological role. For instance, another psychologist noted that a particular officer seemed intent on sabotaging the programme work that they were there to do. They explained that:

> Every single time the PO that was in charge of my officers that were doing the group was on leave or off shift the other PO, who was the security PO, would take everybody away from the group. You need to go down the landing, you need to do this, you need to go here, you need to go there and then we were left with no tutors. Couldn't do the group work.

Another common complaint was that wing staff would deny the psychologists working space on the wings. A number described how some officers would always say that rooms the psychologists were about to use for interview purposes were busy or about to be used and that they would need to come back later. One noted that when they had gone to the wing to interview a prisoner, they found that the office they had booked had '*been filled up with confiscated cell furniture*' rendering the office unusable. Another variation described by nearly half of the sample was officers denying psychologists access to prisoners at given times, or misdirecting prisoners to other areas of the prison when they had appointments due on the wing with psychologists. One particular psychologist captured this when they said that:

> One SO, whenever I had to go on his wing he would find some excuse why I couldn't use the office to interview someone. Or I would find out he had sent them to healthcare or education. He just interfered all the time. All the time. The other staff were alright ... if he wasn't on. If he was on it was like they were all in on it. I felt like "Come on, you're actually getting in the way of my job now". But every time!

Isolational Dominance by Uniformed Staff

Isolational forms of dominance are where the principle agent withdraws or withholds their power, creating a vacuum which both evidences and reinforces that power. This type of behaviour had a number of manifestations. One psychologist described often being left in the airlock in the gate house while the gate staff took their time doing other things. At first, they had not thought much of this but over time had realised this was down to a particular officer:

> It only ever occurred when one of the ... more traditional officers was on. I know he thought psychology a waste of time in the

prison. He didn't like me being there. He made that clear. But doing that was ... you know, just petty.

Other psychologists also described gate staff causing them delays and minor hassles by ignoring them or denying them speedy entrance to the prison. For instance, this psychologist explained how some gate staff would delay them getting into the prison in the morning by pretending to be busy with other duties:

It wasn't like I could say anything because they'd pretend to be busy. You can't complain if people are busy. But ... and here's the thing, I knew they were doing it on purpose ... I could tell. Also, it would be like nearly every time. They'd leave me hanging there. Often it was only when another staff member came through that they would then [let me in] ... and I could carry on.

This type of 'blanking' behaviour was not limited to gate staff and entrance into the prison. It could also occur in other areas of the prison, as this psychologist noted:

I remember one time I was trying to work with one lifer, clearly a staff favourite, I had recommended that he needed to do more work before parole and ... and after that every time I would ask the wing staff for information, or to keep him back for an appointment or whatever they would just ignore me, or not answer questions or ... bloody mindedness.

Another participant relayed a similar experience whereby the wing staff had refused to collaborate with them, after they had written a negative report on a favoured prisoner. They explained they were exposed to various blanking behaviours and staff would *'pretend I wasn't there, that they couldn't hear me'*. All of these behaviours meant that psychologists had to begin to navigate the prison in different ways and under-manage the staff in order to just perform their duties effectively. However, in terms of isolational dominance this is immiserating but somewhat harmless behaviour. It does impact on performance and increased emotion work but it did not pose a threat. Whereas other reported behaviours were more serious in nature.

Other members of staff are reliant upon the uniform body for security and protection. The withdrawal of protection acts as a powerful reminder of the vulnerability of the individual, and of the power of the uniformed body. One psychologist had noted that they had become aware of this issue when they had been accosted by an irate prisoner whilst walking through the wing. They noted that the prisoner was being very aggressive and threatening but the officers had all walked away or returned to the office:

I realised I was on my own. I had this very large, very angry prisoner shouting at me but the staff had all gone. Nothing

> happened, I managed to talk him … I got him to sit down and talk to me but … for a moment I thought … when the staff had walked away I was like … "Uhm, I'm in real trouble here".

The psychologist noted that there was nothing malicious in the officer's behaviour here it was *'just one of those things'* but nevertheless it was sufficient to highlight the vulnerability of being alone in the prison. Another psychologist relayed a similar experience when they had been threatened by a violent sex offender:

> … I've been threatened in that situation previously umm … you know … "wait and see what happens now you've done this" and "may God help you, you … C word. I'm gonna make sure you pay" umm, that was quite nasty and … the officer who was with me just walked away. In the middle of it. That stayed with me for a long time umm … especially when [the prisoner] was released. I followed that case quite closely, yeah. It got to me, I felt abandoned …

Many participants were unsure whether or not uniform staff would protect them. One said explicitly they were not sure that staff would *'come to [their] aid'* or if they did that they would *'come quickly'*. Whilst others hoped that staff *'professionalism would trump their feelings'* if and when a worst-case scenario occurred. For one psychologist, this particular issue had been made evident to them when early in their career they had made a complaint against a member of uniformed staff over an instance of witnessed racism. They explained that after putting the complaint in a senior manager in the prison had taken them aside for a chat and asked them if they were sure *'you want to go ahead with the complaint?'* because doing so might mean that some officers *'may not have your back'*. They noted that prior to this they had not given much thought to their safety in the prison but after that *'felt really unsafe everywhere'*. The support and protection of staff could be removed (intentionally or not) and that this could have a significant impact on the manner in which psychologists subsequently responded to the prison.

Psychologists also relayed moments whereby staff had deliberately put them into dangerous or potentially harmful situations. Nearly all of these involved situations that involved volatile or violent prisoners and had a very similar theme. For instance, these two psychologists relayed two very similar events that occurred in very different prisons:

> This was a long time ago now but … I had to do feedback on a parole assessment with this one person where I was recommending that he needed to do more work before release. He had no single female contact on his record but when the officer bought him to the interview room he just left me with him … nothing happened

but ... you know? And I'm sure he only did that because he didn't like us and could get away with it.

I was working with one lad who had been convicted of a very violent rape and he was not to be left alone with women, the staff had not told me that his behaviour was becoming increasingly troubled and that they had been having problems with him that morning ... so when he was bought to the interview room the staff just ... they just shut the door behind him, locking me in with him ..., now nothing happened and it turned out that his father was very ill and he was upset so we spoke about that and he was fine but when we left the room I could see the staff members smirking ... like they thought it was funny and ... and you don't expect a colleague to put you in that situation.

These were not atypical accounts. One participant explained that how wing staff had failed to mention to them that the prisoner they were to interview was in a very distressed state, had been threatening staff, and then tried to lock them in the office with the prisoner. Nearly all those who had experienced such situations felt that not only were staff showing the psychologists how vulnerable they were but also testing them in some way. This individual stated that they felt like the officers were seeing if they '*had the mettle*' to cope with violent, or dangerous prisoners. A sentiment echoed by others. One psychologist noted that when they had raised concerns about being left in this way the uniform staff had subsequently been very dismissive of them. Another too noted this:

I was on a wing once when some prisoners started fighting. Very scary. I retreated out of the way to the games room which was a gated room just to one side of the wing, by the servery. After a few minutes the staff put one of the prisoners in the games room and locked the gate. He was still being very aggressive and destructive but he was between me and the gate. Afterwards the wing staff were very dismissive of my concerns and said that I should be able to take care of myself.

As Kauffman (1988) and Liebling et al. (2011) note, two of the fundamentals of officer and staff culture is the notion that that you do not leave a fellow officer in trouble and that you actively show concern for a colleague's welfare. However, the behaviour being displayed here is a clear breach of these norms. As an out-group, psychologists are not afforded the same courtesies, protections, or even recognition. This withdrawal of staff norms and power isolates the psychologist within those spaces dominated by the uniform staff. This not only emphasises the power of the uniform in-group but also reinforces the outsider status of the psychologist.

We have seen in this chapter that psychologists are themselves subject to the wider structures of power in the prison in varying ways. Above and beyond the

matrices of employment rules and regulations which shape the working environment are interpersonal power dynamics, from territorialism to varying formulations of impositional and isolational dominance, that shape the occupational
reality of psychologists. These behaviours, mainly by the uniformed body, can
have a negative impact on prison psychologists and contribute to those factors
which are associated with high levels of attrition in the psychology body. For
those that remain and *'tough it out'*, these dynamics compound the type, level, and
degree of navigation work that psychologists must undertake in order to maintain, or retain, professional efficacy within the prison.

Chapter 8

Gender, Sexism, and the Prison

> In my experience prisons are ... there's a lot of sexism. Its better
> than it was when I first started, all those years ago. Its still a daily
> thing though.
>
> –Trainee Psychologist

Psychologists working in prisons are overwhelmingly female (Crewe, 2009).
Correspondingly, the majority of those who participated in this study were those
who identify as female. This chapter is concerned with examining the experiences of
these individuals. The aim is to explicate how the explicitly gendered, and dominant
masculinity, cultures of the prison can impact upon and affect psychologists
personally and professionally. This chapter also explores how exploring the
gendered realities of female psychologists in the prison can introduce a further facet
of vulnerability that goes beyond contesting disciplinary discourses and practices.

Organisations can be gendered in at least three ways: the first is when gendered
assumptions about roles, suitable practices, and moral behaviour comprise the
fabric by which the organisation arises or is constructed (for a discussion on how
this relates to prison see Carlen (1982)); the second is when an organisation's
structure perpetuates, through inherent or systemic practice, certain forms of
gender beliefs; the third is when the organisation, and the cultures it engenders,
limits or constrains either people, practices, or dialogue because of gender (Acker,
1990). Organisations cannot be seen in gender-neutral terms for they, to a greater
or lesser degree, fall into one of these three categories. Both Britton (2003) and
McMahon (1999) note in the prison all three of the above factors hold true. The
very nature of the prison is heavily influenced by gendered assumptions surrounding the incarceration of men and the constraint of traditional masculinities.
Furthermore, the masculine cultures produced within the prison serve to constrain
and limit the development of differing or alternative gender beliefs and practices
(Feinman, 1994).

The quasi 'closed' nature of prison institutions often exposes gender processes
that may be hidden in more open organisations (Britton, 2003). This is in part, she
argues, because of the sense of 'totality' (see also Goffman, 1961) that institutions
such as the prison represent. She notes that though the prison may be a micro-
cosm of its symbiote society, this does not preclude distinct cultures and practices
emerging from within which can either create new forms of gendering or serve to

Forensic Psychologists, 165–182
Copyright © 2021 Jason Warr
Published under exclusive licence by Emerald Publishing Limited
doi:10.1108/978-1-83909-960-120200009

highlight extant forms of gendered nuances (Jenne & Kersting, 1998). For instance, as Crawley (2004) highlighted, female uniformed officers are aware that their performance *as officers* can often be judged by the manner in which they utilise, or become subject to, female stereotypes and constructed femininity norms. As a result of this women officers are often forced to subvert or dismantle these stereotypical and gendered perspectives as they relate to the peculiarities of their work.

The prison is widely perceived as a 'male' environment where the intrinsic cultures perpetuate hegemonic masculinities which are played out against a backdrop of masculine-orientated situational control measures such as bars, gates, locks, patrol dogs, guards, etc. However, as Britton (2003) argues, though the prison may well be constructed in such a way that male-orientated gender assumptions are both inherent and perpetuated, this is only an aspect of the complex reality whereby matrices of masculinities and femininities strive, buffer, and exist in conflict with each other to produce the cultures and practices that exist within the modern heterosocial prison. This increased heterosociability of the prison in the modern era has not diminished the gendered nature of the organisation but has instead served to expose some of the gender practices and biases that exist within the prison and, perhaps, in wider society (Feinman, 1994). For instance, as McMahon (1999) notes, historically women working in men's prisons tended to occupy or were assigned to 'female roles' – clerical, nursing, treatment, therapy, etc. She argues that this in itself highlights the largely gendered nature of the prison and the struggles that women face whilst working within it. It is to this issue that this chapter now turns, exploring how gendered cultures constrain and affect the lives of female forensic psychologists.

One of the core questions posed was: what it was like to work in such a male-dominated organisation? For the older and more experienced participants, and those who were consulted for historical context, this question evoked memories of an extremely gendered and gender hostile past where the problems of sex discrimination and gender bias had dominated their occupational reality. However, they also held that this reality was consigned to a bygone age:

> It's not as bad as it used to be. When I first started it was different ... there were not that many women working in [name of prison] then so it was a bit of a culture shock I think for some of them. You used to get comments ... hostility even but it's not like that now, it's much better.

> Years ago ... when you had that ... you know ... ex-army kind of culture, it was bad but not now.

> I remember speaking to one of my older colleagues about it and they told me some ... real ... stories about back when she had started ... I'm so glad it's not like that anymore.

> Prison officers are male and female so it is not that it is completely male dominated anymore.

This past was often associated with the imported legacies of hyper-masculine staff culture that had at one point been the norm amongst the uniform body (see Liebling, Price, & Shefer, 2011). As one psychologist noted '*walking into a staff room was like walking into a barracks*'. This generation of psychologists had seen reductions in the prevalence of gender hostility and improvements in occupational experiences as that tradition of officer culture had atrophied. Nevertheless, for the majority of the female participants in this study, those still working at the coal face, as it were, these issues continued to be a daily reality. The types of behaviour that these women were subject to fell into three categories: constraints and burdens experienced, sexism and gender hostility, and unwanted sexualised interactions.

Gendered Constraints and Burdens

Nirmal Puwar, in her book *Space Invaders: Race, Gender and Bodies Out of Place* (2004), argues that one of the many constraints faced by women entering into spaces with historically entrenched masculinities is the expectation and necessity of managing their own femininities. These male-dominated spaces are not neutral – they are laminated with gendered expectations, norms, rules, cultures, behaviours, and even smells that distinguish them as the domains of men. When women transmurally breach the walls of these spaces they must then navigate these confluences of gendered practices and processes by careful management of their womanhood. A process that often begins before they actually cross the redoubt of the prison wall. Many of the participants in this study explained this process and related a sense of trepidation from entering the male world of the prison. As these explained:

> When I first started at [name of prison] it was like a lot of male officers and all male prisoners and so it was a bit daunting.

> You have to prepare yourself to be surrounded by men all day, it can be … challenging.

One participant explained that she would have to brace herself, '*take a deep breath*' and '*get her shit together*' before entering the prison and the '*world of men*' that lay beyond the gate. Another stated that when preparing for work she had a '*little ritual*' that she followed every morning before entering the prison:

> It's a little bit silly and I feel embarrassed telling you this but … I have this little ritual that I do when I get to the prison. I sit in my car, I prepare myself for the day ahead, make sure my outfit is suitable, my hair is up, etc … I get into my professional space up here [pointing to head] … then when I get out of the car I am [name] the psychologist not [name] me! I do that because [name] me wouldn't … she's not acceptable in there but the psychologist is …

When asked to elaborate, she explained that, outside prison, she was quite a '*girly girl*' but had learnt very early on that she needed to suppress that part of herself within the prison. She went on to note that as a woman she was quite a '*tactile and touchy-feely kind of person*' but found that her normal sense of tactility was abhorred in the prison so that she had needed to learn how to repress this side of herself. This ritual of redressing, changing her comportment, altering her interactions with others, and the way she feels that she must become a different woman in order to operate in the male prison is part and parcel of the constraints that the gendered environment imposes. Women need to manage their female self. Cleveland, Stockdale, and Murphy (2000) note that these constraints on physical aspects of femininity, especially appearance, in the occupational space are so ingrained in the gendered workplace that they can become, eventually, both self-imposed and self-perpetuated as well as being internalised and enforced by other women.

This goes beyond the normal development of a professional self. Skovholt and Ronnestad (1995) argue that the development of a 'professional self' relates to the emergent professional identity and skill development that a person may go through in the course of their professional career. This is a normal, pro-social and healthy development that gradually takes place over time. However, what is being described here is a perceived necessity to develop a defeminised professional façade in order to be accepted by and within the prison. As another psychologist noted '*I can't take the woman I am out here, in there*'. In that sense, the gendered nature of the prison results in a constraining of both the psychological and physical identities of female psychologists. Others made reference to similar processes of gender neutralisation:

> I had ear rings and they said, I shouldn't have earrings and I should not have long hair because somebody could grab me by the hair, do me harm; grab me by the earrings and do me harm. So now I cut my hair short and don't wear jewellery.

> I guess one must be mindful ... mindful of working in a male environment and being aware of that and being aware of the differences in terms of being a relatively young woman, working in that kind of environment ... yes you have to be careful how you look.

Some of these constraints, such as appropriate dress and comportment, were firmly entrenched in the thinking of many participants, particularly those who had worked in more than one establishment or who had been 'in service' for more than 5 years. One expressed amazement that one of her younger colleagues wore long skirts and boots, which she felt was inappropriate for wearing in a prison. Another recalled that when she arrived for work in a tailored, skirted suit she was told by her female line manager not to dress like that again as it was neither appropriate nor safe to be dressed in '*such a manner*'. This is consistent with what Puwar (2004) notes about gendered dress norms being imposed, even by other women, on women in the workspace. Certain forms of dress, if they emphasise the feminine, can be a source of censure in the gendered workplace. One very senior participant interviewed for historical context acknowledged the peculiarity of this situation. She related a story about how she had advised a junior member of the team not to wear skirts around the prison but could not think of a clear reason for her position. She explained that she had always been advised to wear trousers and shoes that she could '*run and kick in*' and had just accepted that as the way it should be and had passed that on to those she managed.

Cleveland et al. (2000) note that the justifications for such dress norms can be difficult to articulate upon closer examination. Often, these dress norms go beyond the realm of occupational safety, terms in which they are often couched, but rather attach to gender biases, if not misogyny. For instance, the wearing of high heels on a building site would be clearly inappropriate in terms of safety but make-up not. Yet they note that women are often castigated or commented on in the work place for wearing make-up or having their hair down and displaying forms of femininity where the question of safety does not arise. The judgement and constraint is a normative one about their womanhood.

Working with male prisoners and especially men who had been convicted of sexual offences added extra burdens of managing their femininity. One psychologist noted that you had to be '*really, really careful*' when choosing your work outfit if you were doing group work or 1-to-1 work with men convicted of sex offences as you didn't want to be a '*trigger for anyone*'. Whilst another, when discussing dress and behaviour, explained that:

> ... you have got to be mindful of what you wear, you have to be mindful of your boundaries, being professional. Not being overly familiar – in terms of how you speak, interact and dress. You are not being friendly – there might not be anything behind that – I am not saying I have to stop being over familiar I mean have to be mindful of that. Mindful of my role that I am not there to be friendly or someone's friend. What you are wearing – how you ... I know I keep talking about [name of prison] but that is when I was working with sex offenders and people who have committed sexual crimes and yes, you have to be... careful.

Working with such stigmatised populations seemed to have vicarious consequences for the gendered judgements that psychologists were subjected to. For instance, and I will return to this point below, it was common for psychologists to report that uniform officers would gossip about them having sexual relationships with prisoners, other officers, and even each other. For one psychologist, who worked exclusively with prisoners convicted of sex offences, this gossiping added to the constraints over dress norms as they did not wish to be seen to be dressing provocatively in any way. In order to avoid compounding the gossip, she would avoid wearing anything that could, in any way, be perceived as provocative; and thus, only wore '*loose trousers and a baggy jumper*' to work.

A further factor to be considered here is how gender expectations can also constrain, or impact on the quality/nature of, the relationships that female psychologists develop within the prison. Both McMahon (1999) and Britton (2003) argue that therapeutic work within the carceral is often perceived as 'women's work'. The notions of care, support and, to some extent, rehabilitative work become cast through a gendered lens. The fact that female psychologists were engaging in what some other staff perceived as 'women's work' had a number of consequences. The first was that it could lead to alienation from those women who performed front line and more traditionally perceived 'male' roles. In this regard, a number of psychologists spoke of strained relationships with the female prison officers. One psychologist captured this when they noted that '*because we're not frontline staff I think the female officers look down on us*'. For another psychologist, this was bought into relief during a training session when she was paired with a female officer who refused to work with her, requesting to work with a male officer instead as they '*knew what was what*' and '*did proper prison work*'. What we see here is female prison officers adhering to the same gendered tropes of prison work and judging and reacting to psychologists because of those tropes (see Rader, 2007). This could be difficult for some psychologists as it hampered their relationships both intra- and extramurally with female members of staff with whom they might otherwise form closer working relationships, or even friendships.

A number spoke of the difficulty in overcoming the gender bias that male prisoners, especially older ones, may have when confronted by young professional female psychologists (see also Crewe, 2009). For the participants in this study, these issues were particularly pertinent when working with sex offenders either in a one-to-one type capacity or, before they were abandoned/rebranded/relaunched, on various SOTP type courses. One described a situation whereby on a course there were a number of South Asian men who would not speak to her about their offences and would only direct comments to the male facilitator on the programme. She explained that it was the first time in her life where she had experienced men just refusing to talk to her. This had quite an impact on her as it led to feelings of self-doubt and professional insecurity as she explained: '*It made me question what I was doing … could I do it?*' Another described some of the tensions caused by being a young woman working with older men convicted of sex offences:

> Oh yes, I am conscious…and I think maybe earlier on … I am 29 now, a bit older than when I started, and being a younger female in a male prison working with some men who are older than my dad and thinking how would my dad feel if someone his daughter's age approached him and was trying to talk to him about his sex life. And I think being mindful of that, being really aware of that and sensitive to it is important.

There were gendered considerations here that affected women's professional practice that did not pertain for male facilitators. Though this may relate to wider gendered practices and biases in the community, the prison forces female psychologists to confront these attitudes and norms in a more concentrated way than beyond the wall.

Sexism in the Workplace

Though often thought to be consigned to the past, all of the female participants described instances of open gender hostility. This hostility took a number of forms but that most often commented upon was the overt hostility that was communicated to them from staff regarding their place and status within the prison:

> ...[we were called] Fools ... or young girls that knew nothing and were putting them [the officers] at risk by being on the wings. Or they are just eye candy.

> You know – 'you should not work here. You are a woman, we don't want to let you in. this is a maximum-security prison'.

> I have been called everything from a man-hater, I think there are still half a dozen lifers that go around calling me that lesbian that hates men kind of thing – there are all sorts of kind of – and I know some of that came from staff. I heard them.

This gender hostility was not hidden but overt and was often said directly to the women concerned, as one noted it was always '*right to my face*'. Others pointed out that this overtness is what made it striking as it was done in front of others and without sanction or censure. One psychologist had noted that a '*particularly obnoxious*' officer had said to her that '*cunts like her*' should not be allowed to work in prisons and that the others officers there, including women, had just laughed along. When she had complained about this it had been written off as '*that's just him*'. One participant described a situation that was almost identical to some of the isolational dominance behaviours described in the previous chapter but which in this case was marked by overt misogyny:

> ... when I moved from [X prison] to [Y prison] it was to run the [omitted][1] programme and there were lots of problems in that prison at that time ... the staff were very sexist and anti what we were trying to do ... I go to meet with the first group, who were all long term high risk prisoners, the ... the officer who had shown me where the room was ... he was very misogynistic, I'd had a run in with him before, him saying nasty little things ... anyway, he introduced me to the room and then shut and locked the door behind him as he left. I was ... errm 'what?' ... all the men turned

---

[1]The name of this course has been omitted as it would identify which prison this occurred in and thus who the psychologist in question is.

to stare at me, it was very uncomfortable. I noticed there was not enough chairs so said I would go and get some more ... turned and unlocked the door and walked into the corridor ... the officer and his cronies were waiting and smirking. I know they only did that to see what I would do, it was a test to see if the little woman could cope in their world ...

Others described encountering forms of sexism in differing contexts:

I remember the sexism from my induction to security talks because the only women they had been used to were admin, teachers and there were always the stories about you know how many teachers have had affairs with prisoners that was it.

If I am being honest I think there are some very strong feelings about women working in the Prison Service from some people but not lots ... it tends to be security ... those working in the segregation unit ... you know the type ...

Some prisons are worse than others ... for instance when I worked in [X prison] it had ... what I would call an old POA culture, it was all security and ... and it was very sexist, very anti women, very anti ... well anything that didn't support them.

Security briefings were identified as a distinct site of hostility where great emphasis would be placed on sexual relationships between female psychological and educational staff and prisoners rather than others. One psychologist highlighted this point when they said that a security officer had pointed directly at her when talking about the 'grooming' of staff by prisoners. The officer had said to the room that it was people like her who *'ended up in compromising positions'*. This psychologist noted that she had felt humiliated and offended at the time but had been too junior and naive to tackle the officer or to do anything about it afterwards. A circumstance that she still regretted.

The experiences of male and female psychologists who had worked in the same establishment differed considerably and highlighted gender biases. One female participant explained that a prison she had once worked in had quite a traditional masculine culture and was an unpleasant place to work as a psychologist. She noted that the sexism and the misogyny were both overt and pervasive. She noted that:

The other thing I thought was how aggressive the prison officers were. They were very sexist and they said things like – you should not be here, you are a woman.

However, a male psychologist who had worked in the same establishment in an overlapping period expressed a very different perspective on the occupational cultures. When asked about how he thought he and others from his team were viewed by the uniformed staff in that prison he said '*I don't get a strong sense that a lot of staff have an opinion either way*'. When probed further, he noted that there was a degree of distance between the uniformed and non-uniformed body but that:

> ... I have never had seriously negative reactions, I have never had officers be derogatory or unprofessional towards me in any way ... I think that is perhaps a reflection of the prison because it is quite a pleasant place to work.

In light of that last comment, and knowing the experience of the woman who I had interviewed before him, I went on to ask him:

> Interviewer: Do you think your experience is typical?
>
> Psychologist: ... here it is I think, yes ... the prisoners in there and the staff, I suppose I expected them to be more ... more aggressive and hostile. And I think it was both the staff and prisoners I expected that from. So, I guess the short answer would be it was not as bad as I thought it would be. Not at all. As I said it's a pleasant place to work.

This situation was replicated with another pairing of psychologists. In this case they worked in the same prison but at different time periods. The woman some five years before the male psychologist had joined the service. She described the culture in that prison as '*traditional and sexist*' as well as being '*intimidating*'; whereas he described the same environment as '*open and friendly*' and the '*best place he'd ever worked*'. Of course, it is possible that in the intervening 5-year period there was a sea change in the staff who operated in the prison which reduced the nature and extent of the sexist culture that was experienced by the woman. However, the likelihood of the staff changing so significantly in this particular prison, which is not known for the plasticity of its staff culture, at that particular pre-benchmarking time, to account for such a profound change is slim.[2] What is more likely is, as Vartia and Hyyti (2002) argue, that of all forms of workplace bullying it is only sexual harassment and gender bullying that women both recognise and report significantly more than their male counterparts. Not being subject to it, non-participant male members of staff rarely become aware of the pervasiveness of gender hostility and the impact that this can have on their female colleagues.

A deeper form of gender hostility and harassment reported by female psychologists concerned being subjected to unwanted sexualised commentary and sexual overtures. In the previous chapters we saw that workplace hostility and

---

[2]The prison in question is an old Victoria prison with a long history of entrenched traditional, officer culture.

bullying can include any behaviour that is designed to belittle, intimidate, immiserate, hurt, or marginalise. Much of what we have seen in this chapter constitutes such behaviour; however, with what follows there is little doubt that such behaviours do constitute a form of workplace violence. Di Martino, Hoel, and Cooper (2003) note that the definition of 'workplace violence', though somewhat broad and culturally complex, includes behaviours that constitute bullying and harassment (including gender and sexual harassment). McMahon (1999) notes, within her study of female correctional officers working in a Canadian male prison, that her participants were subject to high rates of sexual harassment. Likewise, Britton (2003) found similar themes arising from her research on women working within carceral settings. This sexually hostile behaviour can be classified in the following ways: 1. Teasing and insults; 2. Offensive and sexual comments; 3. Rumour mongering and gossip about women's sexuality and sexual behaviour; 4. Sexual propositioning; and 5. Sexual assault and rape. I shall take each of these classes of behaviour in turn and describe the relevant accounts within my study.[3]

We saw in the previous chapter the role that 'banter' can play both in immiserating others, and masking forms of intimidation. However, many of the women in this sample felt that the teasing and insults that they were subject to went beyond 'banter', and was directed at them because they were women. For instance, one woman noted that when she was beginning her career, the officers in the next-door office would always play tricks on her and her female colleagues. However, she noted that the teasing and insults were only targeted at the female members of staff, never the male members of staff, and were primarily sexualised in nature. She said that it was not the sort of behaviour that she could moan about, as that would open her up to more ridicule, nor was it serious enough to warrant a formal complaint. Nevertheless, it began to cause distress to her and her female colleagues as they felt they were being harassed. Other participants described how forms of teasing and banter would devolve into more offensive and sexualised commentary:

> It's banter isn't it? Sometimes it goes beyond that though. Don't get me wrong most of them are ok but there's one, I go on his wing a lot in the course of … and he's really bad. He stares all the time and his banter is all sexual and quite nasty.

> I've felt objectified … sexually by prison officers a lot as well. I think they've all got like … little names for each one of us. I catch them sometimes. I don't know what mine is but I've heard them talk about one of my colleagues. Really degrading and

---

[3]It was as this topic came up in our discussion that the individual who withdrew from the research decided to terminate the interview. One other person also mentioned unwanted sexual attention but explained that they did not wish to discuss this 'on tape' as it were. Field notes.

disrespectful things about her. They probably talk about me like that too when ... [I'm not there].

I think the hostility is quite underground if you like. The kind of comments, sexual comments, banter whatever, it is really there all the time but people don't often actually come out with it so you just have to be quick witted or deal with it in your own way.

Most psychology staff are young women and ... umm, most prison officers are old men, they leer at you and they make comments. They think it's funny ...

Such sexualised commentary often made these psychologists feel both uncomfortable and miserable within themselves and within the workplace. One noted it made it difficult for her to come into work. However, none explicitly perceived such behaviours as bullying. I asked one psychologist if she felt as if she was being bullied, we were surrounded by safer custody posters which claimed that bullying could include any of the behaviours which she had just described, and her response was a resounding '*God no*'. Another responded in the following way to my suggestion that perhaps her experience constituted bullying:

Interviewer: Obviously as you said banter is an important part of, especially if you work in quite a stressful environment, it's like a catharsis ... but you intimated there that it steps over the boundary of acceptable banter into a kind of negative ... sexist ...

Psychologist: Mm ... mm.

Interviewer: ... I mean have you ever experienced ... I mean have you ever felt like targeted by people, or bullied ... or something ...?

Psychologist: No, definitely not.

Lewis (2006) in her study '*Recognition of Workplace Bullying: A Qualitative Study of Women Targets in the Public Sector*' notes that it is often the case that women who are subject to bullying in the workplace, even if they recognise it occurring to others, minimise the significance of the behaviours that they themselves are subject to. They become, through processes of personal coping, professional preservation, and organisational socialisation, accepting of the bullying behaviours and cultures. To challenge the very values and culture of the organisation within which they are employed represents a challenge to their own sense of professional and personal self. As Liefooghe and Mackenzie (2001) argue this situation almost demands processes of minimisation (or neutralisation) in order to maintain an investment in, and commitment to, the workplace and the profession. This was evident in these accounts. They sometimes acknowledged the consequent immiseration, but not in such ways that forced them to confront the role of the prison's/prison officer's culture in that immiseration.

These issues of sexism in the workplace allowed degrees of minimisation to occur. Lewis (2006) points out that when it comes to more serious or predatory sexist behaviours minimisation ceases to be viable and the acknowledgement and recognition of bullying becomes inevitable. With regard to this study when it came to sexualised behaviour the 'line' between what is acceptable and what was not could be quickly drawn.

Sexualised Gossiping and Propositioning

One of the more insidiously sexist behaviours that women can be confronted with in the prison is the malignant rumour-mongering about sexuality and sexual behaviour (McMahon, 1999). Britton (2003) argues that often women become the focus of such gossiping when they do not conform to gender stereotypes or breach some aspect of the masculine culture of the prison. Both McMahon (1999) and Britton (2003) note that the most common forms of this behaviour range from the re-casting of behaviours to malicious rumour spreading concerning sexual proclivity/orientation, promiscuity, and inappropriate behaviour within the prison – especially with prisoners. This becomes a discreetly harmful practice in the prison where relationships are necessarily close and professional scrutiny/ judgment are primary factors.

Two of the female psychologists interviewed noted that they had heard rumours about themselves being gay. Both laughed this off as being silly but somewhat intrusive. Others spoke of being victims of malignant rumour-mongering. A further two psychologists noted that they had heard of themselves as being labelled as 'men haters' and 'lesbians' by both prisoners and staff. Another pointed out that she had heard officers say that *'all the psychologists are dykes'*.[4] However, the rumour-mongering went beyond sexuality to commentary about sexual behaviour. One psychologist claimed explicitly that she had become aware of officers casting assertions on her and her colleague's relationship with a uniformed officer with whom they liaised. She explained that they were saying as he *'got to work with all the women'* then he must be *'having sex with them all'*. This psychologist noted that such rumours were rife and persistent – so much so that they were common knowledge amongst the psychology team who were the subject of the gossip. Another stated that she had been asked by a departmental colleague if the rumours that she was having an affair with a particular male officer were true. It was not. She said that she was taken aback that this gossiping, of which she had been unaware, had even penetrated through to her own colleagues in the psychology department.

McMahon (1999) noted that if a woman had a relationship with another officer then this could amplify the rumours, causing male officers to re-cast her as someone who was easy and, as Rader (2007) notes, could affect how other female officers judged them. One psychologist related having been out for a drink with a male uniformed officer, very early on in her career, which had

---

[4]Offensive colloquialism for a gay woman.

caused a number of rumours to be spread around the prison about her. Such rumours had caused her a number of problems, in part because the person she had gone for a drink with was married to another prison officer and thus had evoked hostility from that member of staff. Also, this had led to issues of being seen as fair game by other male staff and of being shunned by female officers and other female staff. She noted that she was naive and that she should never have gone for a drink with him. Since that event she explained that she had been careful to erect barriers between herself, her professional self, and the wider prison in order to protect herself from such a situation from occurring again.

Other participants also reported the need for keeping private and professional lives very separate. Though many did not give specific reasons for this one did note that the need to have '*distinct lives*' was in order to protect themselves from this rumour-mongering which could have very negative consequences not only on their occupational lives but also on their professional credibility. This psychologist went on to note that if the rumours got so bad that they permeated through to the general prisoner population then that could, in some ways, '*undermine your position*'. As Britton (2003) argued, rumour and innuendo could impact on a woman's standing in the prison. This was an issue that these psychologists were concerned about. For women, their perceived expertise was vulnerable to gendered judgements, especially about sexual behaviour, and as such needed to be carefully navigated and potentially mitigated. The easiest way for female psychologists to do this was to establish a distance in the proximal relationships between them and male members of staff. For example, one of the psychologists mentioned that being able to socialise with colleagues would make the workplace a '*nicer place to be*' but that, on balance, it was '*not worth the hassle*'. When asked to explain she stated that if you did socialise with the prison officers outside of the working day you would constantly have to be on guard so as not to be perceived in certain ways. She explained that:

> If you go out for a drink, or whatever, then tongues start wagging … yap yap yap. You know you're going to get hit on all the time … that happens anyway but you don't want to … you know, add to it. So it's best not to. It's best to stay away.

This last quote highlighted a further aspect of the environment that female psychologists were subjected to: unwanted sexual attention (e.g. impositional flirtation) and outright propositioning. Of those that spoke of this type of behaviour it was evident that this behaviour was, at best, an annoyance and, at worst, a significant cause of stress and anxiety. Notably too, they made, like the women in Britton's (2003) study, a distinction between the behaviour of the prisoners with whom they worked and that of staff:

> A lot of the men that we work with are long termers and so … you know … you get comments. I don't take it personally … it's quite sad really.

> The men that I work with on the [name of course] ... well of course
> you get the odd comment. It's to be expected really ... you just ...
> you just brush it off and continue.

> You do get things said ... things that are inappropriate, but ...
> with the prisoners you ignore it because, you know? But with staff
> it's different ... I never expected it from them ... and yeah, that can
> take you aback.

> They're worse than the lads we have on the [SOTP] course. The
> way they behave towards us women is disgraceful sometimes.

This last psychologist recounted a number of instances of harassment by male
uniformed staff. She found their behaviour, misogyny, and sexism so pervasive
that she was adamant that many of them would score sufficiently high on the Risk
Matrix 2000 that they would be considered as having a 'high risk' of future sexual
and/or violent offending.[5] Many participants reported feeling that many of their
male uniformed colleagues believed them to be both sexually permissive and
available. Some noted that this seemed to be the case even when it was either
evident, or it had been made clear, that this was not so. As these two noted:

> The problem I had with staff more was just being asked out the
> whole time. There was kind of an element of fair game because you
> were a female and who cares what your domestic situation is and I
> think that says a lot about prison staff dynamics and how
> incestuous it is.

> ... early on I got cracked on all the time. ... they made it difficult. I
> had a partner then but that didn't seem to matter. It made me feel
> uncomfortable coming into work. I never socialised with them
> outside of the work because of that ... even now I don't.

Britton (2003) argues that within predominantly masculine gendered environments, some men will perceive women as having *made* themselves available
simply by entering into the masculine domain. However, other commentators,
most notably Jenne and Kersting (1998), highlight the power dynamic involved in
this form of sexual harassment and note that men who revel in such dynamics
may seek employment in correctional settings for this reason. However, such
displays of sexual assertiveness on behalf of male officers seemed to have little to
do with actual heterosexual desire and more to do with the imposition of hegemonic masculinity. As one psychologist noted:

---

[5]This psychologist thought that all male staff should undergo the same risk assessments that
prisoners were subjected to as they felt there was little difference between the prisoners and
the officers. They also explained that doing some of the sex offending courses would be of
benefit too.

> What makes it worse is you know it's not genuine. When an officer does that … it's not genuine … even if it was that would still be … but when they hit on you all the time they're just trying to put it on you. It's pathetic. It's about power and how threatened they are by us.

Another psychologist pointed out that one of the prisons she had worked in was oddly intimate and incestuous. She explained that many of the staff, both front line and administrative, in her prison were '*involved*' in tangled '*webs of affairs*'. She explained that it seemed to be the norm in that prison – over and above that she had witnessed elsewhere. However, this complex and entrenched amorosity meant that often officers felt that they could proposition a female member of staff without recourse:

> The whole time I was there I felt like I was dodging lecherous men. Not the prisoners, the officers. Even the married ones were … it was all of them. They acted like there were no boundaries. It was really shocking. I'd never … you don't see that. If I had to go on to the wing I would try and do so when they were busy so I didn't have to be confronted by it.

This woman, like others, felt that she needed to carefully navigate the prison environment in order to protect herself from unwanted sexual attention. This was a common theme given by the female psychologists. Though none referred to their behaviours in such explicit ways, nearly all spoke of adopting behaviours that enabled them to navigate, manage, or mitigate the sexism and gender hostility that shaped their occupational lives.

Coping Strategies

Experiences of sexism and gender hostility necessitated a range of coping strategies that added to both the emotional and emotive labour that female psychologists needed to perform. The strategies adopted were individuated ones rather than collective coping mechanisms. These women were on their own and developing strategies for themselves rather than in conjunction with their colleagues. There were a range of coping strategies that female psychologists employed; these largely fell into two broad categories which I define as: armouring and avoidance.

Most of the participants had a somewhat fatalistic attitude to the sexism that they were subject to. It seemed to be expected as a norm for working in a male environment, as this psychologist noted:

> You have got to be sufficiently robust to be able to work in a male environment but that is the same if you are a single female in a building site area – it is just a male environment.

Another noted that they had worked behind the bar in a Conservative Club during their time at university and the sexism and sexual objectification they suffered there was similar to what they experienced in the prison but that this was '*just what working around men is like*'. This sense of resignation regarding the gendered and sexist working environment seemed to be pervasive and led to individuals having to formulate mechanisms for dealing with a hostile workplace. As this psychologist explained:

> Where you get comments and ... knowing how to handle them or sexualised comments from prisoners or other members of staff and thinking about how to respond to those. ... I still might get some now but I suppose I can ... I am a lot.... I handle it completely differently, but I spent a lot of time thinking about that.

Armouring

Armouring involved developing a thickened façade in order to deflect sexism. The first was a form of emotional labour whereby women would attempt to harden themselves to the gendered hostility so that it would not get to them, or that perpetrators would not see the affect that such sexism had on them:

> You find yourself being confronted by these ... comments, from staff as well as prisoners, and you just learn to ignore them, you get ... you've got to grow a thick skin to work here I think.

> I quickly got used to the level of just cat calls out of windows and the comments in offices. You develop a thick skin.

One psychologist linked this armouring to her routine for preparing to enter the prison. She explained that outside of the prison such sexism and sexual objectification would '*really get me down*' but that when she put on her psychology outfit/self this allowed her to '*brush it all off*' and not '*let it get to me*'. Another gave a similar account explaining that when she put on her professional persona she felt '*stronger and more able to cope with the horribleness*'. Here then the professional identity and the adoption of that particular narrative allowed them to armour themselves against the gender hostility which they were forced to experience. This strategy allowed them to manage their emotional experiences in such a way that it allowed them to not only maintain efficacy in their working lives but also mitigate the harms they felt. However, this internalised approach to coping meant that entrenched work place sexism was not being challenged.

This is where an externalised form of armouring occurred. Some of the psychologists noted that they had '*toughed it out*' by becoming combative. They had learnt to '*give as good as they got*' which earned them a modicum of peace. Britton (2003) noted that often female staff would demonstrate their 'toughness' in the verbal cut and thrust of the prison environment in order to show male colleagues that they could handle the prison. Such displays of masculinity performance by women allowed them to show that they were really one of the men. Though not going so far as that, this form of armouring meant that female psychologists could counteract the sexism in various ways. For instance, this psychologist noted that when some male staff would try to belittle her due to her gender she would, verbally, '*cut them down to size*'. She gave an example when she explained that one time when working with someone convicted of a sex offence the male staff in the wing office accosted her:

> ... as I was passing the door one said, you know you are wasting your fucking time seeing him and he is only seeing you for what you have got, that I have not got. And I turned around and said, "what do you mean – brains?

She noted that she would always riposte when confronted by sexist comments, even when she didn't feel like it. This allowed her to feel '*more protected*' in the prison. By acting in this way, she guarded herself from the harms that were pushed on to her. Another psychologist explained that she used her '*expertise*' to formulate a similar system of put-downs. She related a story of a time when after having been commented on by a number of officers on a wing she had turned to a female colleague and explained that sexism was really the immature response to '*genital insecurity*'. She noted that after a number of such encounters and responses she was left alone. From that point on the she explained that she felt much more secure in the prison and that working in the prison became much more pleasant. What these examples highlight is a particular form of Emotive Labour whereby the psychologists are attempting to either subvert or control the emotion states of the officers who are subjecting them to the sexism in order to minimise or eradicate its occurrence. However, such armouring tactics were not always suitable or viable for some of the female psychologists. In such cases the most common coping strategy was simply one of avoidance.

Avoidance

Some female psychologists took to avoiding, as much as was possible, those officers who were most likely to subject them to unwanted sexual attention and/or sexist commentary. By attempting to avoid these officers they saved themselves the emotional labour of having to filter and sift the sexism and the emotive labour of the riposte. However, this tactic generated a different form of labour. Women who wanted to avoid being confronted with such behaviours engaged in process of mapping the environment in order to navigate the potential harassment hot spots. For instance, one psychologist noted that if certain officers were on she would avoid going through their wing and would take a longer route to get to/ from the psychology department. Another explained that instead of taking notices or messages to the wing directly she would use the internal mail so as to avoid having to confront the landing staff. One participant explained that she would carefully time when to enter a wing as it had got to a stage where she could not bear to confront a certain cohort of wing staff. She explained that:

> I try to avoid the officers on E wing as much as possible. There's a little knot of them who are very aggressive. If I need to go on E wing I will wait until lock up or unlock starts so I know that the officers are busy on the landings.

Another expressed a similar timing strategy by noting that there were points in the core day regime where she *'could get in and out without the staff noticing'*. Another explained that previously if she'd had correspondence to deliver she would *'wait until the bulk of staff had gone off for lunch or evening lock up'*, when the wings would be quiet. This meant that she often ended up working later into the evening than her colleagues just so that she could avoid the harassment that she had at times been subjected to. Here then we see not only a spatial labour but a spatio-temporal labour whereby women are having to calculate what time and by what route they can access certain areas of the prison.

There were a number of similar scenarios described all of which involved varying forms of space/time avoidance. However, such strategies were not always reliable. For instance, the psychologist who waited for staff to go off the wing found that, during a reconfiguring and relocating of OMU, her psychology team were relocated from their office in a corridor to an office on the wing that she most wanted to avoid. Being permanently located in the very locale that she had sought to avoid and being confronted by those staff on a daily basis meant that she had needed to adopt a different set of coping strategies which involved both forms of armouring. She noted that this had been a *'nightmare'* and that she had *'dreaded coming to work'* but had resolved that they would *'not get to her'* and that she would now *'give them as good as she got'*.

In this chapter we have seen how the very gendered nature of the prison and the relationships that occur within impact on the behaviour and experience of female psychologists. All those interviewed noted that the prison as a gendered space constrained or placed burdens upon them in some way or another. This had a significant effect on the way that all female psychologists in this sample operated as professionals and performed their occupational selves. From constraints on dress and physical appearance to the unwanted and overt sexualisation of the spaces in which they moved and worked female psychologists had to navigate the prison differently from their male peers. This added an extra dimension to their operational lives that was both beyond the experience of, and largely unacknowledged by, their male colleagues. Rather than being an element of psychological practice consigned to the past this was still the daily reality of those interviewed and necessitated the development and maintenance of armouring and avoiding coping strategies.

Chapter 9

The Paradox of Being Vulnerable Adjuncts

In philosophy and formal logic, a paradox is a state, or a set of propositions, which despite there being sound reasoning, evidence, and argumentation leads to a conclusion that seems illogical or self-contradictory (Poundstone, 1988). Often found lurking within the pages of abstract philosophy texts and puzzle grimoires, the paradox can often be written off as a mere quirk of language – an amusement. However, as Sainsbury (2009) notes, the humble paradox is a much more serious matter than it is often given credit for in the popular imagination. For they have often lain at the heart of advancement in knowledge. The author argues explicitly that '*Historically, they are associated with crises in thought and with revolutionary advances. To grapple with them is not merely to engage in an intellectual game, but is to come to grips with key issues*' (p. 1). Now, I do not claim to be making any revolutionary advances in this book (I am not quite that arrogant), and I am not entirely sure there is a crisis of thought when it comes to the issue of power, but the simple fact is that that there is a paradox in how forensic psychologists exist as both powerful and yet vulnerable individuals within prisons. Tackling this paradox, I argue, does allow us to come to grips with, and increase our knowledge of, some of the key issues within the contemporary prison.

Forensic psychologists comprise a niche but disproportionately powerful staff group within the prisons of England and Wales. They are, by both discipline and occupation, a significant factor in the contemporary penal landscape where they wield a diffuse yet inescapable and unchecked form of disciplinary power. Forensic psychology has, in the last three decades, influenced, informed, and underpinned both prison practice and penal power. Psychologists themselves have become a mainstay of the lifeworld of the prison. Yet, despite being perceived as powerful they themselves feel both vulnerable and alienated from the prisons in which they operate. This paradoxical position of being a vulnerable wielder of extreme penal power, reflective of Muir jr's (1977) discussion of the police and power, has been one core focal point of this book. Exploring this issue allows us to disentangle the Gordian Knot of power that exists within these complex institutions. It allows us to move beyond explanations of penal power that are solely dependent upon dyadic mechanisms of interaction to explicate how the entanglements of power operate within the institution. It also allows us to explore in more depth how disciplinary symbols operate, materially, within the contemporary prison.

Forensic Psychologists, 183–191
Copyright © 2021 Jason Warr
Published under exclusive licence by Emerald Publishing Limited
doi:10.1108/978-1-83909-960-120200010

The examination of the power of psychologists furthers our understanding not only of power within the prison but also how medicalisation processes both relate to power in our society and become embedded within our institutions. In this regard, the self-perpetuating logics of medicalised processes, categorisation, treatment, evaluation, become the same processes which underpins psychology in the prison and thus determines not only its longevity but also its symbolic interactivity. This also establishes the grounds for the disciplinary capital of psychological expertise within the prison. This analysis of how their disciplinary 'expertise' both contributes to and is entangled with the interests of the prison extends Bourdieu's (1986) concept of multiple forms of 'capital'. Here the capital is disciplinarily symbolic and gains both exchange and legitimation value within the scripturally dominated bureaucracy of the modern prison. However, this is not a power that is separate or distinct from other forms of power within the prison. Operating where it is, it is necessarily, and contiguously, influencing and being influenced by those other forms. This also helps us to understand the complexities of their power in relation to their practice. By exploring how the predicates of psychological power are influenced by other forms of disciplinary and penal power we can begin to understand how professional practice within the prison, that would be questioned or opposed in other psychological settings, emerges. This is a distinct problem for forensic psychologists working in prison and one that has been little explored.

Power is a fundamental aspect of the prison lifeworld. The discipline of psychology itself operates as an element of that system of power. Psychologists become net contributors, as both embodiments of their discipline and as experts within the institution, to the matrices of power which underpin the contemporary prison. This is a simple reality, a brute fact. Yet nearly all participants neutralised or attempted to shed, in one way or another, the power that they had as psychologists. Even where there was some acknowledgement of their authoritative position, there existed a reluctance to accept just how profoundly powerful they were, what the implications of their role could be, and the manner in which they could affect the lives of those incarcerated. In some ways this is related to not seeing the product of their labour, and thus having direct evidence of their influence. Nevertheless, these processes of neutralisation tell us of the reality of that power. If it did not exist then the need for neutralisation would not exist. However, it also reveals some issues with regard to ethical practice, especially in terms of the dual relationship issue. For forensic psychologists operating in the prison, the dual relationship problem goes beyond the simplistic notion of a care/control dichotomy that nurses in the prison may experience. Psychology, as a discourse, is a predicate of the prison's disciplinary power and therefore practitioners both create and wield a great deal of disciplinary capital within the prison. Theirs is necessarily a practice geared to the interests of the institutions they serve. This nuanced relationship blinded many to the coercive nature of their profession and the implications that this could have for those in their care.

In fact, it seemed difficult for many to truly accept that their professional psychological practice served the interests of the prison, and the discipline of psychology, first and foremost. The people, the humans, with whom they work are by their very practice rendered lower in the hierarchy of service user. Some of the psychological types, especially the Functionalists and Utilitarians, openly admitted to utilising prisoners as a means to a psychological and disciplinary end, rather than treating them as an end in and of themselves. A process that reveals that their practice was more concerned with the institutional and professional discourses of risk and its management rather than what any of us would usually understand as rehabilitation. Here existed a disjunct between what they thought of their practice and the reality of their practice. This conflation of risk/ rehabilitation often resulted in not just an ethical blindness to the consequences of that practice but a moral blindness to the very people who were subject to their power. Forensic psychology, for all its rhetoric of care, is often insensitive to the prisoners who are rendered bureaucratised entities in the trade of their disciplinary capital. In such situations the very concept of care becomes sacrificed on the altar of penality.

The combination of the power of psychology and this lack of awareness results in a situation where coercive practice no longer becomes seen through the same ethical lens as it is in other psychological contexts. It may well be that the development of psychological practice within the prison, and its enmeshing with other forms of power, in many ways contributes to these processes of neutralisation and displacement. What was evident though was that the notion of personal power was uncomfortable for many. That is something that needs further exploration. Is it to do with training, management, the individuals attracted to psychological practice, or the very discipline itself? These questions, unfortunately, lie beyond the scope of my findings. However, what is clear is that such neutralisation, ethical, and moral blindness can have implications for the way that psychological services are utilised in the prison, and what practices are acceptable when prisoners can be used to reach a psychological end. This ethical complexity also has implications for how prisoners experience the psychologists with whom they interact, how psychologists are managed within carceral settings, how junior members of staff are trained, and how ethical guidelines are produced by governing bodies.

There is of course the flip side to this coin of power. Not only did psychologists act as producers and amplifiers of disciplinary power within the institution but also they were themselves rendered subaltern to wider structural and interpersonal influences within the prison. Psychologists spoke of systems of power that went beyond the complex structural matrices of employment rules and regulations and the manifest systems of situational control that define the prison. Instead, they focussed on more interpersonal and interactional forms of constraint and influence. The first of these offers a novel explanation of the complicated dynamic between space and staff relationships. Territorialism within organisations is often a benign facet of the workplace as it allows employees to personalise their workspaces and create havens for themselves and their colleagues. However, the accounts given by the participants in this study described a more malign impact. Here, competing disciplinary discourses (especially offender management and security) created territorial boundaries that seemed designed to impede and constrain psychologists personally, professionally, and spatially. This is especially pertinent where psychology departments have been relocated either to administrative areas of the prison or to regional offices beyond the prison walls. This territorial precarity contributed a great deal to the negative experiences that psychologists experienced, as it compounded other, more direct, examples of interpersonal power and dominance.

Both the impositional and isolational forms of dominance identified here absolutely shaped the occupational reality of psychologists working in prisons. These behaviours, identified as coming mostly from uniformed staff, are directed at both emphasising the power of discipline staff and also highlighting the vulnerability of the psychologists. This last issue is of particular importance in terms of our understanding of power in prison. That it is more keenly felt when it is withdrawn highlights an interesting perspective on the performativity of power by the uniformed body. By wilful inaction and wilful isolation, they are able to demonstrate and communicate their power and the relative powerlessness of others. Each iteration of these forms of dominance compounded the stress and anxiety that psychologists feel. It adds to the hostile environment that many feel they are working in, and can have significant negative effects on the ability of prison psychologists to operate efficiently within their host institutions. Indeed, more than half of those interviewed had said they had considered leaving the service in the year prior to interview, and some have indeed subsequently left. However, even for those that remain and 'tough it out', these dynamics compound the type, level, and degree of navigation work, and emotive/emotional labour that psychologists must undertake in order to maintain, or retain, professional efficacy within the prison.

There was, however, one area of interpersonal power that was particularly unique to the women who participated this study. Every female participant noted that the highly gendered nature of the prison, and the hegemonic masculinities to which they were subject, constrained or placed burdens upon them in some way or another. Whether this was with regard to sartorial choices, relationships within the prison, or the physical navigation of space within the prison, there were few areas of their occupational lives that were not, in some way, impacted by gendered concerns. These everyday and routine burdens had a significant effect on all female psychologists in this sample as it affected the way they felt they could operate as professionals within the prison. The most significant and wearying behaviours to which psychologists were subjected were the unwanted and overt sexualisation of the spaces in which they moved and worked, which necessitated the development and maintenance of strategies of both armouring and avoidance. Facets of womanhood that are, we must acknowledge, all too depressingly common. HMPPS Equality Policy Statement notes that the organisation '... *is committed to fairness for all ... We insist on respectful and decent behaviour from staff, prisoners and others with whom we work. We recognise that discrimination, harassment and bullying can nevertheless occur and we take prompt and appropriate action whenever we discover them*' (Ministry of Justice, 2012, p. 4). Yet, the women who participated in this study were still subjected to such behaviours and were still discouraged from entering into any formal means of redress. That fact speaks volumes about the adhesiveness of these hegemonic and gendered influences in the late-modern prison.

The analysis of these power dynamics that psychologists experience and the inherent paradox that this seems to present also allow us to move beyond the merely dyadic and structural formulations of power that characterises much of the extant literature on sociality and power (see Dowding, 1996; Stewart, 2001; Wartenburg, 1990; Wrong, 1995). Here there is a quintic of interweaving structural, discursive, spatial, gendered, and interpersonal power that directly impacts on the daily lives of individuals who are themselves arbiters of aspects of that power. This complicates our understanding of the directional flow and nature of constraints. Power here is not just coming from above, it is not simply imposed. Rather what we witness here is matrices of power that are both diffused and in constant flux. Differing combinations of power are constantly and simultaneously combining or competing with one another in order to produce a wide variety of effects and constraints. This highlights how entanglements of power can enmesh those who are net contributors to elements of that power in ways that they are not entirely aware of, only minimally able to mitigate, and which fundamentally shapes their own actions. The traditional distinctions between adjunct and subaltern are not only blurred but so too are the normal conceptions of power in context. This then necessarily alters how we go about conceptualising, understanding, operationalising, and researching questions of power.

Though this paradox has been a central focus of this book, it has not been the only one. It has also explored how this staff population experiences the prisons in which they work. It has shown that psychologists operating in prisons are not a homogenous population, obviously, but one with distinct moral and professional orientations. It has also discussed how these different occupational positionalities can inform both differing practices and result in differing occupational experiences. It has discussed how the notion of emotion work needed to be extended beyond the confines of emotional labour to include emotion work that is explicitly intended to evince responses in others. Each of these issues has implications for the way in which we understand the prison, prison work, psychological work, prison staff, and relationships between prison staff.

The typology posited emerged from, and was dictated by, the responses of psychologists who participated in the initial study. They were classified into four master categories dependent upon their moral and occupational outlook: Humanists were those focussed on a hominine approach to psychological work which balanced both 'rehabilitative' and welfarist principles. They were concerned with working with people and saw themselves as being there to help. Functionalists were concerned with wider criminal justice outcomes and thus focussed on rehabilitative goals as they related to public protection ideals. It was this group who most exemplified the fact that practices of rehabilitation in the late-modern prison had become concerned with the mitigation of risk rather than providing any direct rehabilitative (positive or progressive) benefit for those inside. Their sense of occupational self revolved around facilitating desired change in 'offenders' and thus they saw themselves through a medicalised/interventionist lens. Utilitarians had a more embedded moral outlook which meant that they perceived punitivity as a welfarist good. This meant that they saw both the prison and their psychological practice, regardless of harshness, as operating for the greater good of both society and, as a consequence, the prisoners themselves. Lastly, the Retributivists (both the Cynic and the Idealist) perceived the punitive elements of psychological practice as a means of achieving public protection. In this they focussed their practice on enabling the prison and the criminal justice system to achieve the desired disciplinary ends. Each of these standpoints shaped not only how psychologists interpreted their role but also how they approached and performed that role within the prison. These standpoints went to the heart of their professional identities and informed their ontological security.

What the typology tells us is that there is significant variation in approaches to psychological work in prisons. Individuals prioritise different elements of psychological practice, including risk assessment and offending behaviour work, depending upon which master status they happen to adhere to. Given this occupational reality, it seems inevitable that prisoners may well receive very different, and occasionally competing, psychological inputs (and outputs) from those forensic psychologists with whom they engage. This potentially poses three distinct yet related problems: firstly, delivering a cohesive psychological service needs a greater consideration of the moral and occupational positionality of the staff. Secondly, if prisoners are experiencing differential practice, which results in differing requirements for psychological work, then this could lead to significant confusion about their carceral lifecourse and thus alienation from psychological expertise and practitioners. For those people serving very long and indeterminate sentences, whose carceral trajectory can very much be dependent upon their relationships and work with forensic psychologists (see Crewe, Hulley, & Wright, 2020), this can have long-term detrimental consequences. This is something that needs to be considered by those responsible for the delivery of those services. Lastly, as psychological reports have been shown to have a significant impact on parole board decisions, differing perspectives and focusses within psychological reports to parole boards can have adverse effects on that decision-making process.[1] This last is perhaps something that needs careful research.

Psychologists working in prisons felt a distinct need to differentiate between the internal and external forms of emotion work that was necessary in order to maintain efficacy in the workplace. In the traditional literature on emotion work, especially in carceral settings, the focus has been on emotional labour. This is usually described as those internal emotion processes that involve the faking of emotions that are not felt, the hiding of emotions that are felt, and active emotion regulation so as to be able to meet workplace expectations. This was certainly true, and a significant daily practice, for the psychologists involved in this study.

---

[1]The recent controversial Worboys case is a prime example of this. In the judgement made by the High Court regarding the judicial review bought by two of his alleged victims, it was made clear that the reports presented to the parole board by four different psychologists had contradictory and competing focusses that went beyond just adversarial perspectives (see https://www.judiciary.gov.uk/judgments/the-queen-on-the-application-of-dsd-and-nbv-ors-v-the-parole-board-of-england-and-wales-ors-and-john-radford/).

However, it was also evident that a fundamental aspect of the emotion work that psychologists were undertaking was concerned with altering the emotion states of others. This external emotion work involved the three following processes: evocation – the process of inciting emotion responses in others; deflection – the processes of altering the nature and course of emotion responses in others; and inversion – the processes of changing negative emotion responses in others to ones that are positive or meet the ends/needs of the psychologist. This is what I have referred to as emotive labour. This labour, due to the nature of psychological work, is not just focussed at prisoners and 'treatment' work but becomes a necessary part of navigating interstaff relationships, disputes in the workplace, and the broader more general social world of the prison. It was also found that each of the types described categorically used both emotional and emotive labour in ways that adhered to their positionality. For instance, the Humanists would use processes of deflection to help those they worked with cope with their emotions and the prison, whereas Retributivists might use processes of evocation to force prisoners into confronting the harms they have enacted. In both cases the focus of the emotion work being conducted is focussed on an external one rather than one's own emotion states. This had particular pertinence for those who were forced into careful, and territorialised, navigations of the uniformed body. Many described situations where such emotive work was a daily necessity in order to protect themselves in various ways.

The distinction between emotional and emotive labour not only has pertinence for the understanding of how psychologists operate within the prison but also for other prison, and criminal justice, staff. Hochschild (1983) states that emotion work operates both within and without as, at heart, all emotion work influences others. However, this external work remains implicit to Hochschild account and is carried through into the work on emotional labour that we see with Mann (2004), Mann and Cowburn (2005), Walsh (2009) and even Marroquín, Tennen, and Stanton (2017). However, in this study I have made these processes explicit and explained how they may operate in this context. This expands what we know about emotion work and how it becomes operative within forms of sociality. However, the concept of emotive labour may have pertinence beyond the literature on emotion work and may add to other works on interactions within carceral and/or noncarceral spaces. For instance, Liebling, Price, and Shefer (2011) note that prison officers rely heavily on the relationships they build with prisoners to maintain order. Emotive labour could represent one mechanism by which this is achieved. In de-escalating or diffusing confrontation, prison officers too seem to be engaging in processes of evocation, deflection, and/or inversion. The same is true with other prison staff, nurses, drug workers, probation, etc.

A further issue that results from the variant nature and moral perspectives of psychologists relates to emotion work. Firstly, it is possible that certain 'types' of psychologist are better suited for differing roles within the prison. However, of course, this would need a great deal of careful research and thought before any hint of implementation. However, this may be especially beneficial given that utilising psychologists in such ways that compete or clash with their sense of professional self can negatively impact on their working lives, their perception of the environment in which they work, their profession, and their engagement with prisoners. Such issues may impact on staff attrition; historically a major issue for forensic psychology in prisons. We saw that performing a discordant role can compound the dissatisfaction that psychologists experience and increase the levels and forms of emotion work that they engage in. Secondly, as differing psychologists are utilising forms of emotive labour in different ways, and for differing purposes, there are implications for how effective work is developed and managed. In measuring the efficacy of a programme or offending behaviour course, you would need to establish the relationship between the course format and the types of emotive labour being employed, and by whom, in order to ensure robust measurement of that programme. Thirdly, the processes of emotive labour have implications for the way psychologists work with vulnerable individuals in prison. Given the wide range of vulnerabilities that exist in incarcerated populations, it is necessary that psychologists are, or become, sophisticated emotive labourers in order not to compound problems that prisoners may have.

The conjunction of typology and emotion work was also important in understanding the dynamics of the varying but quotidian occupational experiences of prison psychologists. Whilst it was clear that, for many psychologists, procedural and organisational factors, such as workload, were significant in evoking dissatisfaction, it was relational issues that were central for all types. For example, it became evident that team dynamics, and especially poor leadership within a team, played a significant role in effecting psychological staff. Poor supervision and management impacted on matters ranging from coping with everyday tasks to completing chartership. A compounding factor was when occupational experiences lay outside a psychologist's sphere of direct control. Where this external triggering occupational phenomenon occurred but was not mitigated by supervisors and other team members, then it created the need for emotional labour. These dynamics resulted in the need for psychologists to engage in distinct, but potentially unnecessary, forms of emotional labour that would allow them to cope with the anxiety, stress, and interpersonal conflicts which were commonplace. Yet as was noted by some participants, some of this need for emotional labour could be mitigated through greater access to a wider range of supervisors and senior psychologists.

It is perhaps unsurprising, given what is generally known about work and working life, but for many psychologists, satisfaction derived from a perceived attachment to the product of labour. Where this became problematic was in the scarcity of this attachment. It was clear that psychologists in prisons rarely receive any positive evidence with regard to their labour by seeing what happens to the prisoners with whom they start to work. Partly this was because any particular prisoner would be moved on or would be released and thus the 'product' not witnessed. This was compounded because of the episodic and limited interactive nature of psychological work in the prison in contrast to other psychological settings. This reality had a profound effect on psychology types as this situation eroded not only any sense of achievement but also any confirmation of occupational position. Many were just left with nothing to grasp on to or by which to measure their success. The combination of these issues had a significant effect on individual psychologist's sense of self and place.

As is acknowledged in a wide range of occupational and organisational literature (see Belilos, 1997; Judge & Church, 2000; Mumford, 2011), seeing the fruits of one's labour is integral to a sense of self-worth in the workplace. This sense of self-worth is itself connected to workplace well-being, efficacy, and organisational attachment. The peculiar mechanisms of prison as an industrial workplace undermine these aspects of forensic practice and highlight just how attachment to the products of one's labour is not dependent on a material product/remuneration relationship. Here we see, especially given the variated perspectives attached to the differing typologies, that with forensic psychological work there are elements of symbolic attainment, disciplinary interests, and disciplinary change, in their work with prisoners from which their labour becomes separated. This symbolic interactivity adds to the way that we understand the nature of 'product' in labour relationships and more specifically the type of product (exchange and disciplinary capital too) that the prison is geared towards producing. This suggests that symbolic signifiers of labour then become a fundamental element of the occupational ecology of prisons. However, it is my contention that this is an under-researched and little understood facet of working in prisons, and it demands of us a more sophisticated explanation on the symbolic production, exchange, interactivity, and economy of 'prison work'.

Thus, I come to my last words. My final thought is that this research, long in the making, not only has implications for the way that we understand forensic psychology and its adherents but also for how we consider the prison as an entity within our society. Prisons exist as these edifices of control and dominance which are often pushed to the edges of our social vision. They often remain hidden from the very people they serve. In that reality, ignorance abounds. Within our prisons, and they are ours, we may deny this and we may hide that truth from ourselves, but they emerge from and serve our interests. In them are housed those deemed unworthy, by their own hand, of a seat at our collective table. It is within these lazaretto houses that punishment is enacted and the demands of disciplinary change supposedly met. It is here that we as a society expect those civic revenants to be remade, reformed, and rendered 'safe'. Yet we still have little understanding of how these processes are, if at all, made manifest. Much of this societal expectation falls on the shoulders of psychologists and other specialist staff. By examining how they experience the carceral habitus, it allows us to gain a greater understanding of the prison as an entity and its role in all our lives. More importantly, hopefully, by exploring the realities experienced by those who work there, we learn more about what these stony edifices do to those we consign there.

Thank you.

References

Acker, J. (1990). Hierarchies, jobs, bodies: A theory of gendered organisations. *Gender and Society*, *4*, 139–158.

Adam Smith Institute. (1983). *Omega report: Expenditure and taxation policy*. London: Adam Smith Institute. Retrieved from https://www.adamsmith.org/research/omega-report-expenditure-and-taxation-policy

Adams, J. (1995). *Risk*. London: UCL Press.

Adler, J. R. (2004). Forensic psychology: Concepts, debates and practice. In J. R. Adler (Ed.), *Forensic psychology: Concepts, debates and practice*. Cullompton: Willan Publishing.

Adler, J. R., & Gray, J. M. (2010). *Forensic psychology: Concepts, debates and practice* (2nd ed.). Abingdon: Willan Publishing.

Allen, R. (2013). Paying for justice: Prison and probation in an age of austerity. *British Journal of Community Justice*, *11*(1), 5–18.

Andrews, D. A., & Bonta, J. (1994). *The psychology of criminal conduct*. Cincinnati, OH: Anderson Publishing Company.

Andrews, D. A., & Bonta, J. (1998). *The psychology of criminal conduct* (2nd ed.). Cincinnati, OH: Anderson Publishing Company.

Andrews, D. A., & Bonta, J. (2003). *The psychology of criminal conduct* (3rd ed.). Cincinnati, OH: Anderson Publishing Company.

Andrews, D. A., & Bonta, J. (2010). Rehabilitating criminal Justice policy and practice. *Psychology, Public Policy, and Law*, *16*(1), 39–55.

Anshel, M. H. (2000). A conceptual model and implications for coping with stress events in police work. *Criminal Justice and Behavior*, *27*(3), 375–400.

Arendt, H. (1959). *The human condition*. New York, NY: Anchor Books.

Arendt, H. (1970). *On power*. harmondsworth: Allen lane. The Penguin Press.

Armstrong, R. (2014). Trusting the untrustworthy: The theology, practice and implications of faith based volunteers' working with ex-prisoners. *Studies in Christian Ethics*, *27*(3), 299–309.

Arnold, H. (2005). The effects of prison work. In A. Liebling & S. Maruna (Eds.), *The effects of imprisonment*. London: Routledge, 391–420.

Arnold, H. (2016). The prison officer. In Y. Jewkes, J. Bennett, & B. Crewe (Eds.), *Handbook on prisons* (2nd ed.). London; New York, NY: Routledge, 265–283.

Ashman, I., & Gibson, C. (2010). Existential identity, ontological insecurity and mental well-being in the workplace. *Lancashire Business School* Working Papers: New Series, *1*(3), 1–19.

Atrill, G., & Liell, G. (2006). Prisoners' views on risk assessment. In N. Padfield (Ed.), *Who to release? Parole, fairness and criminal justice*. Cullompton: Willan Publishing.

Bachrach, P., & Baratz, M. S. (1962/1994). The two faces of power. In J. Scott (Ed.), *Power* (Vol. 2). London: Routledge.

Bailey, K. D. (1994). *Typologies and taxonomies: An introduction to classification techniques, sage university paper series on quantitative applications in the social sciences* (pp. 7–102). Thousand Oaks, CA: SAGE Publications.

Bailey, J., McHugh, M., Chisnall, L., & Forbes, D. (2002). *Training staff in suicide awareness*. In G. Towl, L. Snow, & M. McHugh (Eds.), *Suicide in Prisons*. Blackwell Publishers Ltd.

Barnes, S. B. (1988). *The nature of power*. Cambridge: Polity.

Bartol, C. R., & Bartol, A. M. (1999). History of forensic psychology. In A. K. Hess & I. B. Weiner (Eds.), *The handbook of forensic psychology* (2nd ed.). New York, NY: John Wiley & Sons.

Bartol, C. R., & Bartol, A. M. (2015). *An introduction to forensic psychology: Research and application* (4th ed.). Los Angeles, CA: SAGE Publications.

Bauman, Z., & Donskis, L. (2013). *Moral blindness: The loss of sensitivity in liquid modernity*. Cambridge: Polity Press.

Bayer, R. (1987). *Homosexuality and American psychiatry: The politics of diagnosis*. Princeton, NJ: Princeton University Press.

Beck, U. (1992). From industrial society to risk society: Questions of survival. Social structure and ecological enlightenment. *Theory, Culture & Society, 9*, 97–123.

Beck, U. (1992a). *Risk society: Towards a new modernity*. London; Newbury Park, CA: SAGE Publications.

Becker, H. S. (1963). *Outsiders: Studies in the sociology of deviance*. New York, NY: The Free Press of Glencoe.

Beetham, D. (1991). *The legitimation of power*. Basingstoke: Macmillan.

Belilos, C. (1997). *Understanding employee drives and motivations: The first step towards motivation at work*. Vancouver: CHIC Services.

Bennett, J. (2016). *The working lives of prison managers: Global change, local culture and individual agency in the late modern prison*. London: Palgrave McMillan.

Bennett, J., & Shuker, R. (2017). The potential of prison-based democratic therapeutic communities. *International Journal of Prisoner Health, 13*(1), 19–24

Black, M. B. (1963). On formal ethnographic procedures. *American Anthropologist, 65*(6), 1347–1351.

Boothby, J. L., & Clements, C. B. (2002). Job satisfaction of correctional psychologists: Implications for recruitment and retention. In *Professional Psychology: Research and Practice, 33*, 310–315.

Bottoms, A. E. (2000). The relationship between theory and research in criminology. In R. King & E. Wincup (Eds.), *Doing research on crime and justice*. Oxford: Oxford University Press.

Bourdieu, P. (1986/2011). 'The forms of capital' reproduced. In I. Szeman & T. Kaposy (Eds.), *Cultural theory: An anthology* (pp. 81–93). Malden, MA: Wiley-Blackwell Publishers.

Bourdieu, P. (1990). *The logic of practice*. Stanford, CA: Stanford University Press.

Bowers, L., & Friendship, C. (2017). Forensic psychological risk assessment for the parole board. In K. D. Browne, A. R. Beech, L. A. Craig, & S. Chou (Eds.), *Assessments in forensic practice: A handbook* (pp. 103–121). Chichester; West Sussex; Malden, MA: John Wiley & Sons.

Bowles, S., Gintis, H., & Osbourne, M. (2001). The determinants of earnings: A behavioural approach. *Journal of Economic Literature, 39*, 1137–1176.

Boyd, R., & Richerson, P. J. (2005). *The origin and evolution of cultures.* Oxford: Oxford University Press.

British Psychological Society. (2008). *Candidate handbook for the diploma in forensic psychology.* Leicester: Qualifications Office BPS.

Britton, D. M. (2003). *At work in the iron cage: The prison as gendered organisation.* New York, NY: New York University Press.

Brown, G., Lawrence, T. B., & Robinson, S. L. (2005). Territoriality in organisations. *Academy of Management Review, 30*(3), 577–594.

Brown, G., & Robinson, S. L. (2007). The dysfunction of territoriality. In J. Langan-Fox, C. L. Cooper, & R. J. Klimoski (Eds.), *Research companion to the dysfunctional workplace: Management challenges and symptoms* (pp. 252–266). Cheltenham: Edward Elgar Publishing Ltd.

Brown, J., Shell, Y., & Cole, T. (2015). *Forensic psychology: Theory, research, policy and practice.* Los Angeles, CA: SAGE Publications.

Broyles, J. (1975). The fallacies of composition and division. *Philosophy and Rhetoric, 8*(2), 108–113.

Bryons, S. (2008). Prison governors: New public managers? In J. Bennett, B. Crewe, & A. Wahidin (Eds.), *Understanding prison staff* (pp. 213–230). Cullompton; Portland, OR: Willan Publishing.

Burdon, W. M., & Gallagher, C. A. (2002). Coercion and Sex Prisoners: Controlling sex-offending behaviour through incapacitation and treatment. *Criminal Justice and Behavior, 29*, 87–109.

Cane, P. (2016). *Controlling administrative power: An historical perspective.* Cambridge: Cambridge University Press.

Carlen, P. (1982). Papa's discipline: An analysis of disciplinary modes in the scottish women's prison. *Sociological Review, 30*(1), 97–124.

Carlen, P. (2005). Imprisonment and the penal body politic: The cancer of disciplinary governance. In A. Liebling & S. Maruna (Eds.), *The effects of imprisonment.* London: Routledge.

Carlen, P. (2008). Imaginary penalities and risk-crazed governance. In P. Carlen (Ed.), *Imaginary penalities* (pp. 1–25). Cullompton; Portland, OR: Willan Publishing.

Carlen, P., & Worrall, A. (2004). *Analysing women's imprisonment.* Cullompton: Willan Publishing.

Carrabine, E. (2005). Prison riots, social order and the problem of legitimacy. *British Journal of Criminology, 45*(6), 896–913.

Carrithers, M. (1992). *Why humans have cultures: Explaining anthropology and social diversity.* Oxford: Oxford University Press.

Castells, M. (2013). *Communication power.* Oxford: Oxford University Press.

Cavadino, M., Dignan, J., Mair, G., & Bennett, J. (2019). *The penal system: An introduction* (6th ed.). Los Angeles, CA: SAGE Publications.

de Certeau, M. (1988). *The practice of everyday life.* Berkeley, CA: University of California Press.

Chase, S. (1954). *Power of words.* New York, NY: Harcourt, Brace & Company.

Clark, C. (1990). Emotions and micropolitics in everyday life: Some patterns and paradoxes of "place". In T. D. Kemper (Ed.), *Research agendas in the sociology of emotions* (pp. 305–333). New York, NY: State University of New York Press.

Clark, D. (1999). *Risk assessment in prisons and probation, issues in forensic psychology.* London: British Psychological Society.

Clarke, J., & Newman, J. (1997). *The managerial state*. London: SAGE Publications.

Clarke, A. E., Shim, J. K., Mamo, L., Fosket, J. R., & Fishman, J. R. (2003). Biomedicalization: Technoscientific transformations of health, illness and US biomedicine. *American Sociological Review, 68*, 161–194.

Clarke, A., Simmonds, R., & Wydall, S. (2004). *Delivering cognitive Skills programmes in prison: A qualitative study*. London: Home Office Online Report, Accessed on April 27.

Clear, T. R., & Cadora, E. (2001). Risk and correctional practice. In K. Stenson & R. R. Sullivan (Eds.), *Crime, risk and justice: The politics of crime control in liberal democracies*. Cullompton: Willan Publishing.

Clegg, S. R. (1989). *Frameworks of power*. London: SAGE Publications.

Cleveland, J. N., Stockdale, M., & Murphy, K. R. (2000). *Women and men in organizations: Sex and gender issues at work*. London: Lawrence Erlbaum Associates Publishers.

Cohen, S. (2001). *States of denial: Knowing about atrocities and suffering*. Cambridge; Malden, MA: Polity Press: Blackwell Publishing Company.

Collier, D., Laporte, J., & Seawright, J. (2008). Chapter 7 - typologies: Forming concepts and categorical variables. In J. M. Box-Steffensmeier, H. E. Brady, & D. Collier (Eds.), *Oxford handbook of political methodology* (pp. 152–173). Oxford: Oxford University Press.

Collins, R. (1975). *Conflict sociology: Toward an explanatory science*. New York, NY: Academic Press.

Collins, H., & Evans, R. (2007). *Rethinking expertise*. Chicago, IL: University of Chicago Press.

Conrad, P. (2007). *The medicalization of society: On the transformation of human conditions into treatable disorders*. Baltimore, MD: John Hopkins University Press.

Conrad, P., & Schneider, J. W. (1992). *Deviance and medicalization: From badness to sickness*. Philadelphia, PA: Temple University Press.

Cooperrider, D., Whitney, D., & Stavros, J. (2007). *Appreciative inquiry handbook*. San Francisco, CA: Berrett-Koehler.

Coxon, A. P. M. (1999). *Sorting data: Collection and analysis, sage university paper series on quantitative applications in the social sciences* (pp. 7–127). Thousand Oaks, CA: SAGE Publications.

Crawley, E. (2004). *Doing prison work: The public and private lives of prison officers*. Cullompton; Portland, OR: Willan Publishing.

Crawley, E., & Crawley, P. (2008). Understanding prison officers: Culture, cohesion and conflicts. In J. Bennett, B. Crewe, & A. Wahidin (Eds.), *Understanding prison staff*. Cullompton; Portland, OR: Willan Publishing.

Crewe, B. (2007). Power, adaptation and resistance in a late-modern men's prison. *British Journal of Criminology, 47*, 256–275.

Crewe, B. (2009). *The prisoner society: Power, adaptation and social life in an English prison*. Oxford: Oxford University Press.

Crewe, B. (2011). Depth, weight, tightness: Revisiting the pains of imprisonment. *Punishment & Society, 13*(5), 509–529.

Crewe, B., Bennett, J., & Wahidin, A. (2008). Introduction. In J. Bennett, B. Crewe, & A. Wahidin (Eds.), *Understanding prison staff* (pp. 1–11). Cullompton; Portland, OR: Willan Publishing.

Crewe, B., Hulley, S., & Wright, S. (2020). *Life Imprisonment from young adulthood: Adaptation, identity, and time, palgrave studies in prisons and penology*. London: Palgrave Macmillan.

Crewe, B., Liebling, A., & Hulley, S. (2011). Staff Culture, use of authority and prisoner quality of life in public and private sector prisons. *Australian and New Zealand Journal of Criminology, 44*(1), 94–115.

Crewe, B., Liebling, A., & Hulley, S. (2015). Staff-Prisoner relationships, staff professionalism, and the use of authority in public and private sector prisons. *Law & Social Inquiry, 40*(2), 309–344.

Crewe, B., Warr, J., Bennett, P., & Smith, A. (2014). The emotional geography of prison life. *Theoretical Criminology, 18*(1), 56–74.

Crighton, D. A. (2004). Risk assessment. In A. P. C. Needs & G. J. Towl (Eds.), *Applying psychology to forensic practice*. Oxford: Blackwell Publishing.

Crighton, D. A., & Towl, G. J. (2008). *Psychology in prisons* (2nd ed.). Oxford: BPS Blackwell.

Crighton, D. A., & Towl, G. J. (2015). *Forensic psychology* (2nd ed.). Chichester: John Wiley & Sons.

Crow, I., & Semmens, N. (2008). *Researching criminology*. New York, NY: The Open University Press.

Crozier, M. (2010). *The bureaucratic phenomenon*. London: Transaction Publishers.

Dahl, R. A. (1957/1994). The concept of power. In J. Scott (Ed.), *Power* (Vol. 2). London: Routledge.

Dahl, R. A. (1968/1986). Power as the control of behaviour. In S. Lukes (Ed.), *Power*. Oxford: Oxford University Press.

Dale, C., & Woods, P. (2001). *Caring for prisoners*. London: RCN.

Darley, J. M., & Gross, P. H. (1983). A hypothesis-confirming bias in labelling effects. *Journal of Personality and Social Psychology, 44*(1), 20–33.

Day, A., & Casey, S. (2009). Values in forensic and correctional psychology. *Aggression and Violent Behavior, 14*(4), 232–238.

Day, A., Tucker, K., & Howells, K. (2004) Coerced offender rehabilitation – a defensible practice? *Psychology, Crime and Law, 10*(3), 259–269.

Dean, M. (1999). *Governmentality: Power and rule in modern society*. London: SAGE Publications.

Dellana, S. A., & Hauser, R. D. (1999). Toward defining the quality culture. *Engineering Management Journal, 11*(2), 11–15.

Deshpande, R., & Webster, F. E. Jr (1989). Organizational culture and marketing: Defining the research agenda. *Journal of Marketing, 53*(1), 3–15.

Di Martino, V., Hoel, H., & Cooper, C. L. (2003). *Preventing violence and harassment in the workplace*. Luxembourg: European Foundation for the Improvement of Living and Working Conditions. Office for Official Publications of the European Communities.

Dias, C. F., & Vaughn, M. S. (2006). Bureaucracy, managerial disorganization, and administrative breakdown in criminal justice agencies. *Journal of Criminal Justice, 34*(5), 543–555.

Douglas, T. (2014). Criminal rehabilitation through medical intervention: Moral liability and the right to bodily integrity. *The Journal of Ethics, 18*(2), 101–122.

Douglas, M., & Wildavsky, A. (1982). *Risk and culture*. Berkeley, CA: University of California Press.

Dowding, K. (1996). *Power*. Buckingham: Open University Press.

Downes, D., & Hansen, K. (2006). Welfare and punishment in comparative perspective. In S. Armstrong, & L. McAra (Eds.), *Perspectives on punishment*. Oxford: Oxford University Press.

Ducharme, L. J., Knusden, H. K., & Roman, P. M. (2007). Emotional exhaustion and turnover intention in human science occupations: The protective role of Co-worker support. *Sociological Spectrum, 28*(1), 81–104.

Dugdale, R. L. (1877). *The jukes: A study in crime, pauperism and heredity*. New York, NY: GP Putnam and Sons.

D'Emilio, J. (2002). *The world turned: Essays on gay history, politics and culture*. Durham, NC: Duke University Press.

D'Zurilla, T. J., & Nezu, A. M. (2010). Problem solving therapy. In K. S. Dobson (Ed.), *Handbook of cognitive behavioural therapies* (3rd ed., pp. 197–225). New York, NY: The Guildford Press.

Easton, S., & Piper, C. (2016). *Sentencing and punishment: The quest for justice* (4th ed.). Oxford: Oxford University Press.

Einarsen, S., Hoel, H., Zapf, D., & Cooper, C. L. (2002). *Bullying and emotional abuse in the workplace: International perspectives in research and practice*. London: CRC Press.

Etzioni, A. (1961). *A comparative analysis of complex organisations: On power, involvement and their correlates*. New York, NY: Free Press.

Evans, J., & Henson, C. (1999). Incident management. In G. Towl & C. McDougall (Eds.), *What do forensic psychologists do? Current and future directions in the prison and probation services*. Leicester: The British Psychological Society.

Farbar, B. A. (1990). Burnout in psychotherapists: Incidence, types and trends. *Psychotherapy in Private Practice, 8*(1), 35–44.

Farrington, D. P. (1993). Understanding and preventing bullying. In M. Tonry (Ed.), *Crime and justice: A review of research*, Chicago, IL: The University of Chicago Press.

Feinman, C. (1994). *Women in the criminal justice system* (3rd ed.). Westport, CT: Praeger Publishers.

Fitzgibbon, D. W. M. (2007). Risk analysis and the new practitioner: Myth or reality. *Punishment and Society, 9*(1), 87–97.

Fitzgibbon, D. W. M. (2008). Fit for purpose? OASys assessment and parole decisions. *Probation Justice, 55*(1), 55–69.

Fleetwood, J. (2016). Narrative Habitus: Thinking through structure/agency in the narratives of offenders. *Crime, Media, Culture, 12*(2), 173–192.

Føllesdal, D. (1994). Hermeneutics and the hypothetico-deductive method. In M. Martin & L. C. McIntyre (Eds.), *Readings in the philosophy of social science* (pp. 233–246). Bradford Books: The MIT Press.

Forde, R. A. (2018). *Bad psychology: How forensic psychology left science behind*. London: Jessica Kingsley Publishers.

Foucault, M. (1963/1980). *The birth of the clinic*. New York, NY: Vintage Books.

Foucault, M. (1967). *Madness and civilisation: A history of insanity in the age of reason*. London: Tavistock Publications.

Foucault, M. (1978/1991). Governmentality. In G. Burchill, C. Gordan, & P. Miller (Eds.), *The foucault effect: Studies in governmentality*. London: Harvester Wheatsheaf.

Foucault, M. (1979/1977). *Discipline and punish*. London: Allen Lane.

Foucault, M. (1994a). Truth and juridical forms. In J. D. Faubion (Ed.), *Michel foucault: Power – essential works of foucault 1954-1984*(Vol. 3, pp. 1–89). London: Penguin Books.

Foucault, M. (1994b). The birth of social medicine. In J. D. Faubion (Ed.), *Michel foucault: Power – essential works of foucault 1954-1984* (Vol. 3, pp. 134–156). London: Penguin Books.

Foucault, M. (1994c). About the concept of the dangerous individual. In J. D. Faubion (Ed.), *Michel foucault: Power – essential works of foucault 1954-1984* (Vol. 3, pp. 176–200). London: Penguin Books.

Friendship, C., Blud, L., Erikson, M., & Travers, R. (2002). *Evaluation of cognitive behavioural treatment for prisoners*. London: Home Office.

Fulcher, J., & Scott, J. (2011). *Sociology* (4th ed.). Oxford; New York, NY: Oxford University Press.

Gannon, T. A., & Ward, T. (2014). Where has all the psychology gone? A critical review of evidence-based psychological practice in correctional settings. *Aggression and Violent Behavior, 19*, 435–446

Garland, D. (1985). *Punishment and welfare; A history of penal strategies*. Aldershot: Gower.

Garland, D. (2001). *The culture of control: Crime and social order in contemporary society*. Oxford; New York, NY: Oxford University Press.

Garland, B. E., McCarty, W. P., & Zhao, R. (2009). Job satisfaction and organizational commitment in prisons: An examination of psychological staff, teachers and unit management staff. *Criminal Justice and Behavior, 36*(2), 163–183.

Gatens, M. (1996). *Imaginary bodies, ethics, power and corporeality*. New York, NY: Routledge.

Gavin, H. (2014). *Criminological and forensic psychology*. Los Angeles, CA: SAGE Publications.

Geertz, C. (1994). Thick description: Towards an interpretive theory of culture. In M. Martin & L. C. McIntyre (Eds.), *Readings in the philosophy of social science* (pp. 213–232). Cambridge, MA: MIT Press.

Gibson, M. (2002). *Born to crime: Cesare Lombroso and the origins of biological criminology*. Westport, CT: Praeger.

Giddens, A. (1982). Action, structure, power. In A. Giddens (Ed.), *Profiles and critiques in social theory* (pp. 28–39). London: Macmillan.

Giddens, A. (1990). *The consequences of modernity*. Cambridge: Polity Press.

Giddens, A. (1998). Risk society: The context of British politics. In J. Franklin (Ed.), *The politics of risk society*. Cambridge; Malden, MA: Polity Press.

Godelier, M. (1986). *The mental and the material*. London: Verso.

Goffman, E. (1961). *Asylums: Essays on the social situation of mental patients and other inmates*. Garden City, NY: Anchor Books: Doubleday & Co.

Goldsmith, R., & Latessa, E. (2001). Coerced treatment of addictions in the criminal justice system. *Psychiatric Annals, 31*, 657–663.

Gordon, R. (1992). *Basic interviewing skills*. Itasca, Il: Peacock.

Gramsci, A. (2011) *Prison notebooks* (Vol. 1-3) (J. A. Buttigieg, Ed. & Trans.), New York, NY: Columbia University Press.

Gray, B., & Smith, P. (2009). Emotional labour and the clinical settings of nursing care: The perspectives of nurses in East London. *Nurse Education in Practice*, *9*(4), 253–261.

Greenberg, S. A., & Shuman, D. W. (1997). Irreconcilable conflict between therapeutic and forensic roles. *Professional Psychology: Research and Practice*, *28*(1), 50–57.

Gudjonsson, G. (1991). Editorial: Forensic psychology: The first century. *Journal of Forensic Psychiatry*, *2*(2), 129–131.

Haag, A. M. (2006). Ethical dilemmas faced by correctional psychologists in Canada. *Criminal Justice and Behavior*, *33*(1), 93–109.

Habermas, J. (1981). *The theory of communicative action, volume one: Reason and the rationalisation of society*. Cambridge: Polity.

Habermas, J. (1990) *Moral consciousness and communicative action* (C. Lenhardt & N. W. Nicholsen, Trans.). Cambridge, MA: The MIT Press.

Hall, E. T. (1990). *The hidden dimension, anchor books editions*. New York, NY: Random House.

Hannah-Moffat, K. (2005). Criminogenic needs and the transformative risk subject: Hybridizations of risk/need in penality. *Punishment & Society*, *7*(1), 29–51.

Hare, R. D. (1980). A research scale for the assessment of psychopathy in criminal populations. *Personality and Individual Differences*, *1*, 111–119.

Hare, R. D., Harpur, T. J. Hakstian, A. R., Forth, A. E., & Hart, S. D. (1990). The revised psychopathy checklist: Reliability and factor structure. *Psychological Assessment: Journal of Consulting and Clinical Psychology*, *2*(3), 338–341.

Haugaard, M. (1997). *The constitution of power*. Manchester: Manchester University Press.

Henry, O. (2017). Evaluation of the core sex offender treatment programme. *Probation Journal*, *64*(4), 425–427

Hepburn, J. R. (1985). The exercise of power in coercive organizations: A study of prison guards. *Criminology*, *23*(1), 145–164.

Her Majesty's Prison Service and NHS Executive Working Group. (1999). *The future organisation of prison healthcare*. London: Department of Health.

Herrity, K., Schmidt, B., & Warr, J. (Eds.). (2020). *Sensory penalities: Exploring the sensory in spaces of punishment and social control*. Bingley: Emerald Publishing Limited.

von Hirsch, A. (1986). *Past or future crimes: Deservedness and dangerousness in the sentencing of criminals*. Manchester: Manchester University Press.

HMIP. (2006). *An independent Review of a serious further offence case: Anthony rice, her majesty's inspector of probation*. London: HMIP.

Hochschild, A. R. (1983). *The managed heart: Commercialization of human feelings*. Los Angeles, CA: University of California Press.

Hoffman, D. H., Carter, D. J., Viglucci Lopez, C. R., Guo, A. X., Yasir Latifi, S., & Craig, D. C. (2015). *Report to the special committee of the board of directors of the American psychological association: Independent review relating to APA ethics guidelines, national security interrogations, and torture*. Chicago, IL: Sidley Austin LLP.

Home Office. (1959). *Penal practice in a changing society*. London: HMSO.

Home Office. (1966). *Report of the inquiry into prison escapes and security* (Cmnd 3175), London: HMSO.

Home Office. (2003). *Driving delivery: A strategic framework for psychological services.* London: HM Prison Service, NPS, Home Office.

Hood, C., Rothstein, H., & Baldwin, R. (2001). *The government of risk: Understanding risk regulation regimes.* Oxford: Oxford University Press.

Hopkins, P. E. (2007). Positionalities and knowledge: Negotiating ethics in practice. *An International E-Journal for Critical Geographies, 6*(3), 386–394.

Howard, P. D., & Dixon, L. (2012). The construction and validation of the OASys violence predictor: Advancing violence risk assessments in the English and Welsh correctional services. *Criminal Justice and Behavior, 39*(3), 287–307.

Hudson, B. (1987). *Justice through punishment.* London: Macmillan.

Hudson, B. (2003). *Justice in the risk society: Challenging and Re-affirming justice in late-modernity.* London: SAGE Publications.

Hughes, W. (2012). Promoting offender engagement and compliance in sentence planning: Practitioner and service user perspectives in hertfordshire. *Probation Journal, 59*(1), 49–65.

Hurst, N. W. (1998). *Risk assessment: The human dimension.* Cambridge: The Royal Society of Chemistry.

Ignatieff, M. (1978). *A just measure of pain.* New York, NY: Columbia University Press.

Inside time. (2013). Retrieved from http://www.insidetime.org/categories.asp?c=Psychology

Ireland, J. L. (2002). *Bullying among prisoners: Evidence, research and intervention strategies.* New York, NY: Brunner-Routledge.

Ismail, N. (2020). The politics of austerity, imprisonment and ignorance: A case study of English prisons. *Medicine, Science & the Law, 60*(2), 89–92.

Jenne, D. L., & Kersting, R. C. (1998). Gender, power and reciprocity in the correctional setting. *The Prison Journal, 78,* 166–185.

Joffe, H. (1999). *Risk and 'the other'.* Cambridge; New York, NY: Cambridge University Press.

Judge, T. A., & Church, A. H. (2000). Job satisfaction: Research and practice. In C. L. Cooper, & E. A. Locke (Eds.), *Industrial and organizational psychology: Linking theory with practice.* Oxford: Blackwell.

Kant, E. (1785/1998), Groundwork of the metaphysics of morals. In M. Gregor (Ed.), *Cambridge texts in the history of philosophy.* Cambridge; New York, NY: Cambridge University Press.

Kasperson, R. E., Renn, O., Slovic, P., Brown, H. S., Emel, J., Goble, R. ... Ratick, S. (1998). The social amplification of risk: A conceptual framework. In R. Löfstedt & L. Frewer (Eds.), *Risk and modern society.* London: Earthscan Publications Ltd.

Kassin, S. M., Dror, I. E., & Kukucka, J. (2013). The forensic confirmation bias: Problems, perspectives and proposed solutions. *Journal of Applied Research in Memory and Cognition, 2*(1), 42–52.

Kauffman, K. (1988). *Prison officers and their world.* Cambridge, MA: Harvard University Press.

Kemshall, H. (2008). Risks, rights and justice: Understanding and responding to youth risk. *Youth Justice, 8*(1), 21–37.

Kochan, J. (2013). Subjectivity and emotion in scientific research. *Studies in History and Philosophy of Science, 44*(3), 354–362.

Kolind, T., Frank, V. A., Lindberg, O., & Tourunen, J. (2015). Officers and drug counsellors: New occupational identities in nordic prisons. *British Journal of Criminology, 55*, 303–320

Kvale, S. (1996). *Interviews: An introduction to qualitative research interviewing.* Thousand Oaks, CA: SAGE Publications.

Lambert, E. G., Hogan, N. L., Moore, B., Tucker, K., Jenkins, M., Stevenson, M., & Jiang, S. (2009). The impact of the work environment on prison staff: The issue of consideration, structure, job variety and training. *American Journal of Criminal Justice, 34*, 166.

Lange, J. (1931). *Crime as destiny.* London: Allen & Unwin Publishers Ltd.

Lefebvre, H. (1991). *The production of space.* Oxford; Malden, MA: Blackwell Publishing.

Lemert, E. M. (1972). *Human deviance, social problems and social control* (2nd ed.). Englewood Cliffs, NJ: Prentice-Hall.

Levine, T. R., & McCornack, S. A. (1991). The dark side of trust: Conceptualising and measuring types of communicative suspicion. *Communication Quarterly, 39*, 325–339.

Lewis, S. (2006). Recognition of workplace bullying: A qualitative study of women targets in the public sector. *Journal of Community & Applied Social Psychology, 16*, 119–135.

Lewis, D., & Gunn, R. (2007). Workplace bullying in the public sector: Understanding the racial dimension. *Public Administration, 85*(3), 641–665.

Liebling, A. (2000). Prison officers, policing and the use of discretion. *Theoretical Criminology, 4*(3), 333–357.

Liebling, A. (2004). *Prisons and their moral performance.* Oxford: Oxford University Press.

Liebling, A. (2011). Distinctions and distinctiveness in the work of prison officers: Legitimacy and authority revisited. *European Journal of Criminology, 8*(6), 484–499.

Liebling, A., & Crewe, B. (2013). Prisons beyond the new penology: The shifting foundations of prison management. In J. Simon & R. Sparks (Eds.), *The SAGE handbook of punishment and society* (pp. 283–307). London: SAGE Publications.

Liebling, A., Hulley, S., & Crewe, B. (2012). Conceptualising and measuring the quality of prison life. In D. Gadd, S. Karstedt, & S. F. Messner (Eds.), *The sage Handbook of criminological research methods* (pp. 358–372). London: SAGE Publications Ltd.

Liebling, A., Price, D., & Shefer, G. (2011). *The prison officer* (2nd ed.). Hoboken, NJ: Taylor & Francis: Willan Publishing.

Liefooghe, A. P. D., & Mackenzie, D. K. (2001). Accounts of workplace bullying: The role of the organisation. *European Journal of Work & Organizational Psychology, 10*, 375–392.

Litwack, T. R., & Schlesinger, L. B. (1999). Dangerousness risk assessments: Research, legal and clinical considerations. In A. K. Hess & I. B. Weiner (Eds.), *The handbook of forensic psychology* (2nd ed.). New York, NY: John Wiley & Sons.

Lombroso, C. (1876/2006). *Criminal man* (M. Gibson & N. H. Rafter, Trans.). Durham, NC: Duke University Press.

Luhmann, N. (1993). *Risk: A sociological theory.* New York, NY: Aldine de Gruyter.

Lukes, S. (1974). *Power: A radical view.* London: Macmillan.

Lukes, S. (1986/1986). Introduction. In S. Lukes (Ed.), *Power*. Oxford: Oxford University Press.

Lupton, D. (1999). *Risk*. London; New York, NY: Routledge, Taylor & Francis Group.

Mackain, S. J., Myers, B., Ostapiej, L., & Newman, R. A. (2010). Job satisfaction among psychologists working in state prisons. *Criminal Justice and Behavior*, *37*, 306–318.

Mann, M. (1986). *Sources of social power* (Vol. 1). Cambridge: Cambridge University Press.

Mann, S. (2004). People work: Emotion management, stress and coping. *British Journal of Guidance and Counselling*, *32*(2), 205–221.

Mann, R. E. (2016). Sex offenders in prison. In Y. Jewkes, B. Crewe, & J. Bennett (Eds.), *Handbook on prisons* (pp. 246–264). London: Routledge.

Mann, R. E., & Atrill, G. (2007). *Assessing, reducing and managing risk in HM prison service*. London: HM Prison Service.

Mann, S., & Cowburn, J. (2005). Emotional Labour and stress within mental health nursing. *Journal of Psychiatric and Mental Health Nursing*, *12*, 154–162.

Mann, R. E., Howard, F. F., & Tew, J. (2018). What is a rehabilitative prison culture? *Prison Service Journal*, *235*, 3–9.

Mann, R. E., & Riches, E. (1999). HM prison service sex offender programme. In G. Towl & C. McDougall (Eds.), *What do forensic psychologists do? Current and future directions in the prison and probation services*. Leicester: The British Psychological Society.

Marroquín, B., Tennen, H., & Stanton, A. L. (2017). Coping, emotion regulation, and well-being: Intrapersonal and interpersonal processes. In M. Robinson & M. Eid (Eds.), *The happy mind: Cognitive contributions to well-being* (pp. 253–274). Cham: Springer.

Marshall, C., & Rossman, G. B. (2006). *Designing qualitative research* (4th ed.). London: SAGE Publications.

Martin, M. (1994). The philosophical importance of the rosenthal effect. In M. Martin & L. C. McIntyre (Eds.), *Readings in the philosophy of social science* (pp. 585–596). Bradford Books: The MIT Press.

Martinson, R. (1974). What works? – questions and answers about prison reform. *The Public Interest*, *35*, 22–54.

Maruna, S. (2011). Why do they hate us? Making peace between prisoners and psychology. *International Journal of Offender Therapy and Comparative Criminology*, *55*(5), 671–675.

Mason, J. (2002). *Qualitative researching* (2nd ed.). London: SAGE Publications.

Massumi, B. (1993). Introduction to fear. In B. Massumi (Ed.), *The politics of everyday fear* (pp. 3–38). Minneapolis, MN: University of Minnesota Press.

Mathiesen, T. (1965). *The defences of the weak: A sociological study of a Norwegian correctional institution*. London: Tavistock Publications.

Mathiesen, T. (1990). *Prison on trial*. London: SAGE Publications.

McDonald, M., & Fallon, P. (2008). Health professionals in prison. In J. Bennett, B. Crewe, & A. Wahidin (Eds.), *Understanding prison staff* (pp. 349–368). Cullompton; Portland, OR: Willan Publishing.

McGuire, J., & Priestley, P. (1995). Reviewing "what works": Past, present and future. In J. McGuire (Ed.), *What works: Reducing reoffending*. Hoboken, NJ: John Wiley & Sons.

McMahon, M. (1999). *Women on guard: Discrimination and harassment in corrections.* Toronto; Buffalo, NY: University of Toronto Press.

Miller, P., & Rose, N. (1996). Introduction. In P. Miller & N. Rose (Eds.), *The power of psychiatry.* Cambridge: Polity Press.

Ministry of Justice. (2012). *Equalities annual report 2011/12.* London: Ministry of Justice.

Ministry of Justice. (2018). Psychologists in the prison service: Finding the real story inside. *Working in the Prison Service: Blog,* London: Ministry of Justice. Retrieved from https://prisonjobs.blog.gov.uk/2018/05/04/psychologists-in-the-prison-service-finding-the-real-story-inside/

Ministry of Justice. (2020). *Offender management statistics, prison population as of 31st december 2019.* London: Ministry of Justice.

Ministry of Justice. (2020a). *Correctional services accreditation and advice panel (CSAAP) currently accredited programmes – custody,* London: MOJ. Retrieved from https://assets.publishing.service.gov.uk/government/uploads/system/uploads/attachment_data/file/870183/descriptions-accredited-programmes.pdf

Moncrieffe, J. (2007). Introduction: Labelling, power and accountability – how and why our labels matter. In J. Moncrieffe & R. Eyben (Eds.), *The power of labelling – how people are categorised and why it matters* (pp. 1–16). London: Earthscan.

Montada, L. (2001). Denial of responsibility. In A. E. Auhagen & H.-W. Bierhoff (Eds.), *Responsibility: The many faces of a social phenomenon* (pp. 79–92). New York, NY: Routledge.

Moore, R. (2009). Predicting re-offending with the OASys self-assessment questionnaire, Research Summary, 5/09, Ministry of Justice.

Morton, S. (2009). Can OASys deliver consistent assessments of prisoners? Results from the inter-rater reliability study, research summary, 1/09, Ministry of Justice.

Muir, W. K., Jr (1977). *Police: Streetcorner politicians.* Chicago, IL: University of Chicago Press.

Mumford, E. (2011). Job satisfaction – A new approach derived from an old theory. *The Sociological Review, 18*(1), 71–101.

Muncie, J. (1999). Institutionalised intolerance: Youth justice and the 1998 crime and disorder act. *Critical Social Policy, 19,* 147–175.

Murphy, T. (2000). *Coercing prisoners into treatment: A comprehensive state-wide diversion strategy.* In *Paper presented to the society for the study of addiction annual symposium,* Leeds: University of Leeds.

Murrie, D. C., Boccaccini, M. T., Guarnera, L. A., & Rufino, K. A. (2013). Are forensic experts biased by the side that retained them? *Psychological Science, 24*(10), 1889–1897. Retrieved from http://pss.sagepub.com/content/early/2013/08/21/0956797613481812

Neal, T. M. S., & Grisso, T. (2014). The cognitive underpinnings of bias in forensic mental health evaluations. *Psychology, Public Policy, and Law, 20*(2), 200–211.

Newburn, T. (2007). *Criminology.* Cullompton; Portland, OR: Willan Publishing.

Ng, S. H., & Bradac, J. J. (1993). *Power in language: Verbal communication and social influence.* Newbury Park, CA: SAGE Publications.

NOMS. (2015). The offender personality disorder pathway strategy 2015. Retrieved from https://www.england.nhs.uk/commissioning/wp-content/uploads/sites/12/2016/02/opd-strategy-nov-15.pdf

Nye, J. (2004). *Soft power: The means to success in world politics.* New York, NY: Public Affairs.

Nylander, P.-A., Lindberg, O., & Bruhn, A. (2011). Emotional labour and emotional strain among Swedish prison officers. *European Journal of Criminology, 8*(6), 469–483.

Offender Health Research Network. (2009). *A national evaluation of prison mental health in-reach services: A report to the National Institute of Health Research.* London: NHS.

Otto, K. R., & Heilbrun, K. (2002). The practice of forensic psychology: A look to the future in light of the past. *American Psychologist, 57*(1), 5–18.

O'Malley, P. (2005). Governing risks. In A. Sarat (Ed.), *The blackwell companion to law and society* (pp. 292–308). Oxford: Blackwell.

O'Reilly, C. A., III, Chatman, J., & Caldwell, D. F. (1991). People and organizational culture: A profile comparison approach to assessing person-organization fit. *Academy of Management Journal, 34*(3), 487–516.

Pakes, F., & Winstone, J. (2007). *Psychology and crime.* Cullompton: Willan Publishing.

Parole Board. (2013). Retrieved from http://www.justice.gov.uk/downloads/prisoners/parole-board/guidance-on-laspo.pdf

Paull, M., Oman, M., & Standen, O. (2012). When is a bystander not a bystander? A typology of the roles of bystanders in workplace bullying. *Asia Pacific Journal of Human Resources, 50*(3), 351–366.

Phoenix, J. (2009). Beyond risk assessment: The return of repressive welfarism? In F. McNeill & M. Barry (Eds.), *Youth offending and youth justice.* London: Jessica Kingsley Publishers.

Pink, S. (2015). *Doing sensory ethnography* (2nd ed.). London: SAGE Publications.

Pitts, J. (1968). 'Social control: The concept', *international Encyclopaedia of social science* (Vol. 14). New York, NY: Macmillan.

Poundstone, W. (1988). *Labyrinths of reason: Paradox, puzzles, and the frailty of knowledge.* Waterlooville: Anchor Books.

Puwar, N. (2004). *Space invaders: Race, gender and bodies out of place.* Oxford: Berg.

Rader, N. E. (2007). Surrendering solidarity: Considering the relationships among female correctional officers. *Women & Criminal Justice, 16*(3), 27–42.

Radzinowicz, L. (1968). *Radzinowicz report: The regime for long-term prisoners in conditions of maximum security.* London: Home Office.

Rayner, C., Hoel, H., & Cooper, C. (2001). *Workplace bullying.* London: Taylor & Francis.

Renn, O. (1992). Concepts of risk: A classification. In S. Krimsky & D. Golding (Eds.), *Social theories of risk.* Westport; London: Praeger Publishers.

Robert, L. (2009). Regulating prison life: A case study of the inmate disciplinary system. In B. Keirsbilck, W. Devroe, & E. Claes (Eds.), *Facing the limits of law* (pp. 1–17). Berlin; Heidelberg: Springer Berlin Heidelberg.

Robinson, G. (2005). What works in offender management. *The Howard Journal of Criminal Justice, 44*(3), 307–318.

Robinson, G. (2008). Late-modern rehabilitation: The evolution of a penal strategy. *Punishment & Society, 10*(4), 429–445.

Rogow, A. A., & Lasswell, H. D. (1963). *Power, corruption and rectitude.* Westport, CT: Greenwood Publishing Group.

Rosete, D., & Ciarrochi, J. (2005). Emotional intelligence and its relationship to workplace performance outcomes of leadership effectiveness. *The Leadership & Organization Development Journal, 26*(5), 388–399.

Rubin, H. J., & Rubin, I. S. (1995). *Qualitative interviewing: The art of hearing data* (2nd ed.). London: Sage Publications.

Rupert, P. A., & Morgan, D. J. (2005). Work setting and burnout among professional psychologists. *Professional Psychology: Research and Practice, 36*(5), 544–550.

Ryle, G. (1968). *'Thinking and reflecting', the human agent* (pp. 210–226). London: Royal Institute of Philosophy Lectures, Palgrave MacMillan.

Saari, L. M., & Judge, T. A. (2004). Employee attitudes and job satisfaction. *Human Resource Management, 43*(7), 395–407.

Sadlier, G. (2010). *Evaluation of the impact of the HM Prison Service enhanced thinking skills programme on reoffending outcomes of the Surveying Prisoner Crime Reduction (SPCR) sample, HMPS*. London: Ministry of Justice.

Sainsbury, R. M. (2009). *Paradoxes* (3rd ed.). Cambridge: Cambridge University Press.

Salin, D. (2003). Bullying and organisational politics in competitive and rapidly changing work environments. *International Journal of Management and Decision Making, 4*(1), 35–46.

Samenow, S. E. (2004). *Inside the criminal mind: Updated and revised edition.* New York, NY: Crown Publishers.

Scott, J. (1996). *Stratification and power: Structures of class, status and command.* Cambridge: Polity.

Scott, J. (2001). *Power: Key concepts.* Cambridge: Polity.

Scott, D. (2007). The changing face of the English prison: A critical review of the aims of imprisonment. In Y. Jewkes (Ed.), *Handbook on prisons.* Cullompton; Portland, OR: Willan Publishing.

Scull, A. (2006). Power, social control and psychiatry: Some critical reflections. In S. Armstrong, & L. McAra (Eds.), *Perspectives on punishment.* Oxford: Oxford University Press.

Secret Barrister. (2018). *The secret barrister: Stories of the law and how its broken.* London: Picador.

Serin, R., & Amos, N. (1995). The role of psychopathy in the assessment of dangerousness. *International Journal of Law and Psychiatry, 18*, 231–238.

Shingler, J., Sonnenberg, S. J., & Needs, A. (2017). Risk assessment interviews: Exploring the perspectives of psychologists and indeterminate sentenced prisoners in the United Kingdom. *International Journal of Offender Therapy and Comparative Criminology, 62*(10), 3201–3224. doi:10.1177/0306624X17739211

Shute, S. (2007). Parole and risk assessment. In N. Padfield (Ed.), *Who to release? Parole, fairness and criminal justice.* Cullompton: Willan Publishing.

Jonathan Demme (Director). (1991). *Silence of the Lambs* [film]. Demme Productions: Orion Pictures.

Silverman, D. (2010). *Doing qualitative research* (3rd ed.). London: SAGE Publications.

Sim, J. (1990). *Medical power in prisons: The prison medical service in england 1774 – 1989.* Maidenhead: Open University Press.

Sim, J. (1991). We are not animals, we are human beings: Prisons, protest and politics in england and wales 1969-90. *Social Justice, 18*, 107–129.

Sim, J. (2008). Pain and punishment: The real and the imaginary in penal institutions. In P. Carlen (Ed.), *Imaginary penalities* (pp. 135–156). Cullompton; Portland, OR: Willan Publishing.

Sim, J. (2009). *Punishment and prisons: Power and the carceral state*. Los Angeles, CA; London: SAGE Publications.

Simmel, G. (1971). *On individuality and social forms: Selected writings* (D. N. Levine, Ed.). Chicago, IL: University of Chicago Press.

Skovholt, T. M., & Ronnestad, M. H. (1995). *The evolving professional self: Stages and themes in therapist and counsellor development, wiley series in psychotherapy and counselling*. Oxford: Wiley and Sons.

Smith, R. (2003). *Youth justice: Ideas, policy, practice*. Cullompton: Willan.

Smith, M. J. (2005). Empiricism, idealism, realism. In M. J. Smith (Ed.), *Understanding social scientific practice: Philosophy and methodology of the social sciences* (2nd ed., pp.319–367). London: SAGE Publications.

Smith, R. (2005a). Welfare versus justice – again! *Youth Justice, 5*(1), 3–16.

Smith, P. K., & Brain, P. (2000). Bullying in schools: Lessons from two decades of research. *Aggressive Behavior 26*, 1–9.

Soothill, K. (2007). Prison histories and competing audiences, 1776 – 1966. In Y. Jewkes (Ed.), *Handbook on prisons*. Cullompton; Portland, OR: Willan Publishing.

Sparks, R. (2007). The politics of imprisonment. In Y. Jewkes (Ed.), *Handbook on prisons*. Cullompton; Portland, OR: Willan Publishing.

Squires, P., & Stephen, D. E. (2005). *Rougher justice: Anti-social behaviour and young people*. Cullumpton: Willan Publishing.

Stenson, K. (2001). The new politics of crime control. In K. Stenson, & R. R. Sullivan (Eds.), *Crime, risk and justice: The politics of crime control in liberal democracies*. Cullumpton: Willan Publishing.

Stevens, A. (2019). Access denied: Research on sex in prison and the subjugation of 'deviant knowledge'. *Criminology and Criminal Justice*. doi:10.1177/1748895819839740

Stewart, A. (2001). *Theories of power and domination: The politics of empowerment in late modernity*. London: SAGE Publications.

Stoddart, M. C. J. (2007). Ideology, hegemony, discourse: A critical review of theories of knowledge and power. *Social Thought & Research, 28*, 191–225.

Swets, J. (1988). Measuring the accuracy of diagnostic systems. *Science, 240*, 1285–1293.

Sykes, G. M. (1958). *The society of captives: A study of a maximum security prison*. Princeton, NJ: Princeton University Press.

Sykes, G. M., & Matza, D. (1957). Techniques of neutralisation: A theory of delinquency. *American Sociological Review, 22*(6), 664–670.

Tait, S. (2011). A typology of prison officer approaches to care. *European Journal of Criminology, 8*(6), 440–456.

The British Psychological Society. (2010). 'What do forensic psychologists do?', Information on careers and qualifications.

Thoits, P. A. (1996). Managing the emotions of others. *Symbolic Interaction, 19*(2), 85–109.

Tierney, J. (2010). *Criminology: Theory and context* (3rd ed.). Harlow: Pearson Longman.

Timmermans, S., & Gabe, J. (2002). Introduction: Connecting criminology and sociology of health and illness. *Sociology of Health & Illness*, 24(5), 501–516.

Toch, H. (1992). *Living in prison: The ecology of survival*. Washington, DC: American Psychological Association.

Toch, H. (1998). Psychopathy or antisocial personality in forensic settings. In T. Millon, E. Simonsen, M. Birket-Smith, & R. D. Davis (Eds.), *Psychopathy: Antisocial, criminal, and violent behavior*. New York, NY: The Guilford Press.

Towl, G. J. (2004). Applied psychological services in prisons and probation. In J. Adler (Ed.), *Forensic psychology: Concepts, debates and practice*, Cullompton: Willan.

Towl, G., & McDougall, C. (1999). Introduction. InG. Towl & C. McDougall (Eds.), *What do forensic psychologists do? Current and future Directions in the Prison and probation services*. Leicester: The British Psychological Society.

Towl, G., & Walker, T. (2015, July). Prisoner suicide: Public management, punitiveness and professionalism, online first. *The Psychologist*, 28, 886–889. Retrieved from www.thepsychologist.org.uk

Trotter, C., & Ward, T. (2013). Involuntary Clients, pro-social modelling and ethics. *Ethics and Social Welfare*, 7(1), 74–90.

Tyler, T. R. (1998). The psychology of authority relations: A relational perspective on influence and power in groups. In R. M. Kramer, & M. A. Neale (Eds.), *Power and influence in organisations*. Thousand Oaks, CA: SAGE Publications.

Ugelvik, T. (2014). *Power and resistance in prison: Doing time, doing freedom*. Basingstoke: Palgrave MacMillan.

Vartia, M., & Hyyti, J. (2002). Gender differences in workplace bullying among prison officers. *European Journal of Work & Organizational Psychology*, 11(1), 113–126.

Walsh, E. (2009). The emotional labour of nurses working in HM Prison Service. *Journal of Forensic Nursing*, 5(3), 143–152.

Warburton, N. (1999). *Philosophy: The basics* (3rd ed.). London: Routledge.

Ward, T. (2014). The dual relationship problem in forensic and correctional practice: Community protection or offender welfare? *Legal and Criminal Psychology*, 19, 35–39.

Ward, T., & Syversen, K. (2009). Human dignity and vulnerable agency: An ethical framework for forensic practice. *Aggression and Violent Behavior*, 14(2), 94–105.

Warr, J. (2008). Personal reflections on prison staff. In J. Bennett, B. Crewe, & A. Wahidin (Eds.), *Understanding prison staff* (pp. 17–29). Cullompton; Portland, OR: Willan Publishing.

Warr, J. (2014). Expansion in an age of contraction: Does prison size matter? *Prison Service Journal*. 211, 25–30.

Warr, J. (2019). "Always gotta be two mans": Lifers, risk, rehabilitation, and narrative labour. *Punishment & Society*. doi:10.1177/1462474518822487

Wartenburg, T. (1990). *The forms of power: From domination to transformation*. Philadelphia, PA: Temple University Press.

Watkins, R. E. (1992). *An historical review of the role and practice of psychology in the field of corrections*. Ottawa: Correctional Services of Canada.

Weaver, B. (2009). Communicative punishment as a penal approach to supporting desistance. *Theoretical Criminology*, 13(1), 9–29

Webster, S. D., Mann, R. E., Carter, A. J., Long, J., Milner, R. J., O'Brien, M. D. ... Ray, N. L. (2006). Inter-rater reliability of dynamic risk assessment with sexual prisoners. *Psychology, Crime and Law, 12*(4), 439–452.

Weiss, H. M., & Cropanzano, R. (1996). Affective events theory: A theoretical discussion of the structure, causes, and consequences of affective experiences at work. *Research in Organizational Behaviour, 18*, 1–74.

Whitney, D., & Trosten-Bloom, A. (2010). *The power of appreciative inquiry* (2nd ed.). San Francisco, CA: Berrett-Koehler Publishers Inc.

Wilde, O. (1898). Ballad of reading gaol. In J. B. Foreman (Ed.), *The complete works of oscar fingal O'flahertie wills wilde: Stories, plays, poems, essays (Introduced by V holland 91983)*. London: Collins Clear-Type Press.

Williams, B. (1993). *Morality* (Canto Edn). Cambridge; New York, NY: Cambridge University Press.

Wilson, J. C., & Noon, E. (1998). Difficulties in conducting research in forensic psychology. In J. Boros, M. Munnich, & M. Szegedi (Eds.), *Psychology and criminal justice: International review of theory and practice*. Berlin; New York, NY: Walter de Gruyter.

Woodward, R. (2007). Symbiosis: Therapeutic communities within non-therapeutic community organisations. In M. Parker (Ed.), *Dynamic security: The democratic therapeutic Community in prison*. London; Philadelphia, PA: Jessica Kingsley Publishers

Wrong, D. H. (1995). *Power: Its forms, bases and uses*. New Brunswick, NJ: Transaction Publishers.

Yochelson, S., & Samenow, S. (1976). *The criminal personality: A profile for change*. Lanham, MA: Rowman & Littlefield Publishers Inc.

Index

www.ingramcontent.com/pod-product-compliance
Lightning Source LLC
Chambersburg PA
CBHW050352270326
41926CB00016B/3701